BIBLICAL MOURNING

Biblical Mourning
Ritual and Social
Dimensions

SAUL M. OLYAN

OXFORD
UNIVERSITY PRESS

OXFORD

UNIVERSITY PRESS

Great Clarendon Street, Oxford OX2 6DP

Oxford University Press is a department of the University of Oxford.
It furthers the University's objective of excellence in research, scholarship,
and education by publishing worldwide in

Oxford New York

Auckland Bangkok Buenos Aires Cape Town Chennai
Dar es Salaam Delhi Hong Kong Istanbul Karachi Kolkata
Kuala Lumpur Madrid Melbourne Mexico City Mumbai Nairobi
São Paulo Shanghai Taipei Tokyo Toronto

Oxford is a registered trade mark of Oxford University Press
in the UK and in certain other countries

Published in the United States
by Oxford University Press Inc., New York

© Saul M. Olyan 2004

British Library Cataloguing in Publication Data

Data available

Library of Congress Cataloging in Publication Data

Data applied for

ISBN 0-19-926486-4

1 3 5 7 9 10 8 6 4 2

Typeset in Imprint
by Regent Typesetting, London
Printed in Great Britain
on acid-free paper by
Biddles Ltd,
Guildford & King's Lynn.

ACKNOWLEDGEMENTS

IT is a pleasure to recognize the contributions of friends, colleagues, and institutions to the development of this volume. In the fall of 2000, I presented an early draft of a paper that would eventually become the core of Chapter 5 and a section of the Introduction in Brown University's Culture and Religion of the Ancient Mediterranean faculty seminar. I was fortunate to receive valuable feedback from colleagues in the seminar, particularly Susan Ashbrook Harvey, Stanley Stowers, and Jonathan Brumberg-Kraus, and I thank them for their continuing interest in my work. I am especially indebted to Theodore Lewis, David Wright, Susan Ackerman, and Steven Weitzman for their critical reactions to a more developed version of the above-mentioned paper during July of 2001. Each one of them provided me with suggestions and criticisms that helped me to improve my argumentation. I would also like to thank Rainer Albertz, David Frankfurter, Baruch Schwartz, and William Gilders for giving me the opportunity to present material from this book to audiences at Westfälische Wilhelms-Universität in Münster, the University of New Hampshire, the Hebrew University of Jerusalem, and Emory University, and for their critical feedback. I am grateful to my colleagues Susan Ashbrook Harvey and Muhammad Q. Zaman for bringing G. L. Ebersole's article to my attention, and to Benjamin Foster and Edward Greenstein for other bibliographic suggestions. Brown University provided me with a year-long sabbatical, during the course of which this book was written, and I am happy to recognize the university's ongoing support for my work. I am also delighted to acknowledge the interest of my editor, Hilary O'Shea, in this project, and the useful suggestions of the two anonymous readers for the press, which helped me to improve the manuscript at several points. Chapter 4 appeared in a different form in *'A Wise and Discerning Mind': Essays in Honor of Burke O. Long* (ed. Saul M. Olyan and Robert C. Culley; BJS 325; Providence, RI: Brown Judaic Studies, 2000), 181–9.

Sections of the essay have been reproduced here with permission. Finally and foremost, I would like to express my gratitude to my partner Frederik Schockaert for his unstinting personal support, his ongoing interest in this project, and his patience with my Dutch. This volume is dedicated to him.

S.M.O.

Providence, RI, USA
November 2002

CONTENTS

ABBREVIATIONS

The following is a list of abbreviations used throughout the text and notes.

AB	Anchor Bible
ANEP	J. B. Pritchard (ed.), *The Ancient Near East in Pictures Relating to the Old Testament*
AOAT	Alter Orient und Altes Testament
ATD	Das Alte Testament Deutsch
BKAT	Biblischer Kommentar, Altes Testament
BO	Bibliotheca Orientalis
BWANT	Beiträge zur Wissenschaft vom Alten und Neuen Testament
BZAW	Beihefte zur Zeitschrift für die alttestamentliche Wissenschaft
CANE	J. M. Sasson (ed.), *Civilizations of the Ancient Near East*
CAT	M. Dietrich, O. Loretz, and J. Sanmartín (eds.), *The Cuneiform Alphabetic Texts from Ugarit, Ras Ibn Hani, and Other Places*
CBQ	*Catholic Biblical Quarterly*
Cowley	A. E. Cowley, *Aramaic Papyri of the Fifth Century B.C.*
D	Deuteronomistic Work/Deuteronomistic School
EA	J. A. Knudtzon, *Die El-Amarna Tafeln* (2 vols.; Vorderasiatische Bibliothek 2.1–2; Leipzig: Hinrichs, 1907–15)
EJ	*Encyclopaedia Judaica*
EM	*Enṣiqlopedya Miqra'it*
FOTL	Forms of the Old Testament Literature
H	Holiness Source/Holiness School
HAT	Handbuch zum Alten Testament
HSM	Harvard Semitic Monographs
HUCA	*Hebrew Union College Annual*
ICC	International Critical Commentary

JANES	*Journal of the Ancient Near Eastern Society of Columbia University*
JAOS	*Journal of the American Oriental Society*
JBL	*Journal of Biblical Literature*
JPSTC	Jewish Publication Society Torah Commentary
JSOTS	Journal for the Study of the Old Testament, Supplement Series
LXX	Septuagint
MT	Masoretic Text
NJPS	New Jewish Publication Society Version
NKB	L. Koehler and W. Baumgartner, *The Hebrew and Aramaic Lexicon of the Old Testament*
NRSV	New Revised Standard Version
OTL	Old Testament Library
P	Priestly Writing /Priestly School
Q	Qumran sigla:
1QIsaª	First copy of Isaiah: Qumran, Cave 1
RSV	Revised Standard Version
SBLDS	Society of Biblical Literature Dissertation Series
SHCANE	Studies in the History and Culture of the Ancient Near East
Syr.	The Syriac (Pešiṭta) Version
TDOT	G. J. Botterweck and H. Ringgren (eds.), *Theological Dictionary of the Old Testament*
TWAT	G. J. Botterweck and H. Ringgren (eds.), *Theologisches Wörterbuch zum Alten Testament*
Vg.	Vulgate
VT	*Vetus Testamentum*
VTSup	Vetus Testamentum, Supplements
WMANT	Wissenschaftliche Monographien zum Alten und Neuen Testament
ZAW	*Zeitschrift für die alttestamentliche Wissenschaft*

Introduction

Though groundbreaking work on specific aspects of biblical mourning rites has been published during the past fifteen years (e.g. mourning and rejoicing as ritual type and antitype),[1] no adequate paradigm has been developed for understanding the ritual dimensions of mourning as it is represented in biblical and cognate literatures. Nor have scholars investigated the social dimensions of biblical mourning in any serious way. Recent scholarship on death and the afterlife in the Hebrew Bible and ancient Israel has tended to focus more on understanding the extent and nature of ancestor cults, the mechanics of necromancy, patterns of burial practice, and conceptions of the afterlife than it has on comprehending mourning.[2] Furthermore, the

---

[1] G. A. Anderson, *A Time to Mourn, A Time to Dance: The Expression of Grief and Joy in Israelite Religion* (University Park, Pa.: Pennsylvania State University Press, 1991).

[2] On ancestor cults, see e.g. T. J. Lewis, *Cults of the Dead in Ancient Israel and Ugarit* (HSM 39; Atlanta: Scholars Press, 1989); K. van der Toorn, *Family Religion in Babylonia, Syria & Israel: Continuity & Change in the Forms of Religious Life* (SHCANE 7; Leiden: Brill, 1996), 206–35; B. B. Schmidt, *Israel's Beneficent Dead: Ancestor Cult and Necromancy in Ancient Israelite Religion and Tradition* (Winona Lake, Ind.: Eisenbrauns, 1996); and Lewis's recent critique of Schmidt's position in 'How Far Can Texts Take Us? Evaluating Textual Sources for Reconstructing Ancient Israelite Beliefs about the Dead', in B. Gittlen (ed.), *Sacred Time, Sacred Place: Archaeology and the Religion of Israel* (Winona Lake, Ind.: Eisenbrauns, 2002), 189–202. On necromancy, see J. Tropper, *Nekromantie: Totenbefragung im Alten Orient und im Alten Testament* (AOAT 223; Neukirchen-Vluyn: Neukirchener; Kevelaer: Butzon & Bercker, 1989). On burial in Judah, see esp. E. Bloch-Smith, *Judahite Burial Practices and Beliefs about the Dead* (JSOTS 123; Sheffield: Sheffield Academic Press, 1992). On the afterlife, see e.g. N. J. Tromp, *Primitive Conceptions of Death and the Nether World in the Old Testament* (BO 21; Rome: Pontifical Biblical Institute, 1969) and Lewis, 'How Far Can Texts Take Us?', 183–5. A useful bibliography assembled by B. Janowski consisting mainly of German-

major monographic study of biblical mourning rites,[3] published in 1977 and now out of print, suffers from an unfortunate tendency to read the biblical data through the lens of later rabbinic interpretation, thereby limiting its utility.[4] Add to this the fact that specific problems central to our understanding of biblical mourning practices still require serious exploration. For example, the relationship between mourning for the dead and the variety of non-death-related contexts in which biblical mourning rites also occur (e.g. individual or communal petition of the deity) remains for the most part inadequately investigated by scholars.[5] The constraints on mourning witnessed in several

language items published between 1947 and 1987 on death-related topics may be found in C. Barth, *Die Errettung vom Tode in den individuellen Klage- und Dankliedern des Alten Testaments* (2nd edn.; Zurich: Theologischer Verlag, 1987), 197–225.

[3] The recent study of X. H. T. Pham (*Mourning in the Ancient Near East and the Hebrew Bible* (JSOTS 302; Sheffield: Sheffield Academic Press, 1999)) appears at first blush to be comprehensive, but bears a misleading title. Rather than being a wide-ranging investigation, it is a tightly focused analysis of Lamentations 1–2 and Isa. 51: 9–52: 2, with a brief general discussion of mourning in the introduction that pays particular attention to comforting. My thanks to Edward Greenstein for bringing Pham's monograph to my attention.

[4] E. Feldman, *Biblical and Post-Biblical Defilement and Mourning: Law as Theology* (New York: KTAV/Yeshiva University Press, 1977). Many examples of this tendency could be cited, but a few will suffice to make my point. On 64, Feldman asserts that only the Israelite dead defile according to biblical texts, but cites only rabbinic passages to support this claim. In reality, the claim has no biblical basis; biblical texts that speak of such defilement suggest to the contrary that all human corpses pollute (e.g. Num. 19: 11; 31: 19). A second example is Feldman's treatment of the terms אוב and ידעני on 21. Instead of using biblical texts to establish the meaning of these terms in their biblical context, Feldman turns to the rabbis. Feldman also makes a number of other questionable assertions. For example, on 57, he seems to claim that Leviticus 21 indicates that the priest may not become polluted through corpse contact. Yet Lev. 21: 1–2 states plainly that the priest may indeed defile himself for close relatives who have died.

[5] The most thorough study up to now is that of E. Kutsch, ' "Trauerbräuche" und "Selbstminderungsriten" im Alten Testament', in idem, *Kleine Schriften zum Alten Testament*, ed. L. Schmidt and K. Eberlein; (BZAW 168; Berlin and New York: de Gruyter, 1986), 78–95, orig. pub. 1965, and often cited. Kutsch comes closest to developing a comprehensive perspective on the relationship of mourning the dead and other contexts in which mourning rites occur, though our disagreements are significant, as will become evident. See also the discussion of A. Baumann, 'אבל 'ābhal', *TDOT* 1: 44–8, which is briefer, and builds on Kutsch's work. Several scholars have attempted to explain the relationship of

biblical texts (Lev. 19: 27–8; 21: 5; Deut. 14: 1, which proscribe forms of laceration and shaving) have yet to be convincingly explained. Finally, examples of the apparent mixing of mourning rites and the rites of cultic rejoicing (Jer. 41: 4–5; Amos 8: 3), normally antithetical sets of ritual behaviours, also demand serious consideration which they have not as yet received. Thus, a new investigation of biblical mourning that engages these problems is both timely and necessary.

Taking into account social anthropological research on mourning in specific societies and cross-culturally, I have undertaken an exploration of both the ritual and social dimensions of mourning as it is represented in biblical texts.[6] The social and

---

mourning the dead to petitionary mourning. They include T. Podella, *Šôm-Fasten: Kollektive Trauer um den verborgenen Gott im Alten Testament* (AOAT 224; Neukirchen-Vluyn: Neukirchener; Kevelaer: Butzon & Bercker, 1989), 271–3; and E. Gerstenberger, 'Der klagende Mensch: Anmerkungen zu den Klagegattungen in Israel', in H. W. Wolff (ed.), *Probleme biblischer Theologie: Gerhard von Rad zum 70. Geburtstag* (Munich: Kaiser, 1971), 68. E. Lipinski simply asserts that the rites of the penitent were borrowed from the context of mourning the dead, without argument (*La Liturgie pénitentielle dans la Bible* (Lectio Divina 52; Paris: Cerf, 1969), 28–9, 115). Feldman, *Defilement and Mourning*, does not discuss the various mourning types; his focus is mourning the dead. Anderson, *A Time to Mourn*, treats the rites of petitioners when they are relevant to his discussion and mentions the individual afflicted with skin disease in passing, but makes no attempt to identify mourning types in a systematic way or to explore their interrelationship.

[6] It is important to emphasize from the beginning that any reconstruction of mourning in ancient Israel is really a reconstruction of mourning as it is represented in biblical texts, with reference to non-Israelite West Asian textual and pictorial evidence whenever possible. Thus, I refer to 'biblical representations of mourning' throughout this study to emphasize our dependence on the biblical text. Such dependence is disadvantageous for a number of reasons. First, we cannot access ancient practice in any direct way through textual representations, as these are literary creations that may reflect idealization or hyperbole and may serve revisionist or utopian aims. Second, the relevant texts for this study are a mix of prescriptions, prophetic oracles and their framing materials, psalmic poetry of various genres, and narratives, all from a variety of settings and time periods, making comparison and generalization difficult. Third, many biblical texts are notoriously difficult to date, leaving the scholar at times unable even to compare earlier and later representations of ritual behaviour. Thus, developing a diachronic perspective even on biblical mourning is often an impossible aim, and will therefore not be a central goal of this study. Nonetheless, representations are not generated in a vacuum, and it seems reasonable to assume that our texts might suggest something about mourning as

ritual dimensions of mourning are intertwined and inseparable, in that rites in general are a context for the creation and re-creation of the social order and for its potential transformation.[7] Like other rites, mourning practices provide a ritual setting for the realization, affirmation, re-negotiation, or termination of social bonds between individuals, groups, and even political entities such as states. Thus, one cannot exclude social implications when one ponders the ritual dimensions of mourning just as one cannot avoid thinking about patterns of ritual practice when one contemplates the social dimensions of mourning. My reconstruction of biblical mourning will consider its variety, its ritual patterns, the social links it establishes, perpetuates, and transforms, its temporal structure and the loci in which it does its work. After attempting to provide a 'thick description' of

it was practised, though we must be cautious about what we conclude based on a study of such varied literary representations. On working with textual representations of ritual, see further I. Morris, *Death-Ritual and Social Structure in Classical Antiquity* (Cambridge: Cambridge University Press, 1992), 10–12; S. M. Olyan, *Rites and Rank: Hierarchy in Biblical Representations of Cult* (Princeton: Princeton University Press, 2000), 13–14; D. P. Wright, *Ritual in Narrative: The Dynamics of Feasting, Mourning, and Retaliation Rites in the Ugaritic Tale of Aqhat* (Winona Lake, Ind.: Eisenbrauns, 2001), 3–4, 6; and W. K. Gilders, 'Representation and Interpretation: Blood Manipulation in Ancient Israel and Early Judaism' (Ph.D. diss., Brown University, 2001), 12–16.

[7] On the power of ritual to create social reality, see e.g. E. Leach, *Culture and Communication* (Cambridge: Cambridge University Press, 1976), 77; M. Bloch and J. Parry, 'Introduction', in eid. (eds.), *Death and the Regeneration of Life* (Cambridge: Cambridge University Press, 1982), 6; D. I. Kertzer, *Ritual, Politics & Power* (New Haven: Yale University Press, 1988), 1–2, 12, 14, *passim*; Morris, *Death-Ritual*, 2; J. and J. Comaroff (eds.), *Modernity and its Malcontents: Ritual and Power in Post-Colonial Africa* (Chicago: University of Chicago Press, 1993), pp. xvi–xxi; C. Bell, *Ritual: Perspectives and Dimensions* (New York: Oxford University Press, 1997), 82–3; R. A. Rappaport, *Ritual and Religion in the Making of Humanity* (Cambridge: Cambridge University Press, 1999), 23, 34–5, 75–7, 107–8; and Wright, *Ritual in Narrative*, 32, 46, 137, 227. Throughout this work, I speak of rites realizing and communicating, making and marking, creating and publicizing. I do so to emphasize the dual function of ritual, which I view as both a creative and communicative phenomenon. Ritual is not simply a mirror reflecting a somehow pre-existing social order. Through rites, the social order is continually brought into being anew, with the statuses and identities of participants and relations between them affirmed or reconfigured. Far from being a mode of impeding social transformation, rites have the power to realize such change.

biblical mourning,[8] to represent it in all its complexity, I will bring my observations to bear on theoretical discussion in social anthropology about mourning in individual societies and in cross-cultural perspective. Theoretical models such as Arnold van Gennep's *rites de passage*[9] have the potential to enhance our understanding of phenomena on the ground or in the text by making new connections, raising new questions, or pointing to new avenues of inquiry. But they must be continually subject to critique, and potentially, revision or even rejection, on the basis of close analysis of the data of newly considered individual societies or populations within societies.[10] Thus, theoretical models ought to function as useful stimulants for our research, and our research ought potentially to contribute to the ongoing assessment and shaping of the theoretical models themselves. At all events, theoretical models must never be permitted to pre-determine our conclusions.[11]

My investigation of biblical mourning is divided into five chapters, not including this Introduction and the Conclusion. Chapter 1 has mourning the dead as its focus. Chapter 2 follows with an in-depth exploration of what I call petitionary mourning, the mourning rites employed by individual and communal supplicants in time of need. In Chapter 3, I investigate mourning in non-petitionary and non-death-related contexts (mourning and communal or individual calamity, mourning and skin disease). Chapter 4 provides an analysis of the texts that

---

[8] On 'thick description', see C. Geertz, 'Thick Description: Toward an Interpretive Theory of Culture', in idem, *The Interpretation of Cultures* (New York: Basic Books, 1973), 3–30.

[9] See A. van Gennep, *Les Rites de passage* (Paris: Émile Nourry, 1909). For an English translation, see *The Rites of Passage* (trans. M. B. Vizedom and G. L. Caffee; Chicago: University of Chicago Press, 1960).

[10] An excellent example is Bruce Lincoln's critique of the *rites de passage* model with respect to women initiates (*Emerging from the Chrysalis: Rituals of Women's Initiation* (New York: Oxford University Press, 1991), 99–104). See also the recent critical assessment of the model in R. Grimes, *Deeply into the Bone: Reinventing Rites of Passage* (Berkeley and Los Angeles: University of California Press, 2000), 336–7.

[11] A tendency witnessed all too often among some scholars who have embraced social scientific approaches to the study of the Bible. On the appropriate use of social scientific materials in biblical research, see the instructive comments of R. R. Wilson, *Sociological Approaches to the Old Testament* (Philadelphia: Fortress, 1984), 28–9.

constrain mourning behaviour by proscribing rites of laceration and shaving for priests (Lev. 21: 5) and for Israelites in general (Lev. 19: 27–8; Deut. 14: 1). Finally, in Chapter 5 I explore the implications of Jer. 41: 4–5 and Amos 8: 3, texts in which mourning and rejoicing are fused in the exceptional context of temple destruction and its aftermath. The remainder of this Introduction is divided into three parts. In the first part, 'Mourning in Social Science Discussion', I begin to engage some of the more important social anthropological research on mourning. In the second part, 'Mourning and Rejoicing as Ritual Oppositions', I illustrate the antithetical relationship of biblical mourning rites and rites of cultic rejoicing elaborated most effectively by G. A. Anderson. Building on Anderson's presentation, I incorporate my own further observations and add a number of additional, relevant texts for consideration. In the third part, 'Identifying Types of Mourning', I justify my use of the term 'mourning' for ritual behaviours not directly linked to the death of an individual. I also treat in brief several points of contrast and similarity among types of mourning (locus, presence or absence of pollution, time period, ease of reversibility) in anticipation of more detailed consideration in the following chapters.

MOURNING IN SOCIAL SCIENCE DISCUSSION

At the turn of the last century, Émile Durkheim's student Robert Hertz published a pioneering, comparative study of the death ways of a number of societies practising forms of double burial. In this essay, he argued that mourning behaviour, as well as conceptions of death itself and the status of the corpse and soul, are social productions.[12] For data, Hertz used reports on particular indigenous Indonesian cultures as well as comparative material from New Zealand, Madagascar, and elsewhere. Though a mourning rite such as weeping may appear at first blush to be nothing more than an individual act, argued

---

[12] 'Contribution à une étude sur la représentation collective de la mort', *L'Année Sociologique*, 10 (1905–6), 48–137. Though dated 1905–6, the volume appeared in 1907. For a translation into English, see 'A Contribution to the Study of the Collective Representation of Death', in R. Hertz, *Death and the Right Hand* (trans. R. and C. Needham; Glencoe, Ill.: Free Press, 1960), 27–86.

Hertz, evidence suggests that such behaviour is shaped by social expectations. He came to similar conclusions about attitudes toward the corpse and its treatment in the societies he studied, and notions concerning the fate of the dead person's soul. In the data that Hertz examined, he found a striking correspondence between the status of the corpse and that of the mourner, on the one hand, and the status of the corpse and that of the soul of the dead, on the other. Just as the body does not go immediately to its final resting-place in the belief of societies such as the Dayak of Borneo, so the soul does not go immediately to its final destination in the land of the dead. Just as the corpse is polluted and repellant according to the beliefs of some Indonesian cultures, so is the mourner, with mourning lasting until the corpse has disintegrated, leaving only the bones. The symmetry between the mourner and the corpse led Hertz to view the mourner as a socially dead individual, cut off from communal life. Hertz concluded that mortuary practices address a number of social requirements. Among the most important, the dead person must be detached socially and then reintegrated as a non-living member of society. In so doing, the social order is reconstituted.

Hertz's emphasis on the social dimensions of mortuary rites continues to exercise influence among anthropologists. In fact, two of the most important recent extended treatments of mortuary practices from a cross-cultural perspective express profound appreciation for Hertz's pioneering insights.[13] They do so because Hertz was able to bring into relief the degree to which mourning and other death-related practices are shaped by the social contexts in which they occur. Hertz's passing observation that emotional displays in mortuary settings are social productions serving social functions rather than spontaneous expressions of feeling adumbrates much subsequent scholarship (e.g. Hertz's teacher Durkheim's famous discussion of mourning among native Australians and A. R. Radcliffe-Brown's much-cited study of weeping among the Andaman Islanders).[14] An acknowledgement of the part played by social

---

[13] P. Metcalf and R. Huntington, *Celebrations of Death: The Anthropology of Mortuary Ritual* (2nd revised and expanded edn.; Cambridge: Cambridge University Press, 1991), 33–7, 79–107; Bloch and Parry (eds.), *Death and the Regeneration of Life*, 2–6.

[14] É. Durkheim, *Les Formes élémentaires de la vie religieuse: Le Système*

context in the shaping of emotive expression in ritual has become a routine starting point for those who treat mourning, including biblical scholars who embrace an anthropological perspective.[15]

Recent discussion of ritual and the emotions among social anthropologists has tended to focus on whether the emotional displays common to mourning and other ritual contexts cross-culturally are entirely the product of ritual action or whether the emotions and ritual have a mutually influential relationship.[16] I have embraced the latter perspective in this study because of its greater explanatory value, for it is not clear to me that rites always and in every instance successfully create expected emotional responses in individuals. At times, they certainly do. Joab and Judah's lamentation and weeping over Abner in 2 Sam. 3: 31–7 is an excellent biblical example of rites apparently creating a contextually demanded response. Jer. 9: 16–17 (Eng. 17–18), a text that explicitly acknowledges the role of dirge singers in causing the tears of others to flow, is yet another instance of this phenomenon. Ethnographic evidence from a variety of cultures provides similar cases of ritual action eliciting contextually demanded emotional responses from participants.[17] But in other cases, rites fail to create the expected emotive response, as Neh. 8: 9 shows. In this instance, people weep, probably out of fear, in a ritual context devoted entirely to joyous expression; in response, their leaders suppress their unsuitable ritual behaviour. A second biblical example of the failure of rites to elicit an appropriate emotional reaction among participants is Ezra 3: 12–13. In this narrative, though many witnessing the establishment of the rebuilt temple in Jerusalem shout joyfully,

---

totémique en Australie (Paris: Librairie Générale Française, 1991), 662–72; A. R. Radcliffe-Brown, *The Andaman Islanders* (Cambridge: Cambridge University Press, 1933). See the assessments of the approaches of Durkheim and Radcliffe-Brown in Metcalf and Huntington, *Celebrations of Death*, 43–53; and G. L. Ebersole, 'The Function of Ritual Weeping Revisited: Affective Expression and Moral Discourse', *History of Religions*, 39 (2000), 233–8. I am indebted to my colleagues Susan Ashbrook Harvey and Muhammad Q. Zaman for bringing Ebersole's article to my attention.

[15] e.g. Anderson, *A Time to Mourn*, 3–9.

[16] Bloch and Parry, *Death and the Regeneration of Life*, 3, 5–6, for the former view; Metcalf and Huntington, *Celebrations of Death*, 2–5, for the latter.

[17] Radcliffe-Brown's work on this subject is perhaps the most well-known example.

as would be expected, others weep, apparently in disappointment. An interesting example of inappropriate emotional display from another cultural context is the Javanese girl famously described by Clifford Geertz who cries at the funeral of her father, though such activity is forbidden in her culture.[18] As with Neh. 8: 9, persons in positions of authority suppress her contextually inappropriate emotional response. Thus, biblical texts and contemporary ethnographic observation suggest that along with the emotion-shaping potential of ritual action, we must also recognize that the individual may harbour non-conforming feelings that may overwhelm the power of rites to create emotional responses in participants.[19] Furthermore, evidence from particular cultures, including biblical representations of mourning, suggests a role for feelings of grief and their articulation in particular cultural contexts that is unrelated to the power of rites to generate emotive responses. Feelings of grief may or may not be universal in death contexts; certainly, grief's sanctioned expression in mourning settings is not consistent cross-culturally. Yet a variety of biblical and other West Asian texts represent bitterly sorrowful mourners (e.g. Gen. 37: 34–5; 2 Sam. 19: 1 (Eng. 18: 33); Gilgamesh), and other texts express concern that the emotional anguish of such individuals be contained (Sir. 38: 16–23). Such persons obviously require little help attaining the culturally prescribed emotional response to death. More frequently, their emotional expressions are deemed to require constraint. Thus, we must consider the production of emotive display by means of ritual *in conjunction with* the feelings of individual participants in ritual when we evaluate ritual action such as mourning. An approach that takes into account the individual as an agent allows for the possibility that rites might fail to bring about the desired emotive response in participants or that they might not be necessary to create it. Ritual actors might even be motivated to subvert ritual action in order to achieve their own

[18] *The Religion of Java* (New York: Free Press, 1960), 69–70, 72, brought to my attention by Metcalf and Huntington, *Celebrations of Death*, 60.

[19] Needless to say, non-conforming emotions are also shaped by the particular social and cultural context in question. On the Western tendency to naturalize emotional expression rather than see it as a cultural product, see C. A. Lutz, *Unnatural Emotions: Everyday Sentiments on a Micronesian Atoll & Their Challenge to Western Theory* (Chicago: University of Chicago Press, 1988), 3–13, 209–25, who provides an apt analysis.

ends. Thus, mourning the dead has the potential to be a context in which both predicted and unpredicted action and expression might occur.[20]

What is most crucial to emphasize at this juncture is the recognition that emotive displays in ritual settings have social significance, as Hertz pointed out. The meaning of a ritual act such as wailing or weeping will vary from society to society, and may vary from ritual context to ritual context within a particular social setting. Within a particular ritual context, wailing or weeping may realize and communicate different things, depending on considerations such as who wails or weeps, and when such ritual actions occur. G. L. Ebersole recently published an insightful programmatic discussion of ritual weeping as an issue for the history of religions. I concur with his position on the social dimensions of weeping, and believe that his observations can be applied to other mourning rites as well. As Ebersole has argued, tears may 'serve a variety of social purposes, including marking out social and hierarchical relationships at times, dissolving them at others, inviting or demanding specific social relationships, or marking/protesting the abrogation of social or moral contracts'.[21] This evaluation of rites of weeping captures nicely their potential, and that of other mourning rites, to accomplish any number of social aims, including those that may actually subvert or transgress social norms. Thus, as Ebersole has pointed out, the only way to make sense of a rite such as weeping is to examine it in relation to all aspects of its ritual and larger social context. In order to do this, one must take into account 'the relative social positions of the ritual actors, their audience(s), their interdependencies, and their respective goals.'[22]

Another aspect of Hertz's work that has proved to be of enduring significance was his observation that death is only one particular example of the more general phenomenon of life stage

---

[20] See further Metcalf's critique of the theoretical position of Bloch and Parry, *Celebrations of Death*, 3–5, 6, and Ebersole's criticisms of Durkheim on the emotions of non-Western ritual actors, 'Ritual Weeping', 235–7. I am indebted to both Metcalf and Ebersole, whose discussions were very helpful to me as I formulated the theoretical position outlined here.

[21] Ibid. 214.

[22] Ibid. 240–1.

transitions or passages.[23] This insight was elaborated in a most original manner by Hertz's contemporary, Arnold van Gennep, who published his monograph *Les Rites de passage* in 1909.[24] Van Gennep argued that rites of transition, including mortuary rites, initiations, betrothals, and marriages, are characterized by a threefold structure across cultures. The first phase, separation, is followed by a period of marginality or liminality, during which status change occurs. In the final phase, the participant in transition is reincorporated into society with a new status. Van Gennep noted that his three stages are not elaborated to the same degree in every ritual context: while rites of separation might be emphasized in one type of transition, the liminal phase might be more developed in another. Throughout his work, van Gennep was careful to distinguish social change from physical: social puberty does not necessarily occur at the time of physical puberty; the social death of a person may take place before or after physical death. Van Gennep spoke of the suspension of the social life of mourners during the liminal phase. He suggested that during this transitional period, both mourners and the dead occupy a social locus between the world of the living and the world of the dead, forming their own 'special society'.[25] (V. Turner elaborated extensively van Gennep's observation that the liminal phase of transition rites is characterized by a lack of well-defined statuses among participants, particularly with respect to participants in initiations.)[26] Echoing Hertz, van Gennep observed that in some societies, the liminal period of mourners parallels such a phase in the post-mortem career of the dead, and noted the role kinship might play in shaping mourning behaviour.[27] With respect to the *rites de passage* in general, he concluded that it is their function to mitigate the effects on

[23] 'Contribution à une étude sur la représentation collective de la mort', 128–9.

[24] See above n. 9 for complete citation.

[25] *Les Rites de passage*, 211. 'Pendant le deuil, les vivants et le mort constituent une société spéciale, située entre le monde des vivants d'une part et le monde des morts de l'autre . . .'.

[26] 'Betwixt and Between: The Liminal Period in Rites de Passage', in idem, *The Forest of Symbols: Aspects of Ndembu Ritual* (Ithaca: Cornell University Press, 1967), 95–7 and 'Liminality and Communitas', in idem, *The Ritual Process: Structure and Anti-Structure* (New York: Aldine De Gruyter, 1995), 95–6.

[27] *Les Rites de passage*, 211–12.

society and the individual of the disturbances caused by life stage transitions, including death.[28]

Van Gennep's tripartite schema, especially as it has been applied to initiations and death rites, has exercised considerable influence on subsequent research, in particular his notion of a liminal or marginal phase, as reworked by Turner with respect to initiations.[29] It is not uncommon today to find the theoretical work of van Gennep cited as a point of departure or reference in research that focuses on transitions, including death and mourning.[30] Those writing on mortuary rites as rites of transition have, in the main, focused on applying the *rites de passage* model to the societies they study and assessing its explanatory utility.[31]

For the biblical specialist seeking to engage van Gennep's and Hertz's ideas as a means potentially to add depth and nuance to our understanding of biblical mourning, the best approach is first to undertake a detailed, careful study of mourning in its biblical representations. From such an investigation, it will be possible to map the complex ritual and social dynamics of biblical mourning. Once this mapping has been done, the validity of claims made by Hertz, van Gennep, and others may be assessed critically. On account of its explanatory power, van Gennep's theory of the tripartite structure of *rites de passage* has exercised considerable influence on the way in which biblical scholars look at mourning rites. In this investigation, I seek to go beyond the well-established identification of the tripartite structure of biblical mourning rites, and consider other aspects of van Gennep's and Hertz's theorizing. For example, Hertz's argument that the mourner experiences social death in Indonesian cultures will be tested against the evidence of biblical materials to see whether the idea has a larger applicability to biblical repre-

---

[28] Ibid. 17.

[29] Turner had little to say about death rites per se. But see his brief comments in 'Introduction', *The Forest of Symbols*, 8–9, on the funeral, which he classified as a type of 'life crisis' ritual along with initiations.

[30] e.g. L. M. Danforth in Danforth and A. Tsiaras, *The Death Rituals of Rural Greece* (Princeton: Princeton University Press, 1982), 35–8, in which Hertz's study is also cited. See also Metcalf and Huntington, *Celebrations of Death*, 108–30, who interact critically but sympathetically with both van Gennep and Hertz.

[31] e.g. Danforth in Danforth and Tsiaras, *Death Rituals of Rural Greece*, 35–69.

sentations of mourning. I shall do the same with van Gennep's assertion that mourners and the dead together form a 'special society', situated between the realm of the living and that of the dead.

MOURNING AND REJOICING AS RITUAL OPPOSITIONS

Thanks especially to the work of G. A. Anderson, it is now widely accepted that mourning and cultic rejoicing are typically represented in biblical and other West Asian texts as antithetical and incompatible sets of ritual behaviours.[32] Mourners for the dead, petitioners of the deity, and others utilize mourning rites at times of potential or actual personal or corporate loss or disaster. They tear their garments, weep, sit on the ground, fast, wail, and toss ashes or dust upon their heads, among other characteristic mourning behaviours. Among those who embrace mourning rites, mourners for the dead, polluted by corpse contact, must also avoid the sanctuary sphere for the period of their mourning.[33] In contrast to those who make use of the rites of mourning, persons who participate in cultic rejoicing anoint themselves, go to the sanctuary in festal attire, offer sacrifices and other offerings, eat, drink, sing songs of praise and dance.[34] Text after text alludes to the transition from mourning to rejoicing or from rejoicing to mourning. A person makes the transition from one ritual state to the other while maintaining carefully the ritual

---

[32] See *A Time to Mourn.* Anderson's work informs my discussion of mourning at many points, though we differ on a number of issues as I intend to show here and elsewhere in this study. Anderson was not the first to observe the antithetical relationship between mourning and rejoicing in biblical materials. Among earlier scholars, see e.g. F. F. Hvidberg, *Weeping and Laughter in the Old Testament* (Leiden: Brill; Copenhagen: Nyt Nordisk Forlag/Arnold Busck, 1962) 155; G. Vanoni, 'שׂמח śāmaḥ', in *TWAT* 7: 813; M. Gruber, 'Mourning', *EJ* 12: 487.

[33] Evidence for the mourner's pollution includes Lev. 21: 1–4. See my discussion of this subject in Ch. 1.

[34] Rejoicing might occur in ritual contexts other than the sanctuary. These include the pilgrimage route (e.g. Isa. 30: 29); the vineyard at harvest time (e.g. Isa. 16: 10, which alludes to the rejoicing of vineyard harvest festivals); and the locus of sheep shearing (e.g. 1 Sam. 25: 8, 36, which refers to the day of shearing as a יוֹם טוֹב and also speaks of a מִשְׁתֶּה on that day).

distinctions between the two states, as Anderson has shown.[35]
One does not fast or wail when one rejoices in the sanctuary or on
pilgrimage; one does not anoint oneself or sing joyous songs
praising the deity when one sits on the ground to mourn.
The careful observance of the distinct and contrasting ritual
behaviours associated with mourning and rejoicing establishes
and re-establishes a ritual order that emerges out of the very distinctions themselves.[36]

The usual incompatibility of mourning and cultic rejoicing is
well illustrated by three biblical texts. Two describe rites performed in an inappropriate ritual context (mourning when and
where rejoicing is mandatory, rejoicing when and where mourning is required); one tells of the appropriate replacement of one
set of rites with the other. The first text of interest is Neh. 8:
9–12, which describes a celebration of the New Year at a time of
trouble in Jerusalem. According to the narrative, the assembled
people, as a group, perform penitential mourning rites at the
public reading of the book of the Torah. They are told by
Nehemiah, Ezra, and the Levites to cease such inappropriate
ritual behaviour at a time set apart for rejoicing, and to rejoice as
required by the occasion:

'Today is holy to Yhwh your God. Do not mourn and do not weep.' For
all of the people were weeping when they heard the words of the
Torah.[37] Then they said to them: 'Go, eat festival foods[38] and drink
sweet drinks and send portions to him for whom nothing is prepared,
for today is holy to our Lord; do not grieve, for the joy of Yhwh is your

---

[35] e.g. with respect to the petitioner of the psalms of complaint, who can only
vow praise of Yhwh while mourning; the praise itself is expressed only after
deliverance (*A Time to Mourn*, 93). Neither Ezra 10: 11 nor Josh. 7: 19 are
exceptions to this pattern, as the idiom נתן תודה in each instance is to be understood not as 'to give praise' or 'thanksgiving' to Yhwh, but 'to make confession'
to him. On this, see NRSV and G. Mayer, 'ידי ydh', *TDOT* 5: 428, 442.

[36] Without the common, there can be no holy; without the unclean, there can
be no clean. On ritualization creating distinctions, giving rise to differentiation
itself, see C. Bell, *Ritual Theory, Ritual Practice* (New York: Oxford University
Press, 1992), 91.

[37] The penitential reaction of the people was apparently brought about by the
content of the Torah, as J. Blenkinsopp points out. He compares Josiah's
reaction when he hears what is written in the Torah book discovered in the
temple (see 2 Kgs. 22: 11, and *Ezra-Nehemiah* (OTL; Philadelphia: Westminster, 1988), 289).

[38] משמנים literally, 'fat foods'. Cf. משתה שמנים in Isa. 25: 6–8.

refuge' . . . So all of the people went to eat and to drink and to send off portions and to make a great rejoicing (שמחה גדולה), for they understood the words that they [the leaders] had made known to them.

Because it is the New Year, a holy day devoted to celebration, rejoicing behaviours are obligatory for the people as a group regardless of their personal feelings and reactions.[39] Among the many characteristic rejoicing behaviours, those identified in this passage are eating rich festival foods, drinking sweet drinks, and sending portions of these celebratory items to those people who lack them. In this narrative, all expressions of grief and mourning are successfully suppressed by the community leadership; these must cease because they are ritually inappropriate for the occasion, as the text states repeatedly: 'Today is holy . . . Do not mourn'; 'eat festival foods . . . for today is holy . . .'.[40]

Another text that suggests the opposition of mourning and rejoicing behaviours is Isa. 22: 12–14. Here, in contrast to Neh. 8: 9–12, a series of mourning rites are required. Israelites are ordered to mourn by Yhwh himself, probably for petitionary purposes, at a time when the nation's survival is threatened, but the text suggests that they do precisely the opposite of what Yhwh commands them:

> The Lord Yhwh of Hosts called on that day
> for weeping and lamentation,
> and for the bald spot and the girding of sackcloth.
> But instead there was joy and rejoicing,
> the slaying of oxen and the slaughtering of sheep,
> the eating of flesh and the drinking of wine.
> 'Let us eat and drink, for tomorrow we die.'

---

[39] As Anderson observes, rejoicing refers to a particular ritual state characterized by a set of distinct rites often associated with temple worship, so it can be commanded (see e.g. Deut. 12: 7, 12, 18; 14: 26; 16: 11, 14, 15; 26: 11). On rejoicing as a ritual state 'defined principally by distinct behaviors', see Anderson, *A Time to Mourn*, 14–15, 19–26.

[40] The text says that the public reading of the Torah on this occasion took place in the square before the Water Gate (Neh. 8: 1, 3). Though there has been some debate about the location of the Water Gate, Neh. 12: 31–43 (esp. v. 37) implies that the Water Gate and its square have some connection to the Temple. Further support for this may be found in the narrative of 1 Esdras 9: 38, 41, which parallels Neh. 8: 1, 3. Here, the Water Gate of Nehemiah 8 is the 'East Gate of the Temple' (v. 38).

This defiant refusal to enact the required and appropriate ritual response to impending disaster, and its substitution with con- textually inappropriate and opposed ritual behaviour, is described as an unforgivable iniquity (עון) by the text in v. 14. The statement of the people, 'Let us eat and drink, for tomorrow we die,' suggests that they are aware that their survival is threatened, and that their behaviour is ritually inappropriate for the occasion, but they persist in rejoicing for the sake of indulgence.[41]

A third example of the separation and contrast between rejoic- ing and mourning behaviours is Isa. 35: 10 (= 51: 11). This text, which describes the anticipated joyful return of exiled Judaeans to Jerusalem, envisions a trouble-free pilgrimage-like journey of the unpolluted on a holy way:

> The redeemed of Yhwh shall return,
> they shall enter Zion with a joyful cry,
> and eternal rejoicing shall be upon their heads.[42]
> Joy and rejoicing shall overtake (them),[43]
> Suffering and groaning shall flee.

The final two cola of this verse are particularly interesting, as they contrast a quasi-personified rejoicing (שמחה) and joy (ששון) with a quasi-personified suffering (יגון) and groaning (אנחה), both associated elsewhere with mourning.[44] In the triumphant return of Yhwh's redeemed from Babylon to Jerusalem, the rejoicing of restoration shall replace the mourning of exile, which shall itself be utterly removed from the scene according to this text. As circumstances shift, ritual behaviour follows suit.

---

[41] כי, 'for', 'because', marks the explanation for the contextually inappro- priate behaviour, suggesting that the speakers are aware that their ritual response requires justification.

[42] As Anderson has argued, this is most likely a reference to anointing (*A Time to Mourn*, 47).

[43] I read ששון and שמחה as subjects governing the verb ישיגו. LXX καταληψεται αυτους suggests a similar understanding, with 3 m.pl. object suffix on the verb form in the Vorlage. This interpretation is preferable to that which understands the returning Judaeans as the subject of the colon, since it is clear that יגון and אנחה are the subjects governing the verbal form נסו in the parallel colon. For the alternative interpretation, see e.g. NRSV, NJPS.

[44] On the root אנה associated with mourning, see esp. Isa. 24: 7; Ezek. 9: 4; Lam. 1: 4, 21; on יגון and mourning, see Esther 9: 22. Anderson, *A Time to Mourn*, 70, notes the association of the root אנה and mourning.

Isa. 35: 10, the last example of the incompatibility and opposition of mourning and rejoicing, also illustrates an important pattern found in a variety of biblical texts: the transformation, often sudden, of mourning into rejoicing or rejoicing into mourning.[45] A number of texts that anticipate an impending punishment for Israel or Judah, or describe the punishment fulfilled, narrate a transformation of the characteristic rites of cultic rejoicing into familiar mourning rites. Often the verb הפך, 'to turn' or 'transform', is employed to communicate the sense of wholesale change:

> I shall turn (והפכתי) your pilgrimage festivals into mourning,
> and all your songs into a dirge.
> I shall put sackcloth on every loin,
> upon every head a bald spot . . .
>
> (Amos 8: 10)
>
> The joy of our hearts is ended,
> Our dance has been turned (נהפך) into mourning.
> (Lam. 5: 15)
>
> The new wine has dried up,
> the vine has withered.
> All who were glad of heart (שמחי לב) groan (נאנחו).
> The joy of timbrels has ended,
> The din of the exultant has ceased,
> The joy of the lyre has stopped.
> (Isa. 24: 7–8)[46]

Texts describing the transformation of mourning behaviours into rejoicing are equally common, and also often employ the verb 'to turn' or 'transform' (הפך). These occur in materials anticipating or describing Israel's salvation, or that of a suffering petitioner, by Yhwh:

> Then the virgin shall rejoice with a dance,
> and young men and elders together.

---

[45] Ps. 30: 6b (Eng. 5b) suggests the potential for rapid transformation: בערב ילין בכי ולבקר רנה. The same phenomenon is evidenced in Mesopotamian literature (e.g. Ludlul bēl nēmeqi ('I will praise the Lord of Wisdom') 2. 41–2, in W. G. Lambert, *Babylonian Wisdom Literature* (Oxford: Clarendon Press, 1960), 40, 41).

[46] Isa. 3: 24–6 is another text that describes movement from rejoicing to mourning.

I shall turn (והפכתי) their mourning into joy,
I shall comfort them and make them rejoice free of[47] their suffering.

(Jer. 31: 13)

You turned (הפכת) my lamentation into dancing,
you removed my sackcloth and girded me with rejoicing.

(Ps. 30: 12 (Eng. 11))[48]

Though a number of biblical poetic texts speak of the transformation of one set of ritual behaviours into the other, few
passages provide a detailed narrative of the steps involved in the
transition from mourning to rejoicing or from rejoicing to
mourning. One exception is 2 Sam. 12: 16–20. This prose narrative describes in detail David's penitential petitionary mourning
for his dying son and its cessation at the child's death. The text is
extremely valuable to us, as it narrates in some detail David's
ritual transformation from penitential supplicant to one who
participates in cultic rejoicing: 'David arose from the ground,
washed, anointed himself, changed his clothes, and entered the
sanctuary of Yhwh and worshipped. Then he came to his own
house and called (for food), and food was brought to him and he
ate.' Each of David's earlier ritual actions is reversed as he moves
from mourning back into quotidian life: where he sat on the
ground, he now rises; where he fasted, he now eats. The ritual
state of mourning is left behind with the systematic abandonment of its characteristic and distinct behaviours.[49]

The careful separation and appropriate timing of the contrasting rites of mourning and rejoicing allows for the transition of
persons between the two ritual states. No ritual movement

---

[47] The preposition מן functions here with its privative sense, as W. McKane
has noted (*A Critical and Exegetical Commentary on Jeremiah* (2 vols.; ICC;
Edinburgh: T. & T. Clark, 1996), 2: 788, 795). Cf. similarly, Jer. 48: 45; Job 21:
9, examples listed by B. K. Waltke and M. O'Connor, *An Introduction to
Biblical Hebrew Syntax* (Winona Lake, Ind: Eisenbrauns, 1990), 214.

[48] Other texts describing movement from mourning to rejoicing include Isa.
61: 1–4; 66: 10; and Esther 9: 22.

[49] Anderson also makes this observation in his discussion of this text (*A Time
to Mourn*, 84). David is able to go immediately to the sanctuary as he is evidently
not polluted from corpse contact. Though his petition does not occur in the
sanctuary, other narrative texts describing penitential entreaty suggest that it
could well have (e.g. Ezra 9–10; Joel 1–2). Anderson, in contrast, believes that
mourning per se defiles the petitioner, resulting in his exclusion from sanctified
loci (*A Time to Mourn*, 90, 92, 94, 95). On this, see my discussion in Ch. 2. Many
scholars have observed David's odd refusal to mourn after the child's death.

between rejoicing and mourning or mourning and rejoicing would be possible without two distinct ritual states made and marked by characteristic rites. The texts that I have discussed in this section suggest that rites have an appropriate context (e.g. appropriate timing) and rites 'out of place' are to be suppressed and even punished, as in Neh. 8: 9–12 and Isa. 22: 14. This is because rites performed inappropriately could threaten the integrity of each of the two, distinct ritual spheres, since the rites themselves both realize and communicate the ritual state with which they are associated.[50]

IDENTIFYING TYPES OF MOURNING

The reader will certainly have noticed by now that I employ the English term 'mourning' broadly to describe the ritual behaviour of individuals or groups of persons who do not mourn the dead as well as that of those who do. I speak of the mourning behaviour of petitioners of the deity, of persons afflicted with skin disease, of shamed armies defeated in war, and humiliated individuals who mourn without any evidence of a petitionary intent. This is a conscious choice on my part, which is based on a number of important characteristics about the ways in which biblical texts represent mourning rites. First, biblical representations of mourning the dead employ a distinct and particular vocabulary of mourning which is also used by other biblical texts to describe the ritual activity of petitioners and others who do not mourn the dead. In other words, the texts narrating the mourning rites of penitents, humiliated individuals, and persons seeking a divine revelation, among others, do not use a different vocabulary to describe their behaviour; rather, they utilize the vocabulary of mourning the dead. Three examples illustrate this point well. Ezra 10: 6 describes the ritual behaviour of Ezra, who has undertaken penitential petitionary rites in the Jerusalem temple complex after learning of the extent of intermarriages in the Judaean community: 'Ezra arose from before the House of God and went to the temple chamber of Yohanan, son of Elyashib . . . Food he did not eat and water he did not drink, for he was mourning (מתאבל) on account of the great sacrilege.' Neh.

[50] See further n. 36.

8: 9, a text that I have already discussed, is similar to Ezra 10: 6 in
that people are said to mourn in a context unrelated to death. In
this passage, the leaders of the community tell the people at the
New Year assembly to stop weeping and mourning on a festival
day on which rejoicing is mandatory: 'Today is holy to Yhwh
your God. Do not mourn (אל תתאבלו) and do not weep.' In neither
Ezra 10: 6 nor Neh. 8: 9 has anyone died, yet both texts use a
common form of the verb 'to mourn' (התאבל) to describe the
ritual behaviour of an individual or a group. In both cases, this
ritual behaviour occurs in the sanctuary, a setting completely
divorced from death and from mourning the dead.[51] A third
example of the use of the verbal root 'to mourn' (אבל) in a context
unrelated to mourning the dead is the behaviour of Haman in
Esther 6: 12. After he has been forced to honour his arch-enemy
Mordecai in public, Haman marks his humiliation by retreating
to his home in the guise of a mourner: 'As for Haman, he hurried
to his house in mourning (אבל) and with (his) head covered.'
Forms of the verb 'to mourn' (אבל) are used of ritual behaviour
unrelated to death in a number of other contexts as well. These
include mourning in anticipation of disaster (Jer. 6: 26; Mic. 1:
8); mourning after the destruction of Jerusalem (Isa. 66: 10;
Lam. 1: 4, with the ways of Zion as subject); and mourning in
order to seek divine revelation (Dan. 10: 2–3; cf. 10: 12). Forms
of the verb 'to mourn' (אבל) are not the only mourning idioms
used of the ritual actions of persons who do not mourn the dead.
Other technical mourning terms such as the verb 'to lament' or
'mourn' (ספד) and its derived noun (מספד) also have a broad usage
comparable in range to the verbal root 'to mourn' (אבל) and its
derivatives.[52]

---

[51] Dead bodies, constructed as highly polluting, have no place in the sanctuary. Numbers 19 implies that mourners for the dead and their comforters,
polluted on account of corpse contact or proximity to a corpse, are separated
from the sphere of the sanctuary for a period of seven days and must undergo
elaborate purification rites.

[52] See e.g. Isa. 22: 12; Jer. 6: 26; Joel 1: 13; 2: 12; Mic. 1: 8; Zech. 7: 5; and
Esther 4: 3, texts in which forms of the verb ספד or the noun מספד are used of the
rites of those who do not mourn the dead. The precise meaning of the verb ספד
has not been established. On this, see the discussion of J. Scharbert, 'ספד, sāpad',
TDOT 10: 300. It is possible that the verb means specifically 'to beat the breast'
in at least some contexts (e.g. Isa. 32: 12). It may be that 'to beat the breast' was
its original meaning, as has often been suggested. On this, see further Kutsch,
' "Trauerbräuche" und "Selbstminderungsriten" ', 91–2 (n. 16).

A second characteristic of biblical representations of mourning has led me to speak of the 'mourning' rites of petitioners and others who are unconnected to mourning the dead. It is the fact that the ritual behaviours of mourners for the dead and non-death-related mourners appear for the most part to be the same. In Ezra 9: 3, Ezra reacts to the news of the extent of the intermarriages that he opposes: 'When I heard this report, I tore my garment and my cloak. I tore out some of the hair of my head and my beard and sat down, devastated.' He also fasts as part of his penitential petition (Ezra 9: 5; 10: 6). In Neh. 1: 4, Nehemiah reacts to the sad news he has received on the state of affairs in Jerusalem by sitting, weeping, and fasting; these mourning gestures are accompanied by direct petition to the deity. A third example of non-death-related mourning behaviour is the ritual response of David's daughter Tamar to her rape by her half-brother Amnon: 'Tamar took ashes[53] (and put them) on her head, and the ornamented garment which she was wearing she tore. She set her hand upon her head and walked along, crying out as she walked' (2 Sam. 13: 19). A fourth example of mourning behaviour in a non-death-related context is the collective weeping of David and his men when they discover upon their return to their camp at Ziklag that their wives and children have been taken captive by the Amalekites (1 Sam. 30: 4). No one has died, yet David and his men, Tamar, Ezra, and Nehemiah engage in distinct and easily recognizable mourning behaviours in response to personal calamity, collective disaster, or bad news concerning the community.[54]

A third feature of biblical mourning rites has convinced me that it is most appropriate to refer to the ritual behaviour of petitioners and other ritual actors unconnected to mourning the dead as 'mourning': biblical texts themselves do not hesitate to compare non-death-related mourning rites to the behaviour of those who mourn the dead. For example, Joel 1: 8, addressing Judaeans who are in the midst of a devastating locust attack, commands wailing, a distinct mourning behaviour that the text compares directly to the same mourning behaviour of a widow with respect to her dead husband: 'Wail like a young woman

---

[53] Or dust. On the translation of אֵפֶר, see the discussion in Ch. 1, n. 8.

[54] On the hand on the head as a probable mourning gesture for the dead, see my discussion in Ch 1, n. 12.

girded in sackcloth over the husband of her youth' (אלי כבתולה חגרת שק על בעל נעוריה). Ps. 35: 13–14 is another useful example of a petitioner's ritual behaviour compared to that of a person mourning the dead. In this psalm of individual complaint, the petitioner describes his prayer and petitionary behaviour on behalf of his former friends when they were in trouble, comparing himself to someone mourning the dead: 'As for me, when they were sick, my clothes were sackcloth. I afflicted myself with fasting . . . I walked about like a person mourning (his) mother. I was bowed down low, a mourner' (ואני בחלותם לבושי שק עניתי בצום נפשי . . . התהלכתי כאבל אם קדר שחותי). Jer. 6: 26 is similar, in that it orders the people as a collectivity, who are represented by the figure of a young woman, to mourn like a mother who has lost her only son, after the people have heard the announcement of their impending doom:

> Daughter of my people, gird on sackcloth,
>   Roll in the dust.
> Make for yourself the mourning (אבל) of an only son,
> A bitter mourning (מספד תמרורים).
> For suddenly the destroyer will come upon you.

By comparing non-death-related mourning behaviour directly to the rites of mourning the dead, these three texts view such mourning as a phenomenon intimately linked to mourning the dead.[55]

There are two other aspects of biblical representations of mourning that suggest that the rites of petitioners and others who do not mourn the dead are most aptly described as rites of mourning. These are the non-death-related mourner's frequent expectation of comforters and the separation from rites of rejoicing characteristic of petitioners and others who embrace mourning behaviours but do not mourn the dead. Several texts suggest that petitioners, like mourners for the dead, could expect comforters—family, friends, allies—to join them during their period

---

[55] Extra-biblical texts also attest to this type of comparison. In the Bagohi letter of 407 BCE, Judaeans of Elephantine in Upper Egypt compare the mourning behaviour of their wives three years after the destruction of their temple to that of women mourning their dead husbands: 'Our wives are like widows' (Cowley 31; for the text in Aramaic, see B. Porten and A. Yardeni (eds. and trans.), *Textbook of Aramaic Documents from Ancient Egypt* (4 vols.; Jerusalem: Hebrew University, 1986), I. 72).

of mourning and petition (e.g. Ps. 69: 21 (Eng. 20))) and Ps. 35: 13–14 describes in some detail the supportive actions taken by a comforter for sick friends. A text such as Lam. 1: 2 suggests a role for comforters among those who mourn at the time of calamity. Because comforting the mourner is so central to representations of mourning the dead, it is striking to find the comforter role associated also with forms of non-death-related mourning, and another point in favour of understanding petition and other non-death-related ritual behaviour employing mourning rites as forms of mourning. The final characteristic of petitioning and other types of non-death-related mourning that suggests that such ritual behaviour ought to be described as 'mourning' is the separation, under normal circumstances, of the petitioner and others like him from rites of rejoicing. Though supplicants have access to the temple, in contrast to mourners for the dead who are polluted by corpse contact, like those mourning the dead, they abstain from all participation in rites of rejoicing until they have terminated the period of their petition.

These characteristics of biblical representations of mourning that I have just outlined suggest strongly that in both the rhetoric and the thought of the biblical writers, the rites of petitioners and others who are unconnected to mourning the dead are nonetheless understood as a type of mourning. Their ritual behaviour is characterized using the same vocabulary as that used to describe mourning the dead; the rites themselves are identical to those of death-related mourning; their acts are compared to those of mourners for the dead in several texts; they may expect comforters and they refrain from all rites of rejoicing, like those mourning the dead. Thus, I use the English term 'mourning' to refer to all ritual behaviour which biblical texts construct as mourning. I do this even though the English term is normally less broad in the range of its usage.[56] Here I depart from the practice of E. Kutsch, who argues for a restricted use of the term 'mourning' rather than the broad use that I advocate.[57] I use the

---

[56] Though even the English verb 'to mourn' and its derivatives occasionally have uses outside of death contexts. On this, see the examples in *The Compact Edition of the Oxford English Dictionary* (2 vols.; Oxford: Oxford University Press, 1971), 1: 1864.

[57] '"Trauerbräuche" und "Selbstminderungsriten"', 80–1, 92 (n. 24). Kutsch contends that the petitioner's rites should not be described or understood as mourning. For him, only mourning the dead and mourning disaster are

English term 'mourning' broadly because I believe that this usage best reflects the sense of the Hebrew and avoids imposing on it the notion that only mourning the dead is *really* mourning, an idea that is clearly alien to the biblical text and its usage. Only through a close, contextual textual analysis that avoids imposing ideas alien to the world of the text on the text can we develop a nuanced understanding of mourning as it is constructed in the literary remains of ancient Israel. Beginning with the biblical text's understanding of what constitutes mourning, we can proceed to investigate the relationship the text establishes between the various types of mourning.

There are further implications to the broad construction of mourning evidenced in the biblical text. The fact that petitionary mourning and other, non-death-related mourning behaviour is compared in several texts to mourning the dead is significant in yet another way, for the opposite is never attested. No text compares the rites of mourners for the dead to the rites of petitioners or others who have no direct connection to mourning the dead. This unidirectional mode of comparison suggests that mourning the dead and its attendant rites are somehow paradigmatic in the thought world of the biblical text. Petitionary mourning and similar non-death-related rites appear to be constructed as secondary analogues to mourning the dead, sharing its distinct vocabulary and ritual actions, and comparable to it in a number of ways. Mourning the dead is, in other words, the model for other types of mourning. Therefore, one can never completely dissociate other mourning types from mourning the dead, though death may have no direct and immediate association with such acts as petition of the deity or personal

properly mourning. These points constitute a part of his larger argument that rites employing what I am calling mourning behaviours are all rites of debasement (87–8, 90). Though Kutsch's argument that all such rites have debasement in common is correct in my view, his claim that mourning properly understood is restricted to mourning the dead and mourning at a time of disaster is poorly supported. Any successful attempt to dissociate petition from mourning, as Kutsch has attempted to do, will have to account for the shared constellation of practices, including comforting, that characterize both petition and mourning the dead. It will have to explain their common technical vocabulary (derivatives of both אבל and ספד), the shared pattern of avoiding rejoicing while mourning, and the comparisons made in the text between petition and mourning the dead. Yet Kutsch's paper does not provide any adequate explanation for these common characteristics, if it recognizes them at all.

humiliation in the aftermath of disaster. Exploring the indirect associations between mourning the dead and other types of mourning modelled on it and the implications of such associations will be a goal of this study. Using the English term 'mourning' to refer to the non-death-related ritual practices in question will help to keep their indirect death associations in mind.

Mourning activity as it is represented in biblical texts can be divided into four distinct types. First and foremost is mourning the dead, which is apparently understood to be the paradigmatic type of mourning by our texts. Many passages attest to such mourning behaviour (e.g. Gen. 37: 34–5; 2 Sam. 3: 31–7; Jer. 16: 5–7). The mourner, joined by 'comforters' (מנחמים; Job's friends are the best known example) who are family, friends, or allies, is ritually separated from the sanctuary and from quotidian life for a set period of time, usually seven days. A second type of mourning is that of penitents and other petitioners. Examples of penitential petition include the actions of Ezra and his support group in Ezra 9–10 and those of the whole Judaean community in Joel 1–2. Non-penitential petition is attested in 1 Samuel 1, the narrative of Hannah's prayer and vow; Ezra 8: 21–3, a brief narrative describing a fast to petition Yhwh for a safe journey from Babylon to Jerusalem; and 2 Chr. 20: 1–19, the narrative of King Jehoshaphat's communal fast during a time of military threat, among other texts. Both penitential and non-penitential petition narratives often include or allude to petitionary prayer, as in texts such as Neh. 1: 5–11; Joel 2: 17; Dan. 9: 4–19; 2 Kgs. 19: 15–19; and 2 Chr. 20: 6–12. Under the rubric of petitionary mourning I include many narratives that describe mourning behaviour that anticipates disaster or punishment, as these state or imply a petitionary purpose (e.g. 2 Sam. 12: 16–20; Esther 4: 16). I also classify passages that describe the use of mourning rites to acknowledge submission to or defeat by a more powerful party (2 Sam. 19: 25 (Eng. 24); 1 Kgs. 21: 27–9) as petitionary in intent, since the weaker party's actions communicate a desire for forgiveness and/or acceptance. Among petitionary texts I include narratives in which an individual seeks an oracle or vision from the deity (e.g. Judg. 20: 23, 26–8; Dan. 10: 2–3, 12), as these also incorporate an element of entreaty. In addition to petition narratives, psalms of communal and individual complaint incorporate petitionary elements, and will be included in my analysis of the phenomenon of petitionary mourning. A third type of mourning occurs at the time of a disaster, of either a communal or individual nature, and is not characterized by petitionary elements. Such non-petitionary mourning when calamity occurs is attested in texts such as 2 Sam. 13: 19, David's daughter Tamar's reaction to her rape, and Ezek. 27: 28–36, the envisioned mourning of Tyrians for their destroyed city. Haman's reaction to his public humiliation before Mordecai is a third example of such non-petitionary mourning associated with catastrophe (Esther 6: 12). Non-petitionary mourning at the time of a personal or communal disaster is distinct from all forms of petitionary mourning in that there is no apparent petitionary purpose to it. Rather, it seems intended to mark the calamity, serve as a way to express sorrow and horror, and, where relevant, affirm, renegotiate, or establish social bonds. The mourning of the person who is stricken with skin disease (צרעת) is the fourth discrete mourning type (Lev. 13: 45–6). This individual's mourning behaviour is tied directly to the presence of his disease, and is to be maintained for as long as the disease is present (as implied in v. 46). It is distinct from petitionary mourning in that it does not appear to have a petitionary purpose, and from mourning associated with calamity in that it is but a component of a constellation of behaviours that isolate the diseased person from all others. Thus, four distinct kinds of mourning can be identified in surviving texts, and each of these will be explored in this study.

Though these four mourning types are characterized by the same set of ritual behaviours and though the same special vocabulary is at times used to describe them, they may differ with respect to a number of other characteristics. The locus in which a mourning activity occurs and the extent to which particular mourning types are restricted spatially varies. For example, while mourning the dead probably occurred most frequently in a domestic setting and certainly never in a sanctuary locus, texts suggest that communal petitionary mourning characteristically occurred in a sanctuary setting and individual petition either in the home, in a sanctuary, or wherever the petitioner finds himself. The presence or absence of pollution is yet another point of contrast or similarity among mourning types. While the mourner for the dead is polluted by corpse contact or by being in the vicinity of a corpse and the person afflicted with skin disease is unclean due to his disease, others who utilize mourning rites are generally unpolluted,[58] and therefore, they have unimpeded access to the sanctuary (e.g. the petitioner). A third difference is the length of the period of mourning, which varies depending on the mourning type. The mourner for the dead is obligated to mourn part of a day, one day, seven days, or thirty days, depending on the text. In all cases, there is a set terminus beyond which such mourning may not continue. In contrast, no single, obligatory time frame is imposed on petitioners or others who utilize mourning rites. Some fasts last one to three days; some continue for several weeks. An individual petition may go on until the petitioner's entreaty has been answered, however long that might take. Finally, a fourth difference among mourning types is whether or not the mourning state is immediately or easily reversible. While the mourner for the dead is ritually separated from the sanctuary and polluted for a set period of time, petitioners or non-petitioners who are mourning a disaster such as the destruction of a sanctuary cease mourning at whatever point circumstances warrant it. Therefore, both petitioners and non-petitioners mourning because of a calamity are potentially in a position to abandon mourning and revert to rejoicing at any time, as a number of texts previously discussed illustrate (e.g. Jer. 31: 13; Ps. 30: 6b, 12 (Eng. 5b, 11)). In contrast to the mourner for the dead, the petitioner and the non-petitioner mourning at the time of personal or corporate disaster and loss, the individual afflicted with skin disease mourns as long as his disease is present and he is unclean. Potentially, his mourning could last for the rest of his life, for one of its functions is to isolate him physically and socially from others unaffected by skin disease.

---

[58] On the penitent defiled by sin (e.g. Ps. 51: 4 (Eng. 2)), see my discussion in Ch. 2, nn. 3–4. Num. 5: 11–31 suggests that such defilement does not result in exclusion from the sanctuary.

I

Mourning the Dead

Mourning the dead is but one dimension of a larger complex of death-related practices evidenced in biblical sources and in epigraphic and other archaeological materials. Though we know little of the details of Israelite funerals, depending as we do on the rare, passing description in biblical passages[1], we are fortunate that mourning rites are richly represented in biblical texts, and relevant comparative data also survive in other West Asian sources.[2] In addition to mourning, we now know much more about Judaean burial practices from archaeological excavation and data analysis, and our knowledge of ancestor cults in Israel,

---

[1] The best description of a funeral, as many have noted, is the narrative of Abner's interment in 2 Sam. 3: 31–7. Though we possess no richer representation, this passage nonetheless provides little in the way of detail. Features of the funeral mentioned in 2 Sam. 3: 31–7 include public mourning rites such as weeping and lamentation, mourners following the bier in some kind of funeral procession, burial, and fasting until evening. See further the comments of Lewis, who compares the description of Abner's funeral to that of the funeral of Asa in 2 Chr. 16: 14 ('How Far Can Texts Take Us?', 178–9) and Bloch-Smith, *Judahite Burial Practices*, 148, who reconstructs the 8th-cent. BCE Judaean funeral on the basis of both textual and archaeological evidence.

[2] See e.g. the fragmentary description of the burial of the Babylonian king Nabonidus' mother and the mourning that follows (C. J. Gadd, 'The Harran Inscriptions of Nabonidus', *Anatolian Studies*, 8 (1958), 50, 52, with a translation on 51 and 53; Anderson, *A Time to Mourn*, 77 cites this example and Gadd's article). Also useful is the detailed description of El's and Anat's mourning for Baal (*CAT* 1.5 VI 11–25; 1.5 VI 31–1.6 I 8, translated and discussed by Anderson, op. cit. 60–9 and many others). Danil's mourning for Aqhat is yet another interesting Ugaritic text, mentioning the presence of lamenting women (mšspdt) and weeping women (bkyt) during the mourning period at court (*CAT* 1.19 IV 7–25). Finally, the Ahiram sarcophagus from Byblos portrays mourners (*ANEP* 459). These are but a few examples of materials from the larger West Asian cultural sphere that represent mourning practices.

limited as it is, has been enhanced by more careful recent analysis of biblical texts, West Asian inscriptions, and material evidence from tombs.[3] Ideas about the afterlife are well attested in the Hebrew Bible and in comparative West Asian materials, and Judaean burials also provide testimony to beliefs about post-mortem existence.[4] Thus, though a thorough understanding of the larger complex of Israelite death-related beliefs and practices still eludes scholars, a coherent picture of some aspects of Israelite death ways is within reach, particularly with respect to the textual representation of mourning, since mourning rites are relatively well-evidenced in surviving texts. Unhappily, archaeological data have little to contribute to an effort to recon-struct mourning behaviours, in contrast to their importance with respect to understanding burial practices or beliefs about the afterlife. This is due to the nature of mourning, which leaves behind few material traces, in contrast to an activity such as interment, for which a rich array of evidence survives, from tomb architecture to the treatment of bones to grave goods.

THE MOURNER'S DISTINCT RITUAL BEHAVIOUR

We learn of the rites of mourners from countless biblical passages. Typically, a text might mention one or several of the many attested mourning rites, probably with the intent to suggest a larger combination of practices.[5] For example, in Gen. 37: 34, Jacob is said to tear his garment and don sackcloth when he mourns for his son Joseph. In Deut. 34: 8, the mourning of the people for Moses is characterized by weeping, without mention of any other particular rite. In 2 Sam. 14: 2, the wise woman of

[3] On Judaean burial practices and on ancestor cults, see the works cited in the Introduction, n. 2.

[4] On the afterlife, see the works cited in n. 2 in the Introduction. On grave goods as a class of evidence bearing witness to beliefs about the afterlife, see Bloch-Smith, *Judahite Burial Practices*, 72–108, 140–4, 148.

[5] In other words, the mention of one or two behaviours may well be intended to function as a synecdoche. What combination of practices was usual is of course beyond our ability to know, and what was typical ritual behaviour in one locus or chronological context might not have been so in another place or time. Nonetheless, textual representations of mourning suggest that some combina-tion of tearing the garment, weeping, and one or two other practices was the norm.

Tekoa is ordered by David's general Joab to feign mourning as follows: 'Wear garments of mourning and do not anoint with oil.' On occasion, texts provide a more extensive description of the rites of the mourner. One example is 2 Sam. 1: 11–12, in which David and his men mourn for Saul, Jonathan, and the other Israelites killed at Mt. Gilboa: they tear their garments, weep, fast, and perhaps, lament.[6] Taken together, biblical texts attest to a large number of mourning behaviours. Mourners may tear their garments, put on sackcloth, weep, wail,[7] toss ashes or dust on their heads, roll in ashes or dust,[8] and sit or lie on the ground. They may fast, groan or sigh, move their bodies back and forth (נוד), utter dirges or mourning cries,[9] avoid anointing with oil, lacerate themselves, and manipulate head and beard hair by means of shaving or depilation.[10] Mourners have contact

---

[6] On this possible meaning of the verb ספד, see the discussion in n. 52 in the Introduction.

[7] See Joel 1: 8 for wailing (אלה) as a characteristic behaviour of those who mourn the dead (אלי כבתולה חגרת שק על בעל נעוריה). The evidence is indirect, since the text commands wailing in a context of petitionary mourning, but it compares the petitioner's wailing to that of a young woman mourning her dead husband. Though the verb ילל, 'to wail', is attested only in texts describing non-death-related mourning, the evidence of Joel 1: 8 suggests that wailing of some kind (described by the verb אלה) was not unrelated to mourning the dead. Thus, I must reject the hypothesis of A. Baumann that wailing was an activity characteristic not of mourning the dead, but of collective rites in response to disaster ('ילל yll', *TDOT* 6: 83–4).

[8] Jer. 6: 26 implies that rolling in ashes or dust (אפר) is part of mourning for an only son. On the scholarly debate about the meaning of אפר, see L. Wächter, 'עפר 'āpār', *TDOT* 11: 258 as well as A. F. Rainey, 'Dust and Ashes', *Tel Aviv*, 1 (1974), 77–83.

[9] On the funeral dirge as a distinct literary form, see the influential study of H. Jahnow, *Das hebräischen Leichenlied im Rahmen der Völkerdichtung* (BZAW 36; Giessen: Töpelmann, 1923), and more recently, the discussion of C. Westermann, *Die Klagelieder: Forschungsgeschichte und Auslegung* (Neukirchen-Vluyn: Neukirchener, 1990), 15–20. The preeminent biblical example is 2 Sam. 1: 19–27. On the mourning cry הוי, see 1 Kgs. 13: 30; Jer. 22: 18; 34: 5 and the treatment of W. Janzen, *Mourning Cry and Woe Oracle* (BZAW 125; Berlin: de Gruyter, 1972).

[10] Though some scholars have argued that observing a period of silence is also a behavioural component of mourning, this is doubtful. Recent advocates of a period of silence include Pham, *Mourning*, 29–31, who cites the older work of N. Lohfink, 'Enthielten die im Alten Testament bezeugten Klageriten eine Phase des Schweigens?', *VT* 12 (1962), 260–77. See also Feldman, *Defilement and Mourning*, 97–9 and Lipinski, *La Liturgie pénitentielle*, 32–5. Against this

with the corpse and become polluted thereby. They may walk barefoot, strike the thigh, allow their hair to hang loose and uncovered, avoid washing themselves or their garments, abstain from sexual relations, cover or avoid grooming the moustache or face, and eat foods associated with mourning.[11] Partial or total nudity, the covering of the head, and the laying of the hand on the head were very likely also Israelite mourning practices.[12] Non-Israelite sources from West Asia confirm the widespread utilization of rites such as these outside of Israel.[13]

position, see B. A. Levine, 'Silence, Sound, and the Phenomenology of Mourning in Biblical Israel', *JANES* 22 (1993), 95–6.

[11] Obviously, some of these behaviours are contradictory: one cannot fast and eat a mourning meal at the same time. Therefore, it is likely that evidence for contradictory mourning behaviours reflects the practices of different communities. For fasting as a mourning rite, see e.g. 2 Sam. 1: 12; 3: 35; for the mourner eating mourning foods and drinking drinks, see Ezek. 24: 17, 22 (לחם אנשים?); Jer. 16: 7 (reading *לחם from LXX αρτος); and Job 42: 11.

[12] These rites are attested in biblical texts describing the ritual behaviour of non-death-related mourners and in non-Israelite West Asian materials describing the practices of mourners for the dead. Mic. 1: 8 attests to nudity utilized as a mourning rite in combination with lamentation, wailing, and walking barefoot at the announcement of future catastrophe. In 2 Sam. 15: 30 and Esther 6: 12, the covering of the head functions as a mourning behaviour at a time of personal or corporate disaster and humiliation. In 2 Sam. 15: 30, it is combined with weeping and walking barefoot. 2 Sam. 13: 19 evidences the hand on head as a mourning gesture used along with ashes or dust on the head, the tearing of the garment, and crying out, at a time of personal calamity. Comparative West Asian and Egyptian materials attest to the employment of such mourning behaviours in the context of death. For example, the Ahiram sarcophagus from Byblos (*ANEP* 459) portrays four mourning women with exposed breasts, two of whom place their hands on their heads. Compare the Egyptian scenes of mourning in *ANEP* 634 and 638.

[13] See e.g. the description of the mourning for Nabonidus' mother cited in n. 2. In that text, the mourners apparently allow their hair to grow, weep, abstain from washing, fast, and avoid anointing. They may also lacerate themselves. Because the text is fragmentary, we cannot be certain about the extent of the mourning practices mentioned in it. In the mythological 'Descent of Ishtar to the Netherworld', the heavenly vizier Papsukkal's mourning is described: he dons special mourning garments, weeps, hangs his head, and allows his hair to hang loose (R. Borger, *Babylonisch-assyrische Lesestücke* (Rome: Pontifical Biblical Institute, 1963), 2: 90 for transliteration of the Nineveh Recension; for a convenient translation, see B. R. Foster, *Before the Muses* (2 vols.; Bethesda, Md.: CDL Press, 1993), 1: 407). The richest text for comparison from Ugarit is the description of El's and Anat's mourning in *CAT* 1.5 VI 11–25 and 1.5 VI 31–1.6 I 8. Mourning behaviour here includes descent to the ground, dirt on the

What do these behaviours have in common and how do they function? As has often been noted, some mourning practices are apparently intended to cause discomfort and even pain in the mourner (e.g. the wearing of sackcloth, fasting, depilation, sitting or lying on the ground, walking barefoot, and laceration). Some seem in the main to reverse what biblical texts represent as normal, quotidian grooming behaviours such as anointing, washing, laundering clothes, or binding the hair (e.g. abstention from anointing, ashes or dirt on the head, donning dirty clothes, allowing the hair to hang unbound). Some may have a symbolic significance not easily recoverable (e.g. the tearing of the garment or the covering of the moustache). Finally, some mourning behaviours such as weeping, wailing, groaning, and sighing are intended to display emotional pain. Rites that cause discomfort or pain may have the effect of calling forth a ritually appropriate response to death that may not otherwise become manifest. In other words, one apparent function of mourning rites is to elicit contextually required expressions of grief whether or not the individual is otherwise inclined to express them. Expressions of grief may manifest themselves without external stimulus, or they may be evoked as necessary. Witnessing mourning behaviours such as weeping and lamentation in others may have an effect similar to experiencing painful mourning rites, as Jer. 9: 17 (Eng. 18) suggests.[14] Nothing, however, guarantees that rites intended to elicit a ritual response constructed as appropriate to a death context will be successful in their object.[15] Reversals of day-to-day behaviours, like other mourning rites, function to separate mourners from the rest of society by giving them a distinct appearance, which helps to establish a discrete ritual space for mourning apart both from the

head, donning of sackcloth, laceration, and lamentation. On mourning in Mesopotamian mythological and epic sources, see further B. Alster, 'The Mythology of Mourning', *Acta Sumerologica*, 5 (1983), 1–16. My thanks to Benjamin Foster for providing this reference.

[14] The text speaks of professional mourners summoned at a time of disaster: 'Let them hasten, and let them lift up over us a lament, that our eyes might run with tears, and our eyelids gush water' (ותמהרנה ותשנה עלינו נהי ותרדנה עינינו דמעה) (ועפעפינו יזלו מים).

[15] The relationship between ritual and the emotions has long been of interest to social anthropologists, and has recently received renewed attention from scholars in Religious Studies. See my discussion in the Introduction.

lives of non-mourners and from the rejoicing rites of the temple. Where others bind up hair, mourners allow it to hang loose or shave it; where others anoint the head, mourners abstain from anointing. As a result of a series of distinct ritual actions, mourners, for the period of their mourning, are ritually separated from the larger society. As I discussed in the Introduction, it has been argued convincingly that mourning rites as a series stand in opposition to rites of rejoicing. Thus, mourning practices function to separate the individual mourner or the group from the sanctuary's rejoicing rites. Mourning behaviours with symbolic significance are more difficult to analyse, for it is not always very clear what is being communicated. Tearing the garment may suggest the physical separation of the dead from the living or perhaps the pain of loss suffered by the mourner (cf. Joel 2: 13), among other possibilities.[16] Covering the moustache, face, or head must have some symbolic significance, but these gestures remain obscure to us. In any case, the distinct nature of rites such as tearing clothing contributes to the mourner's ritual separation from day-to-day life and society. The function of actions such as weeping and lamentation appear, at least on one level, to be simple to understand: they may express the pain of loss, as several biblical texts indicate, or create such expression in those not otherwise inclined to feel it.[17] Yet they do much more: they, too, create a distinct ritual state—mourning—and a discrete population that inhabits that state—mourners and those associated with them. In addition to constituting mourners as ritual actors and the distinct ritual state of mourning itself, all of these actions also have the potential to shape social ties, as I shall discuss at the end of this chapter.

[16] H. Z. Hirschberg has argued that tearing the garment may hark back to an older mourning practice of baring the breast. To support this argument, he cites Egyptian reliefs and the images of mourning women on the Ahiram sarcophagus ('אבל', *EM* 1: 43). The point, though interesting, remains a speculation.

[17] Gen. 37: 35 describes Jacob's refusal to stop mourning for Joseph on account of his bitterness. 2 Sam. 19: 1, 5 (Eng. 18: 33; 19: 4), narrate David's inability *not* to mourn his son Absalom, though such mourning is ritually inappropriate in the context of his army's victory. The common expressions 'mourning' or 'lamentation' 'over an only son' (מספד על היחיד, אבל יחיד) are used by biblical texts to describe particularly bitter mourning (e.g. Jer. 6: 26; Amos 8: 10; Zech. 12: 10). See also the expressions מספד תמרורים (Jer. 6: 26) and מספד מר (Ezek. 27: 31).

Do all of these mourning rites share any other characteristic or function in common? Aside from separating the mourner ritually and contributing to the shaping of social relationships, mourning rites also debase the mourner and communicate that debasement, as E. Kutsch has asserted.[18] The notion of biblical mourning rites functioning to debase the mourner finds support in several quarters. Mourning in non-death-related contexts is not infrequently associated with the expression of shame (e.g. 2 Sam. 13: 13, 19; 19: 3–4 (Eng. 2–3); Jer. 9: 18 (Eng. 19); Ezek. 7: 18), suggesting that mourning practices are constructed as self-debasing. Penitents who embrace mourning rites are often said to have humbled themselves by so doing (e.g. 1 Kgs. 21: 27, 29; 2 Kgs. 22: 19; Ps. 38: 7 (Eng. 6)).[19] Non-penitential petitionary mourning practices are characterized in several contexts as rites of self-affliction (e.g. Dan. 10: 12; cf. v. 2) or debasement (Ps. 35: 14; 44: 26 (Eng. 25)).[20] In addition, nudity, probably a mourning rite for those mourning the dead as well as for petitioners, has virtually ubiquitous debasement associations in biblical and other West Asian materials (e.g. Deut. 28: 48; Isa. 20: 4; Amos 2: 16). Finally, the dead in the underworld are portrayed as diminished beings in a number of texts (e.g. Ps. 88: 6, 11–13 (Eng. 5, 10–12)), and if mourners practise a form of identification with the dead, as some scholars have asserted, then mourners, too, debase themselves in order to realize this identification. I shall have more to say about this.[21]

---

[18] ' "Trauerbräuche" und "Selbstminderungsriten" ', 87–8, 90. Kutsch claims that all such practices are 'rites of debasement' ('Minderungsriten'), but provides little argument for his case. My use of the term 'debasement' in this discussion is strictly culture specific: that which biblical texts construct as debasing. Thus, I make no universalizing or essentializing assumptions about which ritual actions are or are not debasing. Aside from Kutsch, others have noted the debasement of the mourner (e.g. Feldman, *Defilement and Mourning*, 94–6).

[19] The verbs used in these passages are שׁחח ('to be low') and the Niphal of כנע ('to humble oneself').

[20] On the verb שׁחח ('to be low') and its debasement associations, see Ch. 2, n. 35.

[21] For a compact review of older scholarly interpretations of the function and significance of mourning rites, see K. Spronk, *Beatific Afterlife in Ancient Israel and in the Ancient Near East* (AOAT 219; Neukirchen-Vluyn: Neukirchener; Kevelaer: Butzon & Bercker, 1986), 33–5.

THE MOURNER'S SEPARATION FROM SOCIETY AND THE CULT

All mourning behaviours function to separate the mourner ritually from society and the cult. In cases where a group or a whole society mourns, the mourning behaviours separate the group from society or society from its routine ritual state (rejoicing). In this section of the chapter, I will explore several aspects of mourning, aside from debasing rites such as weeping and tearing garments, in which the mourner's distinct ritual separation from quotidian life and society is realized and signalled. Four characteristics of mourning will be of interest: the length of the mourning period, the locus of mourning, the mourner's impurity, and the reversibility of mourning.

Texts bear witness to mourning periods lasting less than one day, one day, seven days, and thirty days. The mourning of David and his men for Saul, Jonathan, and the others slain on Mt. Gilboa lasts until evening of the day on which the news was received (2 Sam. 1: 12). Similarly, the mourning of David for Abner lasts until sunset of the day of Abner's funeral, though the text suggests that the rest of David's army had ceased mourning before the day was over (2 Sam. 3: 35). Seven days is the most widely attested mourning period, as many texts indicate (e.g. Gen. 50: 10; 1 Sam. 31: 13; Sir. 22: 12). Some passages speak of a thirty-day mourning period (Num. 20: 29; Deut. 34: 8; cf. 21: 13). Though later Jewish tradition would, to some extent, attempt to harmonize these differences in textual representations of the length of the mourning period, in their original context, they may reflect the practices of different communities in different time periods. [22] Alternatively, the length of mourning may have had some connection to the nature of the mourner's relationship with the deceased (minimal relationship, minimal mourning period) or the status of the deceased (high status, longer period of mourning).[23] In any case, each attested

---

[22] For the rabbinic construction of an initial seven-day mourning period as a component of a fuller thirty-day mourning period, see Feldman, *Defilement and Mourning*, 79–88, who cites relevant texts such as Semahot 7: 8, 9; 10: 12; and b. Moed Q 19b, 23a.

[23] The mourning period of thirty days for Moses and for Aaron may have

Mourning the Dead

mourning period constitutes a discrete duration of time with a definite beginning and end set aside for mourning. Once the time period has elapsed, mourning must end, and the mourners must return to the rhythms and practices of quotidian life. Not surprisingly, texts bear witness to the refusal of some mourners to end the mourning period. In Gen. 37: 35, Jacob, in great pain, refuses to stop mourning for his son Joseph even after many days and even when his other children attempt to force him to stop. In the epic of Gilgamesh, the hero takes mourning to an extreme, replacing day-to-day life with an ongoing state of mourning and isolating himself entirely from society. But these are exceptions in our texts, and such behaviour receives no approbation. The limits placed on the time period of mourning require explanation, though here we are forced to speculate to some extent, given the limited nature of surviving evidence. At a minimum, one can say that the distinct, limited mourning period seems intended to allow for the accomplishment of the things the mourning period must accomplish. Specifically, a limited mourning period might well have been intended to create a controlled and, therefore, socially acceptable context for the expression of grief, if indeed there is grief; a number of texts in fact bear witness to a concern to limit grief to the mourning period (e.g. Sir. 38: 16–23). Another evident purpose of the mourning period is to allow for the concentrated re-negotiation of social roles among survivors. Finally, mourning allows mourners to honour the dead and identify with them. Once accomplished, mourning ceases, and mourners return to quotidian life. I shall take up these themes in more detail further on.

The locus of mourning and the extent to which mourning was spatially limited are difficult to pinpoint precisely but some generalizations are possible. Texts suggest that the mourning of an individual or small group could occur in a single dwelling, possibly the place where the dead person expired. However, it remains unclear whether the locus of the death had a special significance for mourning. Although Num. 19: 14–15 takes up the issue of pollution communicated by a corpse inside a domicile, it suggests nothing whatsoever about whether the place of

some relationship to their high status. On the relationship of status to the length of the mourning period in Mesopotamian sources, see J. Scurlock, 'Death and the Afterlife in Ancient Mesopotamian Thought', *CANE* 3: 1885.

death is the locus of mourning, or whether the corpse might be moved to a different mourning place. The expression 'house of mourning' (בית אבל; Eccles. 7: 2) and 'house of marzeah' (בית מרזח; Jer. 16: 5) are both used of the place of mourning.[24] The mourning of an individual may also occur in a semi-public place such as the upper part of the city gate according to 2 Sam. 19: 1–2 (Eng. 18: 33–19: 1), which describes David's grief over the death of his son Absalom. Job's mourning appears to take place out of doors in a heap of ashes or dirt (Job 2: 8). The mourning of an individual may also occur in a tent on the roof of a house according to Judith 8: 4–5. Another text speaks of corporate mourning by order of King David throughout the city of Hebron (and the Judaean kingdom?) for the slain Abner (2 Sam. 3: 31–7). Though it seems that mourners could be found in many possible loci, the sanctuary and all other sanctified places are clearly out of bounds to those who mourn the dead, since mourners are typically polluted as a result of corpse impurity.[25] That the mourner who has been polluted by a corpse could communicate impurity by means of physical contact (e.g. Num. 19: 22) may have acted to restrict his spatial range further, though this remains unclear. At all events, the mourner's spatial range is limited to the tomb, the house of mourning, and other loci in which his pollution will not be an issue.

According to Numbers 19, physical contact with a corpse, or proximity to a corpse within a structure such as a tent, renders persons unclean for seven days, and therefore unfit to enter sanctified places such as the temple and unable to participate in any rites requiring an unpolluted state.[26] Numbers 19 describes

[24] The ritual actions described of those who enter the בית מרזח suggest a mourning context. The verbs קרח, גדד, נוד, ספד are all used, and the text also speaks of אבל, comforting, and what appears to be food and drink associated with mourning. On this, see further Lewis, *Cults of the Dead*, 89, 137–9.

[25] Among sanctified loci that must remain free of pollution is the war camp according to certain sources. Num. 5: 3 (H) suggests that the required expulsion of persons who have had contact with a corpse—along with two other classes of polluted individuals—is the result of the presence of Yhwh dwelling in the camp and, by implication, the camp's sanctified status. Cf. Num. 12: 14 and 31: 19–24 for similar restrictions on access to the camp as a whole.

[26] On corpse contamination within an enclosed space, see B. A. Levine, *Numbers 1–20* (AB 4; New York: Doubleday, 1993), 466–7. Physical contact with human bones, tombs, and corpses on the open field have the same effect according to Num. 19: 16, as does killing a person according to Num. 31: 19.

elaborate rites of purification that are required of the corpse-
contaminated individual in order to become clean: 'They shall
take for the unclean person some of the dust of the burned
purification offering, and shall set with it living water in a vessel.
A clean man shall take hyssop, dip it into the water, and sprinkle
it . . . upon the unclean person on the third day and on the seventh
day. He shall purify him on the seventh day, and he (in turn) shall
wash his garments and bathe in water, and in the evening, he
shall be clean' (19: 17–19). Along with the impurity of skin
disease (צרעת), pollution from corpse contact requires the most
elaborate purification procedures according to priestly purity
legislation (P and H).[27] Lev. 21: 1–4, a text that limits the mourning possibilities of priests to close relatives alone, makes it clear
that physical contact with the corpse, or at least proximity to the
corpse leading to pollution, was typical for the mourner and
possibly others who join the mourner. A priest 'shall not pollute
himself for a dead person among his relations, except for his next
of kin, who are closest to him: his mother, his father, his son, his
daughter, and his brother. And for his virgin sister who is closest
to him, who has no husband, he may pollute himself.' Ezek. 44:
25–7, another text that speaks of the limitations of priestly corpse
contact, adds an extra week of waiting before the priest who has
become clean may re-enter the temple and take up his cultic
duties. It also requires him to bring a purification offering (חטאת)
to the sanctuary when he resumes his responsibilities. Each of
these texts underscores the serious threat to the sanctuary and
other holy space posed by corpse contamination through their
descriptions of elaborate purification rites (Num. 19: 17–19;
Ezek. 44: 26–7) and the severe limitations on priestly mourning
(Lev. 21: 1–4; Ezek. 44: 25). By implication, texts such as Num.
19: 14 suggest that all who join the mourner in an enclosed space
with the corpse present become polluted as well. Lev. 21: 1–4
hints, through its mention of the potential that one may pollute

---

[27] Numbers 19 is made up of both Priestly and Holiness materials. The
description of the purification rites in vv. 17–19 is to be assigned to the Priestly
Writing; the brief mention of purification requirements in v. 12 belongs to the
Holiness Source. On the division of Numbers 19 into sources, see I. Knohl, *The
Sanctuary of Silence: The Priestly Torah and the Holiness School* (trans. J.
Feldman and P. Rodman; Minneapolis: Fortress Press, 1995), 93–4. On purifi-
cation from skin disease (צרעת), see Lev. 14: 1–32.

oneself for other than immediate relations, that it might not have been unusual for non-priests who are not immediate family to have become polluted by joining the mourner. The pollution of corpse contact or proximity, more than any other characteristic, functioned to separate temporarily mourners, and probably others who joined them during the mourning period, from the rest of the community.

The easy reversibility of most mourning behaviours is sharply contrasted with the difficulty of reversing corpse impurity.[28] While the torn garment may be exchanged easily for non-mourning clothes and loose hair quickly bound up, Numbers 19 suggests that corpse impurity would prevent the mourner from easily reverting to the ritual state of rejoicing. Polluted for seven days, the mourner must wait until the set time period of impurity has elapsed, while undergoing an elaborate and extended ritual process of purification. That the seven-day period of corpse impurity coincides with the seven-day mourning period is hardly surprising, since such pollution contributes to the realization and communication of the mourner's ritual separation. To explain the potential asymmetry between the less common, briefer mourning period of one day and the tradition of seven days of pollution from corpse contact or proximity is difficult. It is possible that corpse impurity in some purity constructions lasted no more than one day, thus coinciding with the one-day mourning period, but this must remain uncertain, given the extant evidence which, though limited, bears witness only to seven-day corpse contamination.

THE MOURNER'S RELATIONSHIP TO THE DEAD

The relationship of the mourner to the dead has elicited quite a bit of attention not only among social anthropologists but also among biblical scholars and specialists treating mourning in ancient West Asian cultures apart from Israel. Among specialists in Israelite and West Asian materials, a number have argued that mourners identify themselves in some manner with the dead.[29]

[28] Shaving and laceration are also mourning rites that are not easily reversed. On these, see my discussion in Ch. 4.

[29] This is not a recent idea among anthropologists. For example, Hertz spoke

Feldman has asserted that mourning law 'has the effect of making the mourner behave as if he himself were dead'. He further claims that the mourner shares no 'community' with others during his mourning, and no 'commonality' with the living. His character as a living person is, according to Feldman, 'suspended'.[30] Thus, in Feldman's view, the mourner's identification with the dead has profound social ramifications in addition to any ritual implications it may have. B. A. Levine and J.-M. de Tarragon argue that the mourner shares an 'intense personal identification with the dead, which evokes the desire to join them in the netherworld'.[31] Anderson speaks of the mourner's behaviour as 'an explicit identification with the plight of the dead' and emphasizes the importance of this identification for his study.[32] Brian Schmidt asserts that mourning rites 'represent . . . in some sense, a convergence of the living's identity with that of the dead', singling out laceration and tonsure as especially powerful agents of identification.[33] Though these scholars and others[34] have spoken of the mourner's identification with the dead, the nature of this identification, often emphasized, has usually not been explained in a clear and cogent manner, and its social significance requires a more careful assessment than it has received up to now.

It seems legitimate to assert that mourners portrayed in biblical and other West Asian texts express identification with the dead through their behaviour. Anderson has argued that

nearly a century ago of such a 'solidarity' between mourner and the dead ('Contribution à une étude sur la représentation collective de la mort', 82).

[30] *Defilement and Mourning*, 93.

[31] 'Dead Kings and Rephaim: The Patrons of the Ugaritic Dynasty', *JAOS* 104 (1984), 658.

[32] *A Time to Mourn*, 69 for this quotation. See 82 for the importance of this conclusion to Anderson's investigation. On 82, Anderson describes the identification of the mourner with the dead differently, leaving out the dead's 'plight': 'The state of mourning itself is closely associated with an identification with the dead.' On 84, Anderson speaks of 'ritual and emotional identification'. On 108, the mourner is said to identify 'for a time' with the dead, and Feldman's study of the identification of the mourner with the dead is cited with approbation (n. 30, 108). I assume that with the mention of 'emotional identification', Anderson again refers to identification with the 'plight' of the dead.

[33] *Israel's Beneficent Dead*, 177–8.

[34] e.g. Spronk, *Beatific Afterlife*, 245–6; Podella, *Šôm-Fasten*, 273.

mourners apparently take on the same physical appearance as the dead. This is suggested by texts such as the epic of Gilgamesh, which describes actions to be avoided by Enkidu so that he will blend in with the dead when he descends alive to the underworld. As Anderson notes, many of these actions that Enkidu is to eschew are precisely those avoided by the mourner (e.g. anointing, the wearing of sandals, engagement in sexual relations). Thus, Gilgamesh is advising Enkidu to take on the appearance of a mourner when he descends to the underworld.[35] Though biblical texts do not make an explicit connection between the appearance of the mourner and the appearance of the dead, it seems very likely that the same correspondence applies, as Anderson suggests. Aside from taking on the appearance of the dead, there is also evidence that mourners imitate the movement of the dead to the underworld by means of a ritual descent of their own to the ground. As a number of scholars have pointed out, El's descent from his throne in the Ugaritic Baal Cycle, followed by easily recognizable mourning rites, reaches a climax with his lament over Baal and this confession: '(To) the place of Baal, I am descending to the underworld.'[36] This notion of ritual movement to the underworld by means of descent to the ground is closely paralleled, as scholars have noted, by the

---

[35] *A Time to Mourn*, 75–6. For the text, Gilgamesh xii 13–27, transliterated, see S. Parpola, *The Standard Babylonian Epic of Gilgamesh* (State Archives of Assyria Cuneiform Texts 1; Helsinki: The Neo-Assyrian Text Corpus Project, 1997), 115. Line 27 characterizes the underworld as a place of lamentation (tazzimtu). Other Mesopotamian texts associate mourning behaviours with the underworld. On this, see above, n. 13. At the turn of the last century, A. J. Wensinck had already argued that mourners 'imitate the dead and take on the appearance of the dead', though his explanation for why they do so—protection from an allegedly dangerous spirit—would find few supporters today. For Wensinck's views and for the quotation from his work, see Spronk, *Beatific Afterlife*, 245.

[36] *CAT* 1.5 VI 24–5. See, among others, Levine and de Tarragon, 'Dead Kings and Rephaim', 656–8 and Anderson, *A Time to Mourn*, 63. The above is my translation of the Ugaritic aṯr b'l ard barṣ. Anderson renders, 'I am descending to the underworld, after Baal.' His rendering is similar to that of others, such as Levine and de Tarragon, op. cit. 657. The difference in translation is based on varying interpretations of the word aṯr, which I take as a noun, 'place', and Anderson and Levine and de Tarragon understand as a preposition, 'after'. Either reading is possible in the context. At all events, El's statement that he is descending to the underworld is without difficulty.

Ugaritic ritual text *CAT* 1.161.[37] This text, apparently a funeral liturgy for the dead king Niqmaddu III of Ugarit, includes the order (to Niqmaddu's successor?), 'Descend to the underworld, be low in the dust' (arṣ rd wšpl ʿpr).[38] These passages shed light on the many biblical texts that speak of the ritual movement of mourners to the ground, where they sit, lie, or roll in dust or ashes. They may also be paralleled by Jacob's words in Gen. 37: 35: 'But I will descend to my son, to Sheol, (in) mourning' (כי ארד אל בני אבל שאלה). Although many scholars have seen this statement as a refusal of Jacob to stop mourning until he himself dies, I believe that it is possible to see in it a refusal by Jacob to stop mourning at the time that his children wish him to stop. He refuses because he wants to prolong his ritual identification with the son whom he believes is dead, which is accomplished through sitting on the ground.[39]

What is the nature of this identification between the mourner and the dead and what is it intended to accomplish? Feldman argues that the mourner's behaviour is like that of the dead, but offers no explanation of why this should be the case. Schmidt refers to a 'convergence' of identities between the mourner and the dead 'in some sense', even referring to this identification as 'unparalleled', but he does not clearly explain exactly in what sense or why this should be so. Levine and de Tarragon speak of an 'intense personal identification with the dead' which motivates the mourner to join the dead in the underworld, but do not

[37] On this, see esp. Levine and de Tarragon, 'Dead Kings and Rephaim', 657–8.

[38] On the identity of the individual or item ordered to descend, see Lewis's summary and evaluation of scholarly views in *Cults of the Dead*, 40–4. Levine and de Tarragon believe that the officiating priest is ordered to descend ritually, and perhaps the king and congregation as well ('Dead Kings and Rephaim', 649).

[39] The text implies that Jacob is seated on the ground when it mentions that 'all his sons and daughters stood up to comfort him'. Cf. the similar usage in 2 Sam. 12: 17, where the elders of David's palace 'stood over him to raise him up from the ground' when they attempt to force him to end his petitionary mourning for his dying child. Those who understand Jacob's words to mean that he will mourn until he dies include Anderson, *A Time to Mourn*, 87; Pham, *Mourning*, 33; C. Westermann, *Genesis* (BKAT 1; Neukirchen-Vluyn: Neukirchener, 1982), 36. But see Lewis, *Cults of the Dead*, 43, for an interpretation similar to mine. Note also Lewis's discussion of the meaning of ארץ in 2 Sam. 12: 16 and Ps. 44: 26 (Eng. 25; ibid. 43–4).

otherwise explain the nature of this identification. Anderson identifies an 'explicit identification with the plight of the dead' on the part of the mourner, though he does not clarify what he means by this. Does he imply that pity for the dead now resident in the underworld motivates these acts of identification? Is this also Levine and de Tarragon's notion of what underlies the mourner's evident identification? Certainly there is a strong textual tradition that the plight of the dead was not to be envied by the living (e.g. Isa. 38: 11, 18–19; Ps. 88: 6, 11–13 (Eng. 5, 10–12); Sir. 22: 11). But does pity explain what appears to be the central thrust of the act of mourning?

No matter what the cultural context, death disrupts the social relationships that existed among the dead and the survivors, and these must be reworked.[40] The socially sanctioned and normative temporary separation of mourners from quotidian social life followed by their aggregation allows mourners and others to recast their social world as one without the dead person as a living member and in which the survivors take on new social roles.[41] The physical remains of the dead are processed through entombment; the spirit of the dead person is relocated to Sheol; the roles and statuses of survivors are renegotiated. Presumably, inheritance is divided among heirs as well. The mourner parallels the spirit of the dead through his physical appearance

[40] The theme of death as disruption of socially constructed worlds is explored in an interesting way by Danforth in Danforth and Tsiaras, *The Death Rituals of Rural Greece*, 30–1. Functionalists have long emphasized the threat death poses to social equilibrium and to authority structures in various societies, and the role of mortuary ritual in restoring equilibrium and buttressing authority. For this approach, see e.g. Radcliffe-Brown, *The Andaman Islanders*, 285, and Bloch and Parry, *Death and the Regeneration of Life*, 41–2.

[41] On the need to restructure social roles after a death from a cross-cultural perspective, see S. C. Humphreys, 'Death and Time', in S. C. Humphreys and H. King (eds.), *Mortality and Immortality: The Anthropology and Archaeology of Death* (London: Academic Press, 1981), 261–83. See also the comments of V. Turner, writing about the Ndembu of Zambia: 'In all life-crisis rituals changes take place in the relationships of all those people closely connected with the subject of the ritual. When a person dies, all these ties are snapped, as it were . . . Now a new pattern of social relationships must be established: if the dead person was, for instance a headman, a successor has to be found for him, his heirs must divide his inheritance among them, someone must be responsible for his debts, the fate of his widow must be decided, and everyone who stood in a particular relationship with him must know where they stand with regard to his heirs and successor' (*Forest of Symbols*, 8–9).

and through his ritual behaviour (e.g. his symbolic movement to the underworld by descending to the ground). He parallels the corpse through his pollution (the corpse is polluted and polluting; the mourner is polluted and polluting).[42] Parallel behaviour (e.g. descent), parallel appearance, and parallel status (e.g. impure, debased) create a symbolic link between the mourner, the corpse, and the spirit of the dead. They now share distinct characteristics for the period of mourning ('presence' in the underworld, similar appearance, pollution, and debasement). Once mourning is over, these shared characteristics disappear. The mourner will leave the state of mourning and no longer resemble the dead physically or in terms of ritual behaviour. He will become pure and fit to enter the sanctuary and to worship, in contrast to the dead, who are forever cut off from Yhwh and the cult (see e.g. Ps. 88: 6 (Eng. 5)), and in contrast to the polluting corpse, which is interred early in the mourning period. There must be more to the temporary connection forged ritually between mourner, corpse, and spirit of the dead than simply identification with the plight of the dead motivated by pity. The symbolic link, so central to mourning, very likely has concrete social consequences. I would like to suggest tentatively that it may be intended to allow for the establishment of a new and mutually beneficial relationship between the mourner and the dead. The old relationship, between two living persons, has been sundered by death. The enactment of identification by means of self-debasing rites re-establishes a social connection between the mourner and the spirit of the dead during the mourning period, a period of transition between the death and the mourner's return to day-to-day life. The mourner honours the dead through performance of his self-diminishing rites of identification.[43] It seems likely that identification, when

[42] Hertz, in his classic essay, developed the idea that the condition of the mourner in Dayak societies parallels that of the corpse in a number of important respects ('Contribution à une étude sur la représentation collective de la mort', 84). His observation suggested to me just such a parallelism in the biblical mourning context on the basis of purity status.

[43] Evidence that persons who participate in rites of mourning honour the dead is found in several texts. According to 2 Chr. 32: 33, Judah and Jerusalem 'rendered honour' to Hezekiah 'when he died' (וכבוד עשו לו במותו). 2 Sam. 10: 3 implies that an ally who sends his representatives as comforters to a court in mourning honours the dead. Cf. Sir. 38: 17, which suggests that the extent of the

enacted, is intended to give positive direction to what must by definition be a transformed relationship. After mourning ends, the link between mourner and dead will continue through the rites of the ancestor cult. Though our knowledge of such ancestral rites in Israel is quite limited, several biblical texts suggest observances that parallel to some extent what we know from other West Asian sources. Survivors invoke the name of the dead (2 Sam. 18: 18), and offer him food offerings (Deut. 26: 14; Sir. 30: 18; Tob. 4: 17), perhaps with the expectation of beneficent intervention in return.[44] Thus, the honouring of the dead by means of identification may model a positive, mutually beneficial future relationship between the mourner and the spirit of the dead, in contrast to an indifferent or possibly negative association.[45] In short, rites of self-debasement in the context of mourning the dead may well be, in a very real sense, an investment on the part of the mourner in his own future and that of his dependants, though this must remain a speculation.

public display of sorrow should be commensurate with the status of the dead (וְשִׂית אֶבְלוֹ כִּיּוֹצֵא בּוֹ); for the Hebrew text of v. 17 with variants listed, see Z. Segal, סֵפֶר בֶּן סִירָא הַשָּׁלֵם (Jerusalem: Mosad Bialik, 1958), 248–9). It is interesting to note that the idiom עָשָׂה כָבוֹד לְ-, 'to do honour for' (2 Chr. 32: 33) is closely paralleled by the idiom עָשָׂה אֵבֶל לְ-, 'to do mourning for' (Gen. 50: 10; Jer. 6: 26; cf. Ezek. 24: 17; Mic. 1: 8, without לְ-). Anderson notes a comparable parallel between עָשָׂה אֵבֶל לְ- and the idiom עָשָׂה שִׂמְחָה (*A Time to Mourn*, 21). On honour in biblical and West Asian contexts, see Olyan, 'Honor, Shame, and Covenant Relations in Ancient Israel and Its Environment', *JBL* 115 (1996), 201–18, with bibliography.

[44] Paolo Xella states that Israelites enjoyed 'a continuous and symbiotic relationship with the dead. They asked them for protection, healing, fertility, and oracular responses in exchange for remembrance and funerary care.' Xella draws on Mesopotamian and other West Asian sources to construct this detailed description of Israelite practice. The picture he draws, though based to a large extent on speculation, is probably not incorrect in some of its details ('Death and the Afterlife in Canaanite and Hebrew Thought', *CANE* 3: 2069). On ancestor cults, see further the items cited in n. 2 of the Introduction.

[45] Though no biblical evidence suggests that ghosts were feared because of their ability to do harm to the living, Mesopotamian data witness just such a concern, and so the possibility of malevolent ghosts among the Israelite dead must be considered. See e.g. J. Scurlock, 'Ghosts in the Ancient Near East: Weak or Powerful?', *HUCA* 68 (1997), 77–96; M. Bayliss, 'The Cult of Dead Kin in Assyria and Babylonia', *Iraq*, 35 (1973), 115–26; and Lewis, 'How Far Can Texts Take Us?', 190–6, who summarizes the Mesopotamian evidence and relates it to Levantine data.

MOURNERS AND THEIR COMFORTERS

Few characteristics of biblical mourning are as intriguing as the act of 'comforting' and the institution of the 'comforter' (מנחם). Comforters and their ritual actions are mentioned frequently in biblical texts, yet it is not always clear what texts mean when they speak of comforting, or who is obligated to comfort whom. Though the contemporary Western reader might be inclined to understand the Hebrew verb 'to comfort' (נחם) to mean simply to console, a careful study of its range of usage suggests that what we understand as consolation (to offer emotional support, encouragement) is but one function of the biblical comforter. And though we tend to understand such actions as voluntary and based on 'genuine' feelings, it is clearly not legitimate to make such assumptions about comforting in its biblical and West Asian context. Several aspects of comforting have been well elucidated by scholars, for example, the role of the comforter in ending the mourner's mourning.[46] But other aspects of comforting, particularly its social dynamics, remain to be explored in greater depth.

A number of texts suggest that all mourners ought to have comforters, and to be without a comforter is a particularly grievous thing. This is emphasized again and again in the first chapter of Lamentations, a text in which Jerusalem, in the figure of a widow in mourning, sits alone, without a comforter (Lam. 1: 2, 9, 16, 17, 21). Friends and family members are expected to play the role of comforter for individual mourners. Job's three friends are probably the pre-eminent biblical example:

When the three friends of Job heard of all this evil that had come upon him, they came, each from his place: Eliphaz the Temanite, Bildad the Shuhite, and Zophar the Naamatite. They took counsel together to come to move back and forth for him (לנוד לו) and to comfort him (ולנחמו). When they raised their eyes from afar, they did not recognize him, and lifted up their voices and wept. Each tore his garment, and they threw dust heavenward upon their heads. They sat with him upon the ground seven days and seven nights, and none spoke a word to him, for they saw that the pain was exceedingly great.   (Job 2: 11–13)

Comforters, as this text demonstrates, participate in the rites of

---

[46] On this, see Anderson, *A Time to Mourn*, 84–7.

mourning with the mourner: they weep, tear their garments, throw dust upon their heads, sit on the ground, and move their bodies back and forth (נוד), all recognizable mourning behaviours. They share the mourner's locus and quite possibly his pollution, and therefore, his temporary separation from the sanctuary.[47] In a word, comforters are individuals who join the mourner for the mourning period, sharing the mourner's appearance, locus, and ritual activity.

A variety of texts suggest several possible meanings for the Hebrew verb 'to comfort' (נחם), and these provide some sense of the range of the comforter's ritual activity. First, 'to comfort' may mean simply to join the mourner in mourning rites, as Job's friends do in Job 2: 11.[48] Isa. 51: 19 communicates this meaning clearly, by paralleling the question 'Who will move back and forth (ינוד) for you?' with the question 'Who will comfort you?'[49] in a discourse on Jerusalem, which has suffered at the hand of Yhwh.[50] Second, 'to comfort' seems at times to mean to impose an end to the mourner's mourning.[51] In Gen. 37: 35, Jacob's children are said to rise up 'to comfort him, but he refused to be comforted', meaning apparently that he refused to end his mourning over his son. In 1 Chr. 7: 22–3, Ephraim mourns, is comforted by his brothers, and has sexual relations with his wife, an act avoided during mourning. Thus, the notation that Ephraim's brothers came to comfort him seems to suggest that they ended his mourning, freeing him to have intercourse with his wife. Comforting, in Isa. 61: 2–3, involves the replacement of mourning behaviours with rejoicing, clearly indicating that 'to comfort' in that context means to impose an end to mourning. Jer. 31: 13 is similar: 'I shall turn their mourning into joy,' // 'I shall comfort them and make them rejoice free of[52] their

---

[47] This would be the case if comforters had contact with the corpse before or during burial, or, following Numbers 19, were in an enclosed space with the corpse before it was buried.

[48] See Anderson, *A Time to Mourn*, 84 for a helpful philological treatment of this 'processual' sense of the verb 'to comfort'.

[49] Here I read with 1QIsaᵃ and LXX *ינחמך for MT אנחמך.

[50] Other examples of this usage of the verb include Lam. 1: 2, 9, 16, 17, 21; 2 Sam. 10: 2; Jer. 16: 7 and others listed by Anderson (*A Time to Mourn*, 84 n. 74).

[51] See ibid. 84–7, from which most of the examples that follow are derived.

[52] See the citations and discussion in n. 47 of the Introduction on the privative sense of מן here.

suffering.' Finally, 'to comfort' is used at times to mean the performance of acts of consolation. Comforters eat food with the mourner in the mourner's house (Job 42: 11; Jer. 16: 7 (?)),[53] give him drink from 'the cup of consolation' (Jer. 16: 7), and attempt to 'restore' his 'spirit'[54] (Lam. 1: 16) by means of speech that strengthens (Job 16: 5). The speech of comforters is characterized as 'tender' in a number of texts (Isa. 40: 1; cf. Ruth 2: 13; Gen. 50: 21)[55] and may involve comparison of the mourner's suffering to that of others (Lam. 2: 13). A goal of comforting is to heal, as Lam. 2: 13 suggests:

> What shall I compare to you, that I might comfort you,
>   Virgin Daughter Zion?
> For great as the sea is your destruction.
>   Who can heal (רפא) you?

To deny or play down a consoling dimension to biblical comforting, as some scholars have done, is clearly without warrant, since quite a number of texts bear witness to it. Such an approach limits our ability to understand comforting as a multidimensional activity.[56]

In addition to the comforting of individuals, the biblical text and comparative West Asian and North African materials bear witness to the role played by comforters in international diplomatic contexts.[57] At the death of a king, allies or vassals may send

[53] The MT ולא יפרסו להם על אבל לנחמו על מת is emended by most scholars to ולא יפרסו לחם על אבל לנחמו על מת on the basis of LXX ἄρτος.

[54] Cf. Lam. 1: 16, in which the comforter is 'one who restores my spirit' (משיב נפשי), to Lam. 1: 19, in which food does the same thing (// כי בקשו אכל למו וישיבו את נפשם), suggesting a sense of strengthening for the idiom 'to restore the spirit'.

[55] Pham emphasizes the consoling dimension of comforting, citing these three texts and noting the parallelism of forms of the verb נחם and the expression דבר על לב (*Mourning*, 31–2).

[56] See e.g. Anderson, *A Time to Mourn*, 84: 'This verb "to comfort" . . . does not connote a simple act of emotional identification. Comfort can imply either the symbolic action of *assuming the state of mourning* alongside the mourner, or it can have the nuance of *bringing about the cessation of mourning*' (italics in the original). Pham's analysis is more balanced, taking into account all three dimensions of comforting (*Mourning*, 27–35).

[57] The classic and oft-cited study is P. Artzi, 'Mourning in International Relations', in B. Alster (ed.), *Death in Mesopotamia* (Mesopotamia: Copenhagen Studies in Assyriology 8; Copenhagen: Akademisk Forlag, 1980), 161–70, initially brought to my attention by Anderson.

representatives to the court in mourning, and these are identified as comforters in 2 Sam. 10: 3. In addition to sending an embassy of comforters to the court of the dead king, a ruler, upon learning of the death of his treaty partner, might fast, weep and lament, declaring a public fast to mark his ally's death, as in EA 29: 55–60.[58] The pattern of mourning in contexts of international diplomacy is thus modelled after the mourning of the common individual, in that treaty partners play the same role that the mourning individual's family and friends play in an individual mourning context.[59] This is not at all surprising, given the common use of familial and friendship-related terminology in treaty idiom.[60]

MOURNING PROFESSIONALS

Both biblical texts and other West Asian materials attest to the institution of the professional mourner. Such mourners, often but not always identified as women, were apparently summoned at the time of a death and engaged to weep and utter laments over the dead. Amos 5: 16 refers to them as 'those expert in lamentation' (יוֹדְעֵי נֶהִי). 2 Chr. 35: 25 mentions Jeremiah's dirge over Josiah and speaks of male and female singers (שָׁרִים and שָׁרוֹת) who intone their own dirges mentioning the dead king. Jer. 9: 16–18 (Eng. 17–19) speaks of the summoning of skilled 'dirge women' (מְקוֹנְנוֹת) to lament over the fall of Judah and Jerusalem:

Thus says Yhwh of hosts: 'Consider carefully, and call for the dirge women, that they might come, and for the skilled women (חֲכָמוֹת) send, that they might come. Let them hasten, and let them lift up over us a lament, that our eyes might run with tears, and our eyelids gush water. For the sound of lamentation is heard from Zion: "How we are destroyed, we are exceedingly shamed, for we have forsaken the land, for they have cast down our habitations." '

[58] For the Akkadian text, see H. P. Adler, *Das Akkadische des Königs Tusratta von Mitanni* (AOAT 201; Neukirchen-Vluyn: Neukirchener; Kevelaer: Butzon & Bercker, 1976), 236. A useful annotated translation appears in W. L. Moran, *The Amarna Letters* (Baltimore: The Johns Hopkins University Press, 1992), 94.

[59] Cf. the formulation of Artzi, 'Mourning in International Relations', 167.

[60] Such treaty language is ubiquitous. See e.g. the use of 'my brother' in the introductory formulae typical of Amarna correspondence between allies, and the comments of Moran, *Amarna Letters*, p. xxiv and n. 59.

Though the focus of this text is lamentation in the aftermath of national disaster rather than after the death of an individual, the passage is suggestive nonetheless about the activity and function of professional mourners in death contexts. It appears that professional mourners were engaged not only to perform mourning in contexts of death or calamity, but to draw out the appropriate ritual response from others gathered to mourn. The lamenting of the dirge women is intended, says the text, to cause tears to flow from the eyes of those present, whether or not members of the assembled body are inclined to weep, for weeping in such contexts has important social functions, as I shall discuss.

Other passages such as Ezek. 32: 16, 2 Sam. 1: 24, and the Kirta epic from Ugarit allude to the role of women in mourning, though it is not clear that these texts speak of professional mourners. In Ezek. 32: 16, the women of the nations are to utter the dirge over the Egyptian Pharaoh presented previously to the prophet himself to intone. The daughters of Israel are ordered to weep for the dead Saul in David's lament over Saul and Jonathan (2 Sam. 1: 24). The Kirta epic also seems to associate dirges with women,[61] and privileges the mourning of Kirta's daughter.[62] Jer. 9: 19–20 (Eng. 20–1) orders women to teach other women lamentation and dirge on account of the widespread death among the populace of Jerusalem at the time of its collapse:

> Teach your daughters lamentation,
> (Let) a woman (teach) her neighbour the dirge.
> For death has come up into our windows,
>   It has entered our citadels,
> To cut off the child from the street,
>   Young people from the squares.

A gendered dimension to mourning emerges out of the many references to women playing the part of the mourner or dirge performer in biblical and West Asian texts. Though texts do not at all suggest that mourning and the composition and performance of dirges are exclusively gendered pursuits, extant evidence does tend often to associate these activities with women. This probably has mostly to do with the construction of gender (women cast as most suited to weep)[63] and the customary

---

[61] *CAT* 1.16 I 3–5, 17–19.   [62] *CAT* 1.16 I 28–30.
[63] See ibid. lines 25–30.

loci (e.g. the home) and social roles assigned to women in the societies that produced these texts.[64]

SOCIAL DIMENSIONS OF MOURNING THE DEAD

Like other ritual settings, mourning the dead is a context for the affirmation, formation, re-negotiation, or termination of social bonds between individuals, groups, and political entities. Social rank may be embraced or rejected by individuals in a mourning context; treaty relationships may be avowed, reworked, or severed by rulers; distinct groups may be created, affirmed, reconstituted, or terminated. A king's authority may be tested by his people's response to his own precedent-setting ritual behaviour. I have suggested that the biblical mourning period may serve as a context to re-establish the link between the mourner and the dead in a reconfigured form; in this section, I will speak of mourning as ritual activity with implications for social relations among living participants. Texts describing public mourning rites at the death of a king or another prominent individual are our richest resource for reconstructing a number of aspects of the social dimensions of mourning. Mourning over common individuals is more poorly documented in its details than is public mourning, but texts suggest that the social dynamics of each are similar. All mourning contexts are settings in which the work of affirming, creating, or transforming social ties is done. I shall first consider several texts that represent public mourning, and then go on to discuss the social dimensions of comforting.

One text that provides a particularly vivid impression of public mourning is 2 Sam. 3: 31–7, an apologetic narrative seeking to distance David from the murder of Abner, Saul's general, by David's nephew and general Joab.[65] Upon learning of Abner's death, David orders public mourning for Abner:

---

[64] On this, see further P. Bird, 'The Place of Women in the Israelite Cultus', in P. Miller *et al.* (eds.), *Ancient Israelite Religion: Essays in Honor of Frank Moore Cross* (Philadelphia: Fortress, 1987), 400–1, 409–10.

[65] On the narrative and its purposes, see P. K. McCarter, Jr., 'The Apology of David', *JBL* 99 (1980), 501–2. The political dynamics that lie behind this text are explored in an interesting way by J. Vanderkam, 'Davidic Complicity in the

Then David said to Joab and to all the people who were with him: 'Tear your garments, put on sackcloth, and lament before Abner.' As for King David, he walked behind the bier, and they buried Abner in Hebron. The king lifted up his voice and wept toward the tomb of Abner, and all the people wept. The king sang a dirge about Abner . . . And all the people continued to weep over him. Then all the people came to make David eat food while it was still day, and David swore (an oath) as follows: 'Thus may God do to me and more if I taste bread or anything else before the setting of the sun.' And all the people understood and it was good in their eyes . . . And all the people and all Israel knew on that day that it was not the king's intention to put Abner son of Ner to death.

We learn much from this text. Clearly, mourning functions here as both an individual and corporate activity utilized to serve the political purposes of a ruler. David's mourning for Abner, and that which he demands of all of the people of Judah, including Abner's murderers, is intended publicly to realize good relations, communicate solidarity, and proclaim regret. The people's weeping in this context is clearly not a spontaneous display of emotion. Required by the exigencies of the situation, perhaps induced by David's example, by other mourning behaviours that create discomfort, and/or by the wailing of professional mourners, it not only honours Abner, but realizes and communicates the people's loyalty to the king and to his political purpose. In addition to this, the collective weeping of David's followers and their other mourning behaviours function to define that group of persons loyal to David over against others who might not harbour such allegiance. Thus, the mourning rites of David and Judah in 2 Sam. 3: 31–7 map several kinds of social relationship at once: David with Saulides and other northerners; David with loyal Judahites; Judahites loyal to David with Saulides and other northerners; Judahites loyal to David with one another, and in contrast to others.

The mourning of David and the people is a public statement of affiliation; it is the ritual behaviour expected of family, friends, and allies. As many scholars have pointed out, typically, the enemy rejoices over the death or defeat of his foe, in contrast to the ally or friend, who mourns or comforts survivors.[66] Thus, to

Deaths of Abner and Eshbaal: A Historical and Redactional Study', *JBL* 99 (1980), 521–39.

[66] On the rejoicing of the enemy, see Anderson, *A Time to Mourn*, 72–3. In

mourn or not to mourn has serious political implications in a
scenario such as the funeral of Abner. Mourning may affirm a
pre-existing relationship, or establish a new relationship
through its very performance. David, through his mourning,
seeks to distance himself and his kingdom from Abner's murder.
His insistence on fasting until sundown convinces the people
that Abner's death was not his idea. But David's mourning over
Abner does more than simply distance him from suspicion. By
mourning over Abner, David is in effect denying that there exists
any alienation from Abner, the House of Saul, and the northern
tribes. He is saying not only that he is not their enemy; he is their
friend. This scenario repeats a similar situation narrated in 2
Samuel 1. There, David, a fugitive from Saul's court and bound
by treaty to Saul's enemy, the Philistine king Achish of Gath,
mourns upon hearing of the death of Saul and Jonathan and
Israel's defeat at the hands of the Philistines on Mt. Gilboa. His
mourning in this text accomplishes several things. First, it is a
political statement of loyalty to Saul and solidarity and affiliation
with Israel, and accompanies David's rejection of the insignias of
kingship brought to him by the messenger who had come from
the scene of battle. Second, David's mourning also represents a
very public rejection of his treaty with his overlord Achish, king
of Gath. The mourning behaviour of David's men not only
declares their affiliation with Saul and Israel, but confirms their
loyalty to their lord, David, and, like their mourning in 2 Sam. 3:
31–7, delimits their circle at the same time. In short, in the two
narratives, David's ritual behaviour and that of the people functions both to reconfigure and affirm political affiliations.[67] In
the case of 2 Sam. 3: 31–7, David's mourning and that of the
people may simply establish in practice the treaty negotiated
between David and Abner before Abner's murder. In the case
of 2 Samuel 1, mourning functions to sever the treaty relationship with the Philistines and, at the same time, create a new

---

Lam. 1: 2, disloyal allies (אהבים) fail to comfort Jerusalem at the time of her
calamity, and are said to have become her enemies.

[67] Ebersole notes the realignment dimension of David's acts in 2 Samuel 1
with respect to Saul and Israel, but seems not to have noticed that such a
reconfiguration also involved public rescission of a treaty. In addition, he
misses the affirmation dimension of the weeping of David's followers ('Ritual
Weeping', 241).

relationship with Saul and Israel. Weeping and other mourning behaviours in 2 Sam. 3: 31–7 and 2 Samuel 1 not only map relations between David and northern interests; they also affirm and publicize the sound relationship of loyalty between David and his men, and function to define the boundaries of their group over against others.

2 Sam. 3: 31–7 illustrates well a hierarchical dimension to public mourning, for it shows that the king's ritual behaviour normally determines that of all who follow him. No matter what others wish to do, and no matter what their private feelings might be, when ordered to mourn and weep over Abner, they do what they are told. By so doing, they realize and communicate their loyalty to David, affirming the reality of his political authority through their ritual actions. Even in cases in which a ruler's behaviour may be ritually inappropriate to the context, his ritual activity nonetheless sets the precedent for his followers who wish to remain affiliated with him. An example of this is the narrative in 2 Sam. 19: 1–9 (Eng. 18: 33–19: 8), a text that describes David's mourning for Absalom in the aftermath of the suppression of Absalom's revolt. David's army has won a victory over the forces of his rebel son. Normally, rejoicing follows such a military triumph, rejoicing presumably led by the king.[68] But in this case, David has allowed his private grief over the death of his son to take precedence over the people's expectation to rejoice in the aftermath of military success. When the people hear that the king is mourning over Absalom, his ritual behaviour determines theirs: 'So the victory (תשעה) on that day was turned to mourning (אבל) for all the army, for the army had heard on that day as follows: "The king is grieving (נעצב) over his son" ' (2 Sam. 19: 3 (Eng. 2)). The text goes on to note the parallel between the shameful mourning of a defeated army forced to flee the enemy and the mourning of David's men, imposed on them by the king's mourning: 'So the army stole into the city on that day, as does an army humiliated when they flee in battle' (2 Sam. 19: 4 (Eng. 3)).[69] In a word, David's army, though

---

[68] Examples of texts associating military victory (תשועה) with rejoicing include 1 Sam. 11: 9, 13–15; 19: 5; 2 Chr. 6: 41. Anderson, *A Time to Mourn*, 21, notes the connection between military victory and feasting.

[69] The shaming dimensions of this narrative are explored in Olyan, 'Honor, Shame, and Covenant Relations', 208–10.

victorious, must embrace the ritual behaviour of a defeated and shamed army on account of the king's ritual acts. Joab, David's general, excoriates David for his inappropriate ritual behaviour in the aftermath of victory, and warns him of potential abandonment by his loyal forces should he continue to allow his private feelings to trump his public obligations. He describes David's acts as 'loving' those who 'hate' him, that is, treating his enemies as if they were his friends, and 'hating' those who 'love' him, namely, treating his friends as if they were his enemies (לאהבה את שנאיך ולשנא את אהביך; 2 Sam. 19: 7 (Eng. 6)). By this Joab means David's acts of mourning for Absalom, David's enemy, and his effective imposition of mourning on his victorious, loyal troops. By so doing, implies Joab, David has broken covenant with his men.[70] In the end, David relents and stops privileging his personal grief. He abandons his mourning, receiving the people in the city gate.

The public mourning described in 2 Sam. 3: 31–7 and 2 Samuel 1 illustrate well the role mourning rites can play in the establishment or the affirmation of social relations among individuals and groups. That public mourning could also serve as a context for terminating social bonds between parties is best illustrated by 2 Samuel 10. In this narrative, David sends emissaries to the court of Ammon at the death of Nahash, the king of the Ammonites. The presence of David's embassy of comforters is intended to affirm the pre-existing treaty relationship between Ammon and Israel at the time of transition to a new ruler in Ammon.[71] David's words in v. 2 make his motivation for sending comforters clear: 'I will be loyal to Hanun, son of Nahash, as his father was loyal to me.'[72] Yet David's covenant loyalty, made

---

[70] On the language of love and hate in covenant settings, see W. L. Moran, 'The Ancient Near Eastern Background of the Love of God in Deuteronomy', *CBQ* 25 (1963), 77–87. Those who love their covenant partner are loyal to the stipulations of the covenant; those who hate their covenant partner have violated treaty requirements. On this, see e.g. Exod. 20: 5–6 (=Deut. 5: 9–10), a text in which Yhwh describes covenant breakers as 'those who hate me', and those loyal to treaty stipulations as 'those who love me'.

[71] As others have noted, the covenant in question is likely one of equals. See Artzi, 'Mourning in International Relations', 162.

[72] Literally, 'I will do covenant loyalty with Hanun, son of Nahash, as his father did covenant loyalty with me' (אעשה חסד עם חנון בן נחש כאשר עשה אביו עמדי חסד). On covenant loyalty (חסד), see the study of K. D. Sakenfeld, *The Meaning of*

manifest through the presence in court of his embassy of comforters, is repaid with a series of hostile acts. The comforters,
thought to be spies, are publicly humiliated in v. 4: 'Hanun took
the servants of David, shaved off half their beards, cut their
garments in half at the buttocks, and expelled them.' The emissaries, deeply humiliated, are ordered by David to remain outside of Jerusalem until their beards have begun to grow back
(v. 5). These acts of aggression against the representatives of
David dishonour David and Israel, and in so doing, effectively
terminate the treaty relationship that had existed between Israel
and Ammon up to that time. The half-shaven beard plays on
beard-shaving as a mourning rite, but distorts it grotesquely.
The cutting of the garment, which results in exposure of the
buttocks and perhaps the genitals, may play on the mourning
gesture of tearing the garment.[73] In any case, as the text notes in
v. 6, the Ammonites, through their aggressive acts, become
'odious' to David. They use the ritual setting of national mourning to terminate their treaty relationship with Israel. David
repays these acts of aggression by attacking and vanquishing
Ammon.

The social dynamics of comforting remain to be considered.
Comforters, by their presence with the mourner and their ritual
actions, realize and communicate their loyalty and affiliation to
the mourner. Like Job's friends, comforters tear their garments,
weep, sit on the ground, and toss ashes on their heads. By sitting
on the ground with the mourner, they join him in his ritual
descent. As I have argued, they may also become polluted from
corpse contact or from proximity to a corpse. Through these
acts of identification, comforters affirm their close ties to the
mourner and project these ties into the future. The ritual
behaviour of the comforter functions to identify him with the
mourner just as the mourner's acts identify him with the spirit of
the dead and his pollution identifies him with the corpse. In
short, comforters honour the mourner through imitative acts of
self-debasement just as the mourner honours the dead through

Hesed in the Hebrew Bible: A New Inquiry (HSM 17; Missoula, Mont.: Scholars
Press, 1978).

[73] Some have speculated that the gestures in this combination suggest castration, although I do not find this convincing. For this interpretation, see P. K.
McCarter, Jr., *II Samuel* (AB 9; Garden City, NY: Doubleday, 1984), 270–1.

such acts. These observations concerning the relationship between mourner and comforter call into question Feldman's assertion that the mourner is socially isolated and without community. Under normal circumstances, biblical texts suggest that nothing could be further from the truth. The mourner is certainly separated temporarily from larger society and cult, but in his separate ritual state, he is joined by comforters, and together, they constitute a distinct temporary community of their own.[74] Those who join the mourner over the dead are his closest social links when he is not in mourning; during mourning, they form his total community. Thus, mourning functions to underscore or bring into relief the mourner's social relationships. Far from being isolated, the biblical mourner is portrayed as surrounded by comforters, both family and friends (e.g. Job). At most, we can grant that the whole circle of mourners and their comforters are socially separated for a temporary period of time, but there is normally no social isolation in mourning. Mourning is a communally oriented ritual context that tends to reinforce and affirm social arrangements more often than it severs or transforms such ties, though it always has the potential to change them. In any case, mourning is a setting in which social relations are formed, confirmed, recast, and dissolved. Such activity would be impossible if the mourner were truly isolated socially as Feldman has asserted.[75]

Given that the mourner is not socially isolated, what then of the notion that the mourner has experienced a social death? As I have mentioned, Hertz characterized mourners in the societies he studied as socially dead: 'Ce sont bien au propre les "gens de la mort"; ils vivent dans les ténèbres, *morts eux-mêmes au point de vue social*, puisque toute participation active de leur part à la vie collective ne ferait que propager au dehors la malédiction qu'ils portent en eux.'[76] What defines social death for Hertz is removal—even temporarily—from the collective life of the community. Others, however, use social death in a different way, to describe the termination of an individual's social identity. This

[74] The emphasis on a lack of comforters in Lamentations 1 implies that it is highly unusual to be alone in mourning.

[75] *Defilement and Mourning*, 93–4.

[76] 'Contribution à une étude sur la représentation collective de la mort', 84–5 (my italics).

is well illustrated by the words of J. Middleton, who speaks of the physically dead among the Lugbara of Uganda: 'Social death . . . refers to the extinguishing of the present social identity of the deceased and its transformation into another. We come here to the transition from a living member of a lineage and neighbourhood into a dead member of these groupings.'[77] Perhaps the best known example of this second and more common use of the concept of social death is O. Patterson's characterization of the slave as a socially dead individual: 'Alienated from all "rights" or claims of birth, he ceased to belong in his own right to any legitimate social order . . . Not only was the slave denied all claims on, and obligations to, his parents and living blood relations but, by extension, all such claims and obligations on his more remote ancestors and on his descendants. He was truly a genealogical isolate.'[78]

Clearly, biblical mourners and their comforters are not socially dead in the way in which Middleton or Patterson employ the concept, for they do not lose their social identity or abandon their social roles.[79] Rather, they continue to occupy their social locus in a mourning context that, if anything, brings their social ties into greater relief. The comforter asserts by his presence that he has an intimate tie of consanguinity or affinity to the mourner. The elder mourning his wife is still the head of household; the king mourning his son remains the king. Yet what of Hertz's notion of social death which he applies to the mourner? Biblical mourners and their comforters are temporarily removed from aspects of collective life in that they cannot participate in the rites of the sanctuary, and mourners do identify with the dead through their appearance and their ritual action. Yet biblical mourners are not completely cut off from society, since a subsection of society—the most significant persons in the lives of mourners—joins them in their mourning. I prefer not to speak of the biblical mourner as 'socially dead', since the concept as it is most frequently used today has implications that clearly do

[77] 'Lugbara Death', in Bloch and Parry (eds.), *Death and the Regeneration of Life*, 141–2.

[78] *Slavery and Social Death: A Comparative Study* (Cambridge: Harvard University Press, 1982), 5. See also 38–45.

[79] Against Feldman, *Defilement and Mourning*, 94, who asserts that the mourner has lost his identity: 'his identity as an individual has melted away . . .'.

not apply to the biblical mourner (e.g. the termination of social identity). In addition, even Hertz's notion of social death is ill suited to describe biblical mourning, since some non-sanctuary-bound aspects of collective life continue for the mourner. Thus, I speak of the mourner's temporary identification with the dead and separation from the sanctuary, but not of his social death.

Van Gennep's assertion that mourners and the dead together form a 'special society' between the realm of the dead and that of the living has some merit when assessed in light of the biblical evidence.[80] The symbolic link of the mourner to both the spirit of the dead and the corpse through shared appearance, behaviour and status lays the groundwork for what might be described as a community of sorts, set apart from the larger society. But the community apart in its biblical representation is more extensive than simply the mourner and the dead. Comforters, who honour the mourner by means of the enactment of identification, also form a central part of this community, playing a significant role in both the ritual and social dynamics of mourning. Thus, modifying van Gennep, one may speak of the dead, the mourner, and the mourner's comforters constituting a distinct community apart from the larger society for the period of mourning.

Conclusions

Mourning, the ritual antithesis of rejoicing, separates the mourner for the dead ritually from quotidian life and the cult. Through their very enactment, the rites of the mourner create and mark a distinct and recognizable ritual state (mourning) and a discrete ritual population (mourners). The ritual separation of the mourner over the dead is accomplished and communicated by means not only of distinct practices such as tearing the garment, sitting on the ground, or tossing ashes or dust upon the head. It is also realized and signalled by a restriction of the mourner's loci of activity to exclude sanctified spaces; by the limited duration of the mourning period (usually seven days); by the mourner's pollution resulting from corpse contact or proximity; and by the mourning state's lack of easy reversibility. The process of ritual separation may be aided by the activities of mourning professionals, often women, whose performance may

---

[80] *Les Rites de passage*, 211.

be necessary to draw out the appropriate ritual response from mourners and those who join them. All mourning rites function to debase mourners and communicate their debasement, as Kutsch has asserted and various texts suggest.

Identification with the dead appears to be the purpose of the ritual separation and debasement of the mourner over the dead. Such identification is established by means of common appearance and behaviour, and shared pollution. The mourner takes on the same appearance as the spirit of the dead and imitates his descent to the underworld ritually; like the corpse, he is polluted. But why identify with the dead in this way? Because mourning is a context for the accomplishment of socially significant 'work' (e.g. negotiating changed statuses), it is unlikely that identification is motivated simply by pity, as a number of scholars seem to suggest; rather, it is more probable that it has concrete social consequences. Though we cannot be sure, it is possible that the symbolic link established by the mourner's honouring of the dead through acts of identification is intended to establish a new, mutually beneficial relationship between the mourner and the dead. In this newly configured association, the mourner invokes the name of the dead and brings him food offerings, perhaps receiving forms of beneficent intervention from the dead in return.

The social dimensions of mourning the dead are many and varied, with mourning emerging in this study as a context both for social continuity and change. Pre-existing bonds between individuals, groups, and political entities are affirmed, renegotiated, or terminated in mourning settings, and new bonds are forged. Discrete social groups are created, terminated, or perpetuated in mourning contexts. Social rank may be conferred or rejected by participants in mourning. Treaties between rulers or political entities may be embraced, reworked, or broken. A king's authority is tested by the ritual response of his followers to his precedent-setting behaviour, bringing into relief the potential, hierarchical dimensions of public mourning. Comforting the mourner has particularly important social ramifications. Comforters, generally the mourner's closest social links when he is not in mourning, honour the mourner by imitating his ritual behaviour. Comforters share the mourner's locus, separating themselves ritually by means of mourning practices. They join the mourner in his ritual descent and very likely in his state of pollution. Aside from being in the company of the mourner for the period of mourning, the ritual functions of comforters include consolation and intervention to put an end to the mourning state when it has reached its conclusion. Through their ritual practices, comforters contribute to the constitution of a distinct, ritually separated community in mourning made up of themselves, the mourner, and the spirit of the dead, a community that functions as the mourner's social world for the period of mourning. Thus, mourning tends to bring into relief and reinforce the mourner's pre-existing social relationships, but allows for change as well, for bonds already established may be transformed or broken in mourning contexts, and new relationships may be created. Though scholars such as Feldman have argued that mourning the dead is a solitary or semi-solitary state, texts suggest that quite the opposite was apparently the norm.

2

Petitionary Mourning

Petitionary mourning is a second, distinct type of mourning activity commonly attested in a variety of biblical texts. As with mourning the dead, entreaty of the deity or, on occasion, a human authority, is frequently characterized by petitioners' employment of easily recognizable mourning behaviours such as tearing garments, tossing ashes or dust on the head, weeping, wearing sackcloth, and fasting.[1] Common mourning idioms such as the verbs 'to mourn' (התאבל) or 'to lament'/'mourn' (ספד) are sometimes used in descriptions of the ritual behaviour of suppliants, and in several texts, petitionary mourning is compared directly to mourning the dead.[2] Evidence also suggests that petitioners, like those mourning the dead, were expected to have comforters, and that they eschewed all rites of rejoicing during the period of their petition. Thus, petitionary mourning shares a number of important characteristics with mourning the dead. Yet petitionary mourning is distinct from mourning the dead in a number of respects as well. First, it has a variety of specific purposes not shared with mourning the dead (e.g. to reverse the deity's decision to punish the people, or to seek Yhwh's guidance by means of an oracle or revelation, or to solicit the deity's help in a situation of personal difficulty). Second, the mourning of petitioners has a common general purpose that is also not

[1] See my discussion of these and other typical mourning practices in the Introduction to this volume and Ch 1. Relevant texts describing such petitionary mourning behaviour include Ezra 9: 3, 5; 10: 6; Neh. 1: 4; 1 Sam. 30: 4; 2 Sam. 13: 19; Joel 1–2, among many others.

[2] For mourning vocabulary used of the ritual behaviour of petitioners, see e.g. Ezra 10: 6; Jer. 6: 26; Joel 1: 13; 2: 12; Dan. 10: 2. For the comparison of petitionary mourning with mourning the dead, see Jer. 6: 26; Joel 1: 8; and Ps. 35: 13–14. These subjects are discussed at length in the Introduction.

characteristic of the rites of the mourner over the dead: to focus the deity's attention on the plea of the petitioner and secure his intervention on the petitioner's behalf. Third, petitioners are frequently unconstrained by temporal limitations, in contrast to those who mourn the dead. And finally, supplicants who employ mourning rites are most frequently portrayed as unpolluted.[3] As a result, petitioners would generally have unimpeded access to the sphere of the sanctuary should they wish to approach Yhwh there, in contrast to those mourning the dead, who are polluted as a result of corpse contact or proximity to a corpse.[4] This

---

[3] Unless they have had contact with polluting persons or things or been defiled in some other way (e.g. through skin disease or, according to some texts, by means of sin). Sources of defilement aside from corpses, bones, and tombs include seminal emission or contact with such (Lev. 15: 16–18; Deut. 23: 10–12 (Eng. 10–11)); menstruation (Lev. 15: 19–24; 18: 19; 20: 18); parturition (Lev. 12: 1–8); genital discharges (Lev. 15: 2–15, 25–30; Num. 5: 2); and skin disease (צרעת; Lev. 13–14; Num. 5: 2). According to Psalm 51, sin has polluted the petitioner (ומחטאתי טהרני // כבסני מעוני; v. 4 (Eng. 2)). This psalm, like the Holiness Source, Deuteronomy, and a number of other texts, recognizes a class of pollution caused by transgressions such as proscribed sexual relations, child sacrifice, consulting mediums, and 'idolatry' (e.g. Lev. 18: 20, 23, 24–5, 27, 28, 30; 19: 31; 20: 3; Deut. 24: 4; Jer. 7: 30; Ezek. 5: 11; 36: 18). Lev. 16: 30 (H) states that through the rites of the Day of Purgation, Yhwh will purify Israel of all their sins (כי ביום הזה יכפר עליכם לטהר אתכם מכל חטאתיכם לפני יהוה תטהרו). The attribution of pollution to the sinner does not appear to be characteristic of all biblical materials concerned with transgression. Many texts speak of transgressors and their rites of expiation without associating their sins with defilement. On this, see further the comments of J. Milgrom, *Leviticus 1–16* (AB 3; New York: Doubleday, 1991), 37, who discusses Lev. 16: 30 and also cites P texts that speak of Yhwh pardoning the transgressions of Israelites rather than purifying them of their sins. (But cf. Num. 5: 11–31, a P text that recognizes impurity caused by iniquity.) A recent study of impurity associated with transgression is J. Klawans, *Impurity and Sin in Ancient Judaism* (New York: Oxford University Press, 2000). Klawans, following scholars such as B. Levine, points out that the pollution of the sinner, in contrast to other types of defilement, cannot be communicated and therefore the sinner understood to be defiled is not excluded from the sanctuary (27, 29, citing Num. 5: 13–14 and Levine, *Numbers 1–20*, 207).

[4] See e.g. 1 Samuel 1; Joel 1–2; 2 Chr. 20: 1–19; Ezra 9–10; Sir. 38: 9–15, among many others. As I have noted, Anderson does not appear to recognize this important distinction between mourners for the dead and petitioners. See *A Time to Mourn*, 90, 92, 94, 95, where he asserts that the petitioner too is defiled and therefore removed from the temple sphere, though he does not indicate clearly in what manner the supplicant becomes polluted nor does he cite evidence to support this claim. It appears that Anderson considers mourning rites

combination of shared characteristics with mourning the dead and distinct features of its own marks petitionary mourning as a discrete ritual activity distinguishable from mourning the dead, and, at the same time, as a type of mourning broadly conceived.[5]

themselves to be polluting and it is their employment that allegedly results in separation from the temple. If mourning rites had such an effect, petitionary mourning would not occur in sanctified settings, as it does in any number of texts. Anderson's assumption that the petitioner is polluted may have been influenced by earlier scholarship. For example, S. Mowinckel argued, with respect to the psalms of complaint, that 'humiliation and mourning imply a state of impurity, because disaster, "curse" has befallen the soul of the person concerned' (*The Psalms in Israel's Worship* (trans. D. R. Ap-Thomas; 2 vols.; Oxford: Blackwell, 1962), 1: 193). A close look at the psalms of complaint, even those that appear to describe a sick petitioner, do not clearly suggest that the petitioner is polluted, with the exception of Psalm 51, which describes a petitioner defiled by means of his transgressions. Excluding Psalm 51, there is in fact none of the distinct pollution and purification vocabulary that one might expect to find if the supplicant were defiled (e.g. derivatives of the roots טמא and טהר). It is certainly possible that some petitioners described in complaint psalms had skin disease (צרעת) or a genital flow (זוב), and were therefore polluted and separated from the sanctuary, but this is a different matter entirely, and even for this there is no clear evidence. On this problem, see the discussion of K. Seybold, *Das Gebet des Kranken im Alten Testament: Untersuchungen zur Bestimmung und Zuordnung der Krankheits- und Heilungspsalmen* (BWANT 5.19; Stuttgart: Kohlhammer, 1973), 54. As mentioned, Psalm 51 casts the petitioner as defiled on account of his sins, but other texts such as Num. 5: 11–31 suggest that pollution due to sin does not limit access to the sanctuary, as Levine, Klawans, and others have pointed out (Levine, *Numbers 1–20*, 207; Klawans, *Impurity and Sin in Ancient Judaism*, 27, 29). Thus, though some texts may suggest that individual petitioners are polluted due to skin disease, a genital flow, or transgression, evidence is lacking to support Anderson's claim that petitioners who utilize mourning rites are defiled thereby and, therefore, separated from the sanctuary sphere.

[5] On petition in Mesopotamian sources, see T. Jacobsen, *The Treasures of Darkness: A History of Mesopotamian Religion* (New Haven: Yale University Press, 1976), 147–64, and the survey of W. H. Hallo, 'Lamentations and Prayers in Sumer and Akkad', *CANE* 3: 1871–81, including bibliography. Primary texts of note include the Sumerian 'A Man and his God' as well as the Akkadian composition Ludlul bēl nēmeqi ('I will praise the Lord of Wisdom'). See S. N. Kramer, ' "A Man and his God": A Sumerian Variation on the "Job" Motif', in M. Noth and D. Winton Thomas (eds.). *Wisdom in Israel and in the Ancient Near East* (VTSup 3; Leiden: Brill, 1955), 170–82 for the text in Sumerian and a translation; for the Akkadian text of Ludlul bēl nēmeqi, see Lambert, *Babylonian Wisdom Literature*, 21–62. On petition in the Aqhat epic from Ugarit, see Wright, *Ritual in Narrative*, 29–41, 157–72. Entreaty in Mesopotamian and Ugaritic texts, as in biblical representation, is frequently

VARIETIES OF PETITIONARY MOURNING
AND THEIR PURPOSE

The mourning activity of petitioners is attested in narrative, prophetic, and psalmic texts, and comes in a variety of forms. Narrative and prophetic representations of both communal supplication and individual entreaty are complemented by the many psalms of complaint, both communal and individual, which possess their own distinct features and may be compared profitably to the representation of petitionary rites in the narrative and prophetic texts. In addition to the useful distinction that one might draw between communal and individual entreaty and between narrative/prophetic representations of petitionary mourning and those of the Psalms, it is also important to note the contrast between penitential and non-penitential supplication.[6] In the following discussion, I shall examine the various types of petition employing mourning behaviours and discuss their individual motivations as well as their common purpose.

Joel 1–2 describes communal rites of penitential entreaty in the sanctuary that temporarily replace the normal rejoicing activities of worshippers. The context of Joel 1–2 is an attack of locust hordes that destroys the produce of field and vineyard thereby causing severe famine (1: 4–7, 10–12, 16–20). As a result, the priests of the temple are ordered to mourn over the offerings now cut off from the sanctuary (1: 13):

> Gird on sackcloth and lament, O priests!
>   Wail, O servants of the altar!
> Come, spend the night in sackcloth,
>   servants of my God!
> For withheld from the house of your God,
>   are cereal offering and drink offering.[7]

characterized by mourning behaviours such as weeping, wailing, the tearing of the garment, and lamentation.

[6] The classic study of penitential rites is Lipinski's *La Liturgie pénitentielle*.

[7] The formulaic nature of this text is nicely explored by V. A. Hurowitz, who demonstrates close and striking parallels between Joel 1: 4–20 and Sargon II's Hymn to Nanaya, including parallel notations that the locust plague has brought to an end the sanctuary offerings ('Joel's Locust Plague in Light of Sargon II's Hymn to Nanaya', *JBL* 112 (1993), 597–603).

The whole of Judah is summoned to the sanctuary for a communal assembly and fast during which Yhwh is to be entreated (1: 14):

> Sanctify a fast![8]
> Call an assembly!
> Gather the elders,
> All the dwellers of the land,
> (to) the house of Yhwh, your God!
> And cry out to Yhwh![9]

The text notes that rejoicing (שמחה) and exultation (גיל) are cut off from the temple of Yhwh with the loss of food (1: 16). In Joel 2: 17, the priests are to petition Yhwh on behalf of the suffering people and land:

> Between the vestibule and the altar,
> Let the priests weep.
> Let the servants of Yhwh say,
> 'Spare your people, O Yhwh,
> Do not make your patrimony into a reproach . . .'

The penitential dimension of this text emerges clearly in 2: 12–13, and the motive for such penitential petition is underscored in 2: 14:

> Return to me with all your heart,
> With fasting, weeping and lamentation!
> Tear your heart, not your garments!
> And return to Yhwh your God,
> For gracious and compassionate is he,
> Patient, loyal, and willing to renounce punishment.
> Who knows? He might turn and relent . . .

Finally, Yhwh does relent; he transforms the people's situation, removing the locust horde. The people will now receive abundant provisions, with which they will be sated. In 2: 21, the

---

[8] The language of sanctification (קדשׁ צום) used of preparation for communal fasting underscores my observation that petitioners at such a fast must meet purity requirements. Cf. the use of this idiom in other texts that speak of preparation for worship or other encounters with Yhwh (Exod. 19: 10, 14; Num. 11: 18; Josh. 3: 5; 7: 13; 1 Sam. 16: 5; Joel 2: 15–16; 2 Chr. 30: 17–18). On communal fasts in general, see Podella, *Ṣôm-Fasten*.

[9] On the communal complaint summons form, see H. W. Wolff, 'Der Aufruf zur Volksklage', *ZAW* 76 (1964), 48–56.

ground is commanded to rejoice and exult; in 2: 23, it is the inhabitants of Zion who are so ordered. Petitionary mourning ends with the change in the community's circumstances.[10]

Joel 1–2 describes the temporary replacement of sanctuary rites of worship with petitionary mourning behaviours at a time of communal disaster. Mourning and supplication, replacing rejoicing, take place within the sanctuary sphere. They are led by the priests themselves, girded in sackcloth, who cry out to Yhwh for mercy in the vicinity of the altar (2: 17). Once Yhwh has determined to end the punishment, and the disastrous situation has passed, mourning ceases and rejoicing behaviour is reintroduced by order of Yhwh (2: 21, 23). The rhetorical contrast of petitionary mourning with rejoicing in Joel 1–2 and their complete separation ritually is precisely what we should expect, given the way in which mourning and rejoicing are typically represented as opposed ritual behaviours. Even if the offerings had been available in the sanctuary, other texts suggest that the fasting congregation would not have partaken of them, for to do so would mean effectively to rejoice and therefore, mix mourning behaviours with rites of rejoicing.[11] This temporary replacement of collective acts of rejoicing by corporate mourning rites in the sanctuary is typical of representations of communal entreaty, as is communal fasting and crying out to Yhwh (cf. e.g. 1 Sam. 7: 5–6; Neh. 9: 1–37 (Eng. 1–38); Jonah 3: 5–10). The call to repentance in Joel 2: 12–13 is paralleled in Jonah 3: 8, and the question 'Who knows? He might turn and relent' of Joel 2: 14 is reproduced almost verbatim in Jonah 3: 9.[12] One element missing from Joel 1–2 but present in some other texts describing communal penitential petition is an explicit confession of sin or a reference to such (e.g. 1 Sam. 7: 6; Neh. 9: 2), though Joel 2: 12–13 does contain the command to repent by means of the enactment of mourning rites. The abandonment of penitential supplication and its replacement with rejoicing might occur once the difficult situation that motivated petition has passed, as in Joel 1–2. Alternatively, it might take place after the passage of a

---

[10] Anderson compares Joel 1: 13–14, 16 to 2: 23, 26–7 as an illustration of the movement from mourning to rejoicing (*A Time to Mourn*, 110).

[11] For other examples of fasts in a sanctuary, see e.g. Judg. 20: 26–8; 1 Sam. 7: 5–6; and Jer. 36: 9. On each of these texts, see my discussion ahead.

[12] Joel 2: 14: מי יודע ישוב ונחם; Jonah 3: 9: מי יודע ישוב ונחם האלהים.

set period of time, as in the case of a calendrical fast day such as the Day of Purgation (or, Atonement) (Lev. 16: 29–34; 23: 26–32). Texts suggest that a desire on the part of the community to convince Yhwh to reverse his negative judgment against them and restore their fortunes typically motivates penitential petition of the communal type.

Like communal penitential entreaty, penitential petition of the individual is well represented in narrative materials. Ezra 9–10 is perhaps the richest example of penitential supplication in the setting of the sanctuary, and because of the context in which Ezra's petition occurs, it may be profitably compared to texts such as Joel 1–2. In contrast to examples of communal entreaty, in which the whole community abandons rejoicing and mourns collectively in the sanctuary, Ezra, the initial petitioner in Ezra 9–10, engages in mourning behaviours individually in the midst of other persons who continue to participate in regular temple worship. The second example of individual penitential petition that I shall discuss is the ritual activity of Nehemiah in Nehemiah 1. Far removed from the sanctuary setting of Ezra 9–10, the context of Nehemiah 1 is the royal city of Shushan in Persia.

Ezra 9: 3–4 narrates Ezra's public penitential mourning in reaction to the news of widespread intermarriages in the Judaean community; it also describes the formation of a significant support group around Ezra, which joins him in his ritual separation. According to 9: 5, Ezra begins to petition Yhwh through penitential prayer at the time of the evening sacrifice.[13] His support group increases in size as bystanders witness his mourning behaviour before the temple and join him ritually by weeping (10: 1): 'While Ezra prayed and confessed, weeping and prostrating himself before the house of God, an exceedingly large assembly—men, women, and children—gathered to him from Israel, and the people were weeping bitterly.'[14] Though Ezra and his supporters are physically present in the same locus as the worshipping community, they have clearly separated themselves ritually from that community through their mourning behaviour and their petitionary stance. After the people's

---

[13] A time of prayer, as Ps. 141: 2 and Dan. 9: 21 suggest. See further the discussion of Blenkinsopp, *Ezra-Nehemiah*, 177.

[14] Reading with Vg.; MT כי בכו העם הרבה בכה.

guilt is confessed and an oath to expel alien wives and their issue is imposed, the text states that Ezra retires to the sanctuary chamber (לשכה) of Yohanan ben Elyashib in which he continues to mourn over the people's transgression, abstaining from food and water (10: 6).[15] That the actions described occur in the sanctuary sphere is indicated by the loci of Ezra's acts of petition and mourning (before the House of God and in the chamber of Yohanan ben Elyashib) and by the mention of the evening sacrifice. But it is a sanctuary sphere in which cultic rites of rejoicing have not been suspended when Ezra petitions Yhwh, as indicated by the mention of Ezra's choice to continue his fast and abstain from eating and drinking. The narrative of Ezra's penitential petition suggests that an individual or small group might engage in entreaty in the sanctuary even while regular praise of Yhwh continues. What makes this possible is the complete ritual separation of petitioners from those engaging in acts of rejoicing. A petitioner such as Ezra fasts and mourns exclusively; there is no mixing of mourning and the sanctuary's rites of praise.

Nehemiah's appeal to Yhwh is described in the first chapter of the book attributed to him. After receiving an embassy from Judah bearing unfortunate tidings regarding the state of Jerusalem and its inhabitants, Nehemiah begins to petition Yhwh on their behalf: 'When I heard these words, I sat down and wept and mourned for days and fasted and prayed before the God of Heaven' (1: 4). Nehemiah's mourning rites are eventually augmented by a penitential prayer in vv. 5–11. In this prayer, Nehemiah confesses his own sins and those of Israel, and asks the deity to receive his entreaty and grant him success. The sequence of Nehemiah's ritual actions is similar to that of Ezra, who also reacts to a report of grievous news concerning the community with mourning behaviour and eventually, a prayer of penitential petition (Ezra 9: 3–15). The major difference is the setting of each narrative: Ezra 9–10 in the Jerusalem temple, and Nehemiah 1 in Shushan. These narratives of individual penitential entreaty suggest that such petition could take place either in the sanctuary or elsewhere, and when it occurs in the sanctuary, regular worship may continue around the petitioner(s).

---

[15] The word לשכה occurs in biblical texts with some frequency. It is used mainly of chambers in a sanctuary complex. See e.g. 1 Sam. 9: 22; Jer. 35: 2, 4; Ezekiel 40 *passim*; Neh. 10: 38, 39; 13: 5.

Like penitential entreaty, non-penitential petition is attested in both communal and individual forms. Examples of communal supplication of a non-penitential nature include 2 Chr. 20: 1–19 and Ezra 8: 21–3; 1 Samuel 1 is a prime illustration of non-penitential petition by an individual. In each of these cases, mourning is an essential component of the ritual behaviour of the petitioners, and in the case of 2 Chr. 20: 1–19 and 1 Samuel 1, entreaty occurs in the sanctuary.

2 Chr. 20: 1–19 describes an obligatory communal fast in the Jerusalem temple called by King Jehoshaphat at a time of national emergency. As the Ammonites, Moabites, and Edomites threaten to attack from En Gedi, Jehoshaphat seeks guidance and deliverance from Yhwh by means of a petitionary prayer in which he rehearses Yhwh's past acts on behalf of the people and expresses confidence in his ability and willingness to save them (20: 6–12). Verse 9, alluding perhaps to Solomon's prayer in 1 Kgs. 8: 28–30, refers to the temple as the site of supplication par excellence for the people. 'If trouble comes upon us,' says the text, 'the sword, judgment, plague or famine, we shall stand before this house and before you, for your name is in this house, and we shall cry out to you from our trouble, and you will hear and save.'[16] Yhwh answers Jehoshaphat's entreaty by means of a prophetic oracle containing assurances and directions for war (20: 14–17). The Judaeans prostrate themselves before Yhwh, and after this, the fast and petition is effectively ended by the Levites, who rise to sing songs of praise to Yhwh (20: 18–19).[17] Clearly, the purpose of this communal petition is to secure Yhwh's guidance and intervention at a time of crisis. The text contains no language of transgression or repentance; there is no confession of sin in Jehoshaphat's prayer to Yhwh. Yet most of the other elements of the communal fast in 2 Chr. 20: 1–19 are similar to those of a penitential fast of the community such as that described in Joel 1–2. The entire population gathers for the petition (20: 13; cf. Joel 2: 16); they fast and cry out (זעק)

---

[16] 1 Kgs. 8: 23–53, Solomon's temple prayer and the paradigmatic Deuteronomistic discourse on entreaty, speaks of the Jerusalem temple as the locus toward which supplication should be directed as well as the locus in which petition is to be made to Yhwh. Its focus, in contrast to 2 Chr. 20: 1–19, is penitential petition.

[17] ויקמו הלוים . . . להלל ליהוה אלהי ישראל בקול גדול למעלה.

to Yhwh that he might reverse their difficult situation (20: 9; cf. Joel 1: 14; Jonah 3: 7); they revert to rejoicing after the crisis has passed.

Ezra 8: 21–3 is a second example of a collective, non-penitential, petitionary fast. In contrast to 2 Chr. 20: 1–19, the fast is set in Babylon rather than in the Jerusalem temple. Yet like 2 Chr. 20: 1–19, there is no indication in the text that a penitential purpose lies behind the entreaty and its accompanying mourning behaviour. Rather, the fast is called by Ezra so that he and his followers might petition Yhwh to grant them safe passage to Jerusalem. The narrative speaks of those participating in fasting and petitioning afflicting themselves before Yhwh in order to secure a trouble-free journey (להתענות לפני אלהינו לבקש ממנו דרך ישרה). The fast was necessary, says the text, because Ezra was ashamed to ask the king to provide a military escort for protection, having boasted about Yhwh's might and his loyalty to those who seek him. The scene ends with the notation that Yhwh was effectively supplicated.

Narrative representation of an individual's non-penitential petition is best illustrated by Hannah's plea and vow in 1 Samuel 1. Hannah, who lacks children, entreats Yhwh for progeny privately at the Shiloh shrine during a family sacrifice (1: 9–10).[18] While weeping and as a component of her petition, she vows a vow: If Yhwh will give her a child, she will dedicate him to serve Yhwh for his lifetime (1: 11). Though she is not a penitent, Hannah's petitionary mourning is similar to that of Ezra in a number of respects. Like Ezra, Hannah mourns and petitions Yhwh in a sanctuary context in which the rites of cultic rejoicing continue to be operative. While she petitions, others are eating and drinking. Like Ezra, her mourning is an individual act. Through Hannah's movement out of the presence of her husband,[19] her weeping, her temporary abstention from food,[20] her prayer of petition, and her vow, Hannah separates herself ritually from her husband and his other dependants, who rejoice

---

[18] On the nature of this זבח הימים, see the discussion of R. Albertz, *A History of Israelite Religion in the Old Testament Period* (2 vols.; Louisville: Westminster/John Knox, 1994) 1: 101, who argues that this yearly, family sacrifice of Elkanah was vow-based. [19] See 1: 9: ותקם חנה אחרי אכלה.

[20] This is suggested indirectly by the notation that she ate after finishing her petition and departing from the presence of Eli the priest (v. 18).

by eating and drinking at their family sacrifice. Once Hannah's petition is complete, she rejoins her husband and the rest of the assembled body ritually by partaking of food, thereby abandoning her mourning actions (1: 18).[21] Hannah's termination of her mourning by participating in rejoicing behaviour is not unlike the end of the communal petitionary fast described in 2 Chr. 20: 1–19: Where Hannah eats in 1 Sam. 1: 18, the Levites sing songs of praise in 2 Chr. 20: 19.

The psalms of complaint (traditionally, psalms of lament), like the narrative and prophetic representations of petition, have the potential to contribute significantly to any reconstruction of penitential or non-penitential petition as it is represented in biblical texts, and so they shall now be considered. Complaint psalms, which for a century have attracted no small amount of attention from specialists, may be divided into two types: communal complaints and individual complaints.[22] Though many

---

[21] The reader might wonder why Hannah is able to separate herself ritually from her family and others observing the rites of a family sacrifice while the congregation of Neh. 8: 9–12 are forbidden by their leaders to weep and mourn during the New Year celebration. Though both texts describe rejoicing contexts, they differ in several ways. Where Hannah and her family have come to Shiloh for a family sacrifice, Neh. 8: 9–12 has as its setting the New Year festival. While Neh. 8: 9–12 states that rejoicing alone is obligatory at the New Year (cf. Deut. 16: 15 והיית אך שמח, said regarding the fall pilgrimage festival), there is no evidence for a similar exclusive requirement for family sacrifices of the sort described in 1 Samuel 1. The Hannah narrative suggests the legitimacy of an individual petition in the context of a family sacrifice, as long as the petitionary mourning activity is not mixed with rejoicing.

[22] A massive secondary literature focuses on the psalms of complaint. Helpful introductions (with bibliography) to issues such as *Sitz im Leben* and genre include E. Zenger, 'Das Buch der Psalmen', in idem. (ed.), *Einleitung in das Alte Testament* (3rd edn.; Kohlhammer Studienbücher Theologie 1.1; Stuttgart: Kohlhammer, 1998), 309–26, esp. 318–20; E. Gerstenberger, *Psalms, Part 1: With an Introduction to Cultic Poetry* (FOTL XIV; Grand Rapids, Mich.: Eerdmans, 1988), 11–14; idem. *Psalms, Part 2, and Lamentations* (FOTL XV; Grand Rapids, Mich.: Eerdmans, 2001), pp. xvii–xxii for an updated bibliography; idem. 'The Lyrical Literature', in D. A. Knight and G. M. Tucker (eds.), *The Hebrew Bible and its Modern Interpreters* (Chico, Calif.: Scholars Press; Philadelphia: Fortress Press, 1985), 409–44; and R. Albertz, *Persönliche Frömmigkeit und offizielle Religion: Religionsinterner Pluralismus in Israel und Babylon* (Calwer Theologische Monographien 9; Stuttgart: Calwer, 1978), 24–7. Individual studies of note include Gerstenberger, *Der bittende Mensch: Bittritual und Klagelied des Einzelnen im Alten Testament* (WMANT 51; Neukirchen-Vluyn: Neukirchener, 1980) and P. W. Ferris, Jr., *The Genre of*

scholars associate the communal complaint with petition at a sanctuary in the context of a fast,[23] the setting of the individual complaint remains much debated, with some commentators arguing for the household as major context, others for the sanctuary, and still others taking other positions.[24] It seems likely that the milieu of individual petition varied, given the evidence of the complaints themselves and narrative or prophetic texts to which they may be compared (e.g. 1 Samuel 1; Nehemiah 1). It is possible that at least some individual complaints find their context in the household, though narrative texts such as 1 Samuel 1 or Ezra 9–10 suggest that the sanctuary could certainly serve as a context for individual entreaty as well.

Psalms of complaint enrich our perspective on the representation of petition by introducing new observations about petitionary ritual behaviour and by confirming aspects of the impression generated by the narrative and prophetic texts already examined. Allusions made to mourning rites associated with supplication of the deity occur in a number of psalms. For example, Ps. 69: 11–12 (Eng. 10–11) mentions the petitioner weeping, fasting, and wearing sackcloth while entreating the deity, and adds that he was reviled for doing so.[25] Ps. 44: 26 (Eng. 25) suggests such mourning rites through a striking image of the prostration of petitioners not unlike what one might find in

---

Communal Lament in the Bible and the Ancient Near East (SBLDS 127; Atlanta: Scholars Press, 1992). On exilic developments pertaining to the complaint psalms, see esp. Albertz, *Die Exilszeit: 6. Jahrhundert v. Chr.* (Biblische Enzyklopädie 7; Stuttgart: Kohlhammer, 2001) 130–5.

[23] See e.g. Gerstenberger, *Der bittende Mensch*, 134; Albertz, *Frömmigkeit*, 27.

[24] The argument for the household as a major context for individual petition was developed by Gerstenberger based on Babylonian analogies. For this position, see Gerstenberger, *Der bittende Mensch*, 134–60, esp. 151–3, and Albertz, *Frömmigkeit*, 26–7 and *A History of Israelite Religion* 1: 100–1, who favours it. As Albertz notes, to speak of a household context as opposed to a sanctuary setting does not exclude a cultic locus per se, since cultic activity characterized both situations (*A History of Israelite Religion*, 1: 281 n. 47). For a summary of other positions, see conveniently Gerstenberger, 'The Lyrical Literature', 429, who notes the continuing popularity of setting the individual complaint in the sanctuary.

[25] Mocking and reviling of the petitioner is a topos throughout the psalms of individual complaint. On descriptions of the activity of enemies in complaints of the individual, see briefly Zenger, 'Das Buch der Psalmen', 319–20.

descriptions of mourning the dead: 'Our soul is low in the dust (עָפָר),' // 'Our belly clings to the earth (אָרֶץ).' In addition, passages such as Ps. 69: 21 (Eng. 20) and Ps. 35: 13–14 mention or allude to a role played by comforters in petitionary mourning, something not clearly evidenced in the narrative and prophetic representations of rites of entreaty. As a result, psalms of complaint provide the scholar with the opportunity to compare and contrast the comforting of mourners over the dead with that of petitioners. Furthermore, complaint psalms serve as yet another source of evidence for the separation of mourning behaviours from the rites of rejoicing. Whenever praise of Yhwh is mentioned in these psalms, it is represented consistently as a future action to take place after the alleviation of the petitioner's difficulties (e.g. Ps. 22: 23–7 (Eng. 22–6); 35: 9–10, 18; 69: 31–7 (Eng. 30–6)), and never as something to be offered at the time of petition.[26]

There is yet another aspect of the richness of the complaint psalms worthy of note. Though they are highly stylized, they may nonetheless provide us with access to the liturgical language of supplication, or at least to literary renderings of such language. Examples of direct pleas to the deity in the psalms of communal complaint include Ps. 44: 24–5, 27 (Eng. 23–4, 26):

> Awake! Why do you sleep, Lord?
> Wake up! Do not spurn (us) forever!
> Why do you hide your face?
> (Why) have you forgotten our affliction and our oppression?
>
> Arise, (be) a help for us!
> Redeem us on account of your covenant loyalty.

A second example, from an individual complaint psalm, is Ps. 22: 20–2 (Eng. 19–21):

> But as for you, Yhwh, do not be far away!
> My help, make haste for my assistance!
> Deliver my life from the sword,
> My only one from the hand of a dog!
> Save me from the mouth of a lion,
> From the horns of wild oxen answer me!

---

[26] A point emphasized by Anderson, *A Time to Mourn*, 91–3. On the vow of praise in the complaint psalms, see further Westermann, *Das Loben Gottes in den Psalmen* (3rd edn.; Göttingen: Vandenhoeck & Ruprecht, 1963), 44–6, 56–9.

The theme of oppression at the hands of enemies in psalms such as these is commonplace, and the animal imagery used here to characterize the petitioner's foes is particularly striking.

As the foregoing survey suggests, petition of the deity and its attendant ritual behaviours have a variety of specific motivations. Petitioners may call upon Yhwh to save them from enemies (e.g. 2 Chr. 20: 1–19), to heal them when they are sick (e.g. Psalm 6), to provide something lacking, such as progeny (e.g. 1 Samuel 1). Yhwh may be entreated to reverse a decision to punish the people or an individual (e.g. Jer. 6: 26; 14: 7–9; 2 Sam. 12: 16–23); to restore the people's fortunes after disaster (e.g. Psalm 79; Lam. 5: 21); or to provide the petitioner with an oracle or vision (e.g. Judg. 20: 23, 26–8; Dan. 10: 2–3, 12). Petitionary mourning rites may be used to acknowledge submission to authority, either divine or human (e.g. 2 Sam. 19: 25 (Eng. 24); 1 Kgs. 21: 27–9), and to indicate repentance for transgressions committed (e.g. Neh. 1: 6).[27] They may serve to secure safe passage on a dangerous journey (Ezra 8: 21). But whatever the specific goal of a particular petitioner, all entreaty shares a common, overriding purpose: to get Yhwh or the human authority to notice the petitioner, receive the plea, and take action on the petitioner's behalf. This sentiment is well-expressed by Ps. 55: 2–3 (Eng. 1–2): 'Give ear, O God, to my prayer!' // 'Do not hide yourself from my petition!' // 'Attend to me and answer me!' Other texts indicate that fasting and other expressions of petitionary mourning are understood to increase the likelihood that the petitioner's plea will be noticed and that action will be taken. In Jonah 3: 7–8, the king of Nineveh orders his people to fast, don sackcloth, call to Yhwh and repent, in order to avoid destruction. In v. 9, the motivation for such ritual action is made clear: 'Who knows? God might turn and relent and turn away from his fierce anger and we will not perish.' 2 Sam. 12: 22 is similar. In this verse, David explains his motivation for undertaking petitionary mourning rites on behalf of his dying son: 'While the child still lived, I fasted and I wept, for I thought, "Who knows? Yhwh might favour me and the child might live."' The words of the people in Isa. 58: 3, part of a larger passage critical of Israelite piety, suggest clearly a

---

[27] On mourning and submission to authority, see Kutsch, ' "Trauer-bräuche" und "Selbstminderungsriten" ', 82–4.

common instrumental purpose to petitionary rites such as
fasting:

> Why do we fast, when you do not see?
> Afflict ourselves, when you do not hear?

The point of self-affliction by petitioners is to get noticed
and elicit a positive, active response from Yhwh or a human
authority. Isa. 58: 5 suggests this by describing the fast both as 'a
day when a person afflicts himself' (יום ענות אדם נפשו) and as 'a day
of Yhwh's favour' or 'acceptance' (יום רצון ליהוה).

LOCUS, TIME PERIOD, AND REVERSIBILITY
OF THE PETITIONARY RITUAL STANCE

In contrast to mourning the dead, which probably occurred
mainly in a household setting and never in sanctified places, texts
represent petitionary mourning taking place in a wider range of
locations. Petition may occur in the sanctuary, as texts such as
Joel 1–2, Ezra 9–10, and 1 Samuel 1 indicate. It may also occur
in the war camp or other public loci where the people might
assemble (e.g. by the River Ahava in Babylon (Ezra 8: 21)). A
number of texts suggest the home as a place for entreaty.
Hezekiah petitions Yhwh effectively from his palace when he is
sick to the point of death (2 Kgs. 20: 2–3 = Isa. 38: 2–3). Hos. 7:
14 speaks of Ephraimites petitioning Yhwh[28] for agricultural
bounty, presumably from their homes: 'They do not cry out to
me with their heart,' // 'But they wail upon their beds (משכבותם).'
// 'For grain and new wine they lacerate themselves,'[29] // 'They
turn aside from me.'[30] Ps. 35: 14 suggests that petition takes place

---

[28] I am not convinced by the arguments of those who attempt to associate the
rites described in Hos. 7: 14 with the worship of Baal. On this, see the cogent
critique of Schmidt, *Israel's Beneficent Dead*, 169–70.

[29] Reconstructing יתגודדו, 'they lacerate themselves', for MT יתגוררו on the
basis of LXX κατετέμνοντο, some Hebrew manuscripts, and the parallelism with
ייליל, 'they wail', as H. W. Wolff has pointed out (*Hosea* (Hermeneia;
Philadelphia: Fortress, 1974), 108). Scribal confusion of dalet and resh would
account for the error; as is widely noted, such confusion is exceedingly common
at many points in the history of the biblical text's transmission.

[30] The mention of 'their beds' suggests a probable domestic locus of petition.
Cf. 1 Kgs. 1: 47, where David is said to worship upon his bed after receiving the
news of Solomon's securing the throne. But see, alternatively, Isa. 57: 7–8,
which associates beds with rites outside the home.

wherever the petitioner goes, given the portability of his mourning behaviour: 'I walked about (התהלכתי) like a person mourning (his) mother.' The entreaties of David and presumably, his supporters, after Absalom's revolt has begun, occur as they flee Jerusalem, walking up the Mount of Olives outside the city (2 Sam. 15: 14–16: 13).[31]

Two additional points of contrast with mourning the dead are the time period of petitionary mourning and the ease with which the petitioner may revert to a ritual stance of rejoicing. While mourning the dead lasts for a set period of time (most commonly, seven days), petition may or may not be temporally restricted. Communal fasts, with an established beginning and end, are commonplace in the biblical text; these might last for one or more days and nights.[32] Daniel's petitionary mourning for the purpose of receiving a guiding vision lasts three weeks according to Dan. 10: 2. But descriptions of or allusions to individual and communal petitions that have no established end point are also attested. Such petitions apparently end when Yhwh has intervened to ameliorate the situation of the petitioner(s) (e.g. Ps. 14: 7) or when the petitioner(s) choose(s) to end the petition (e.g. 1 Sam. 1: 18). A clean petitioner's lack of pollution, in contrast to the mourner over the dead, allows him the option to end his

---

[31] Though the element of supplication in this narrative is admittedly muted given the grave circumstances, it is present nonetheless in David's direct petition to Yhwh in v. 31: 'Render the counsel of Ahitophel useless, O Yhwh!' I read David's statement in vv. 25–6, as fatalistic as it may seem at first blush, to imply that his mourning behaviour, and that of his courtiers and followers, is intended precisely to curry favour with Yhwh under these difficult circumstances. Speaking to Zadok the priest, David says: 'If I find favour in the eyes of Yhwh, he will let me return and see it (the Ark of the Covenant) and its abode. But if he says, "I do not delight in you", here I am; let him do to me whatever is good in his sight.' Finally, 16: 12 may suggest that a petitionary purpose underlies David's rites if by 'affliction' David refers both to his external circumstances and to his acts of self-abnegation: 'Perhaps Yhwh will look upon my affliction and Yhwh will return to me good in place of his (Shimi's) curse today.' (The reading עניי, 'affliction', is supported by MT manuscripts, LXX, Vg., and Syr., and is preferable to MT ketib עוני, 'my iniquity', and qere עיני, 'my eye'. On this, see McCarter, *II Samuel*, 369.) For verbal forms of the root ענה that describe self-affliction by means of rites such as fasting, see e.g. Isa. 58: 3, 5; Ps. 35: 13; Dan. 10: 12; Ezra 8: 21.

[32] e.g. while the two communal petitionary fasts described in Judg. 20: 23 and 26 last until the evening of the day on which they began, the communal fast called by Esther for her benefit is to last three days and nights (Esther 4: 16).

petition suddenly and assume a rejoicing posture simply by reversing his mourning behaviours, as David does in 2 Sam. 12: 20. Because the supplicant is generally not polluted, there is no obligatory wait for purity, nor is there a purification process that he must undergo before he can rejoice. Texts suggest the rapidity that may characterize a shift from petition to rejoicing (e.g. Ps. 30: 6b (Eng. 5b)).

THE ROLE OF SELF-DEBASEMENT IN PETITIONARY MOURNING

Petitionary rites are frequently associated with self-debasement, as various texts show. One such text, 2 Kgs. 22: 11–20, describes King Josiah's response to hearing the content of the book of the Torah found in the Jerusalem temple during its refurbishment. Upon hearing the words of the book, Josiah tears his garments, and orders his courtiers to 'seek Yhwh' (דרשו את יהוה) on his account and on account of the people.[33] His courtiers consult Huldah, a woman prophet who delivers an oracle from Yhwh promising the fulfilment of covenant curses against Judah and Jerusalem. But concerning Josiah himself, she prophesies as follows: 'Because your heart was penitent (רך), and you humbled yourself (ותכנע) before Yhwh when you heard what I had spoken concerning this place . . . and you tore your garments and wept before me, I too have heard—oracle of Yhwh.' Josiah's reward, according to this oracle, is to be a peaceful death without having to witness the devastation to come.[34] Tearing garments, weeping, fasting, and other rites of petition are thus cast as self-debasing acts. To perform these ritual actions in a penitential petitionary context means, therefore, to humble oneself. This association of such rites and self-debasement is present in other texts as well. In 1 Kgs. 21: 27, 29, Ahab's tearing of his garments, wearing sackcloth, fasting, and other mourning actions are equated with self-humbling by the text.

---

[33] The language of 'seeking Yhwh' or 'seeking from Yhwh' (דרש or בקש) in communal and individual petitionary contexts is commonplace. See e.g. 2 Sam. 12: 16; Dan. 9: 3; Ezra 8: 21; 2 Chr. 20: 4 and the discussion of Podella, *Şôm-Fasten*, 237–42, 266.

[34] But cf. 2 Kgs. 23: 29–30!

Self-debasement through rites of entreaty is certainly a strong theme of texts that portray penitential petition, but it is not exclusive to scenarios of repentance. Psalms of individual and communal complaint with no penitential associations also allude to debasing ritual actions on the part of petitioners. Ps. 44: 26 (Eng. 25) is but one example. Toward the end of this communal complaint, the people allude to their self-debasing ritual action of lying on the ground in the dust, an act intended to elicit a favourable response from the deity: 'Our soul is low (שׁחה) in the dust,' // 'Our belly clings to the earth.' Ps. 35: 14 is similar. In this individual complaint, the petitioner tells how he walked around prostrated as a mourner (קדר שׁחותי) on behalf of sick friends. It is striking how similar each of these texts is to Ps. 38: 7 (Eng. 6), which describes an individual sinner's petition: 'I was bowed down, I was exceedingly low (שׁחותי),' // 'All day I walked around, a mourner (קדר).' Both Ps. 44: 26 (Eng. 25) and Ps. 35: 14 use the verb 'to be low' (שׁחה) in their descriptions of the ritual actions of non-penitential petitioners, as does Ps. 38: 7 (Eng. 6) for the penitential supplicant.[35] Ps. 35: 14 employs the noun 'mourner' (literally, 'one who is dark', קדר) in the same manner as Ps. 38: 7 (Eng. 6). On the basis of these texts, there appears to be little distinction made between penitential and non-penitential petition with respect to self-debasement. In characterizations of both types of petition, self-debasement is a prominent theme.

The self-debasement of both penitent and non-penitential petitioner can be explained if we understand debasement to function differently in each type of petitionary scenario. For the penitent, debasement may communicate the acknowledgement of transgression, sentiments such as shame, repentance, and the concession of Yhwh's authority, as various texts suggest (e.g. Lev. 26: 40–2; 1 Kgs. 21: 27, 29; 2 Chr. 7: 14; 12: 6; 32: 26). Implicit in such self-diminishing behaviour is also the hope that Yhwh will take notice and act on behalf of the petitioner, as I have argued. In the case of the penitent, such action might be forgiveness or the reversal or tempering of a decision to punish or destroy. For the non-penitential petitioner, debasement must

---

[35] The verb 'to be low' (שׁחה) has strong diminishment associations across its range of usage. See e.g. Isa. 2: 9, 11, 17; 5: 15, where it is used of the debasement of proud people by Yhwh.

have a function unrelated to the acknowledgement of trans-gression and repentance, though shame is a possible motivating factor, as Ps. 44: 10, 14–15, 16–17 (Eng. 9, 13–14, 15–16) show.[36] The debasement of the non-penitential petitioner through mourning rites is probably best explained as a strategy intended to attract the deity's attention to the petitioner's plight and elicit his positive intervention. Secondarily, it may also express shame if that sentiment is in evidence. Thus, the self-debasement of the non-penitential petitioner is potentially less complex than that of the penitent, for it may only be intended to attract the deity's attention to the petitioner's situation and secure his help to address it.

The self-debasement of the non-penitential petitioner should not give pause. Petition scenarios, including those that lack mourning behaviours, are characterized by acts of relinquishing something of value. Texts portray petitioners who do not utilize mourning rites petitioning the deity by means of vows such as Jacob's vow in Gen. 28: 20–2. In this vow, Jacob promises Yhwh that Yhwh will be his God, that the site of Jacob's dream will become a sanctuary, and that he will give to Yhwh one tenth of all he has, in exchange for Yhwh's protection and support on his journey. Petitioners may utilize offerings to secure the deity's positive action, as David proposes in 1 Sam. 26: 19 when he addresses Saul, who has been pursuing him: 'Now then, may my lord the king hear the words of his servant. If Yhwh has incited you against me, let him accept a sacrifice.[37] But if it is people (who have done it), cursed are they before Yhwh . . .' Each of these scenarios requires the petitioner to give up items of value in order to gain divine notice and elicit positive action from the deity. Self-debasing mourning rites are comparable, in that they strip petitioners of some degree of honour, making them 'low' (שחח, as in Pss. 35: 14; 38: 7 (Eng. 6)) for a period of time for the purpose of ameliorating their situations. In addition, actions

---

[36] The association of shame with mourning behaviours is found in a number of texts aside from those that describe penitential or non-penitential petition. See e.g. texts that mention the mourning of a defeated, shamed army (e.g. 2 Sam. 19: 3–4 (Eng. 2–3)), the mourning of shamed fugitives (Ezek. 7: 18), and the mourning of individuals who have been humiliated (e.g. Esther 6: 12). I shall discuss these texts in Chapter 3.

[37] Literally, 'let him smell a sacrifice' (ירח מנחה), meaning, let Yhwh be appeased by an offering and stop inciting Saul against David.

such as fasting, sitting on the ground, wearing sackcloth, and abstaining from anointing and washing constitute sacrifice of very concrete goods and comforts. Vows and other ways of ceding items of value to the deity in exchange for divine action or intervention may be combined with rites of petitionary mourning, as the Hannah narrative in 1 Samuel 1 illustrates.

PETITIONARY MOURNING AND THE CULT

A striking point of contrast between mourners over the dead and petitioners is the access of the petitioner who meets purity requirements to the sanctuary.[38] Whether the context is a public, communal fast that entirely displaces the rejoicing rites of the temple or an individual or small group petition in a sanctuary context in which rites of rejoicing continue around the suppliant(s), petitionary mourning in a sanctified setting is represented as routine. It is in fact sanctioned and even commanded by the deity according to certain texts (e.g. Joel 1–2). Yet petitioners in the sanctuary are consistently represented as separating themselves ritually from those engaged in rites of rejoicing, never mixing or combining mourning behaviours with rejoicing rites. This pattern of separation seems key to understanding petitionary mourning in a cultic locus.

But what of sacrifices offered in the context of petition? A number of texts mention sacrificial activities in connection with entreaty in a sanctuary context, and these must be explained, given the consistent pattern of separating the rites of mourning from those of rejoicing, and the frequent association of sacrifice with rejoicing. 1 Sam. 7: 5–9 illustrates well the role offerings might play in the context of sanctuary petition:

And Samuel said: 'Gather all Israel to Mispah and I shall pray on your account to Yhwh.' And they were gathered to Mispah, drew water and poured (it) out before Yhwh, and fasted on that day, and said, 'We have sinned against Yhwh' . . . And the Israelites said to Samuel: 'Do not neglect to cry out for us to Yhwh our God that he might deliver us from

---

[38] As I have noted, Anderson believes that petitioners are defiled through mourning activity per se, and are therefore separated from the sanctuary like mourners for the dead, though the narrative evidence suggests otherwise. See further my discussion in n. 4 above.

the hand of the Philistines.' So Samuel took one suckling lamb and offered it up as a whole burnt offering to Yhwh, and Samuel cried out to Yhwh on behalf of Israel, and Yhwh answered him.

1 Sam. 7: 5–9 mentions both the pouring out of water and the burning of a whole burnt offering (עולה כליל) as components of Israel's petition to Yhwh at the sanctuary at Mispah. These ritual acts are combined with fasting and confession of sin in this penitential narrative. A second example of fasting in combination with sacrifices is Jer. 14: 12. In this text, Yhwh speaks of his unwillingness to respond to the petition of the Judaeans: 'Though they fast, I will not hear their cry, and though they offer up whole burnt offering (עלה) and grain offering (מנחה), I will not accept them.'[39] Another illustration of sacrifice in the context of penitential petition in a sanctuary setting is the observance of the Day of Purgation (or, Atonement), as narrated in Leviticus 16; 23: 26–32; and Num. 29: 7–11. Each of these passages mentions required offerings to Yhwh on this day of self-affliction. According to Leviticus 16, purification sacrifices (חטאת) and whole burnt offerings (עולה) are made to the deity on the Day of Purgation; Num. 29: 7–11 adds cereal and drink offerings in addition to whole burnt offerings and purification sacrifices. Leviticus 16 suggests that the function of sacrifices on the Day of Purgation is purgation and expiation, the removal of pollution and transgression through purification and atonement.[40]

Clearly, the sacrifices of the communal penitential fasts narrated in 1 Sam. 7: 5–9 and Jer. 14: 12 and those of the Day of Purgation are central elements of the petitionary enterprise as it is narrated in 1 Sam. 7: 5–9, Jer. 14: 12, and the Day of Purgation passages in Leviticus and Numbers. But the offering of these sacrifices ought not to be understood to constitute an act of rejoicing. On the contrary, the people fast according to 1 Sam. 7: 6 and Jer. 14: 12, and this is probably also the case in texts such as Lev. 16: 29 that command Israel to afflict themselves but do not specify fasting per se.[41] There is no hint in these texts that the

[39] The mention of sacrifices in this verse indicates that a sanctuary locus is assumed for the fast.

[40] On the range of the verb כפר in Lev. 16 and elsewhere, see further the comments of J. Milgrom, *Leviticus 1–16*, 1079–84, and B. A. Levine, *In the Presence of the Lord: A Study of Cult and Some Cultic Terms in Ancient Israel* (Studies in Judaism in Late Antiquity 5; Leiden: Brill, 1974), 56–77.

[41] Fasting is a typical component of self-affliction as it is described in biblical

people partake of the sacrifices in any way, an act central to rejoicing as it is represented in various passages (e.g. Neh. 8: 10, 12; Ps. 107: 21–2).[42] No mention is made of the well-being (or peace) offering (שלמים) or its subtypes (e.g. the thanksgiving offering (תודה)),[43] a portion of which is reserved for the offerer and his dependants.[44] Nor does the distinct vocabulary of rejoicing occur. Petitionary sacrifice involves no element of rejoicing, and therefore the offering of such sacrifices does not challenge the pattern of the ritual separation of mourning and rejoicing activities. Clearly, sacrifice per se does not constitute rejoicing, for a central component of rejoicing is the worshipper's consumption of food and drink.[45]

---

texts, particularly prominent in narratives of communal petition. Note the parallel between fasting and self-affliction in Isa. 58: 3 (עניגו // למה צמנו ולא ראית ונפשנו ולא תדע) and that fasting is a component of self-affliction according to Dan. 10: 12 (cf. vv. 2–3).

[42] On the central role of eating and drinking in rejoicing, see further Anderson, *A Time to Mourn*, 19–26, who includes discussion of relevant rabbinic texts.

[43] I have followed P's classification schema here for simplicity's sake. On P's view of the שלמים and תודה, see Lev. 7: 11–15. P divides the שלמים into three subtypes: תודה, נדר, and נרבה. It seems likely that these were originally independent sacrifices rather than subtypes of the שלמים as P would have it. On this issue, see the analysis of B. Levine, *In the Presence of the Lord*, 45–52, and the discussion of Milgrom, *Leviticus 1–16*, 219.

[44] Judg. 20: 26–8 mentions the offering of עלות and שלמים on a petitionary fast day in the Bethel sanctuary: ויצומו ביום ההוא עד הערב ויעלו עלות ושלמים לפני יהוה. Milgrom reads the text to suggest that the offerings were made in the evening, after the completion of fasting, as an act of rejoicing to end the fast (*Leviticus 1–16*, 217). Lipinski's interpretation is similar (*La Liturgie pénitentielle*, 84). This understanding of the intent of the text is certainly viable. It also relieves the difficulty posed by the notion of sacrificing שלמים during a fast, for how could the public fast and eat at the same time?

[45] Note also the אשם and חטאת sacrifices associated with individual penitential rituals in texts such as Lev. 5: 1–6, 20–6 (Eng. 6: 1–7). As with communal petition scenarios, the prescriptive texts concerning penitential petition feature the offering of sacrifices as a component of the penitential process but make no suggestion that the penitent partakes of any sacrifice during the penitential rites. My thanks to David P. Wright (e-mail of 10 July 2001) for reminding me of these texts.

THE PETITIONER AND DEATH

A common topos in the psalms of complaint and the thanksgiving psalms is the theme of the petitioner, sometimes described as sick, approaching or being present in Sheol, the realm of the dead, or drowning in deep waters.[46] An example of the latter is found in Ps. 69: 2–3 (Eng. 1–2):

> Deliver me, God, for the waters have reached my neck,
> I am sinking in the mud of the deep with no foothold.
> I have entered the depths of the waters,
> The streams flood over me.

Psalm 88: 3–5, 8 (Eng. 2–4, 7) combine imagery of the supplicant's descent to the underworld and that of his drowning, though Sheol imagery predominates:

> Let my prayer come before you,
> Incline your ear to my cry!
> For my soul is filled with troubles,
> And my life approaches Sheol.
> I am reckoned with those who descend into the Pit,
> I am like a man without strength . . .
>
> Upon me your wrath lies,
> You afflict (me) with all your waves.

The imagery of descent to the underworld or foundering in dangerous waters appears to serve a number of purposes. That it is a rhetorical strategy intended to bring the desperation of the petitioner into high relief, as well as the decisiveness of Yhwh's anticipated intervention on the supplicant's behalf (e.g. Ps. 30: 4 (Eng. 3); Isa. 38: 17) is difficult to deny. Such images also accentuate the distance from the deity that the petitioner perceives at the time of his entreaty. These emphases are highlighted

---

[46] The theme of the sick petitioner in the psalms is explored in detail in Seybold, *Das Gebet des Kranken im Alten Testament*. The classic study of the 'rescue from Sheol' topos is Barth's *Errettung vom Tode*. Barth, developing observations of J. Pedersen, challenges the idea that the rhetoric of approaching the underworld is a poetic trope and nothing more. For him, the supplicant's experience of Sheol is as real as that of the dead themselves, though not identical to it. For Pedersen's discussion, which Barth cites, see *Israel: Its Life and Culture* (4 vols.; London: Oxford University Press; Copenhagen: Povl Branner, 1926–40), 2: 466–7.

through both implicit and explicit comparison of the petitioner with the dead, who are frequently described as 'cut off' from Yhwh, as in Ps. 88: 6 (Eng. 5) and similar texts.[47] Such texts characterize being cut off from the deity as an inability to offer him praise, to speak of his acts of covenant loyalty, even to remember him. Yhwh, for his part, does not act on behalf of the dead, and is said to have forgotten them.

Like the dead, the petitioner cannot offer praise;[48] he probably also resembles the denizens of the underworld when he engages in rites of mourning.[49] Yet the petitioner, in contrast to the dead, can vow to praise the deity once he abandons his stance of entreaty (e.g. Pss. 22: 23–26 (Eng. 22–5); 35: 18, 28). Further-more, unlike Sheol's inhabitants, the supplicant of the psalms of complaint speaks often and at times, confidently, of Yhwh's covenant loyalty and his ability to save (e.g. Ps. 35: 9–10). In con-trast to the dead, the petitioner remembers Yhwh, and calls upon him to act for his benefit (e.g. Pss. 51: 3–4 (Eng. 1–2); 88: 3 (Eng. 2)). Yhwh, for his part, acts decisively to rescue petitioners from the underworld (e.g. Ps. 30: 2–4 (Eng. 1–3)), unlike the dead, whom he has forgotten. Narrative depictions of entreaty suggest that the typical petitioner has full access to the sanctuary even while petitioning, in contrast both to the dead who are cut off from the sanctuary forever, and to the mourner over the dead, who is separated from the temple for the period of mourning.[50] In short, the petitioner's comparison of himself with the dead in psalms of complaint is rather imperfect and asymmetrical. There are a few points of contact between the petitioner and the dead, but as many or more points of contrast. The petitioner, in a number of important respects, is not at all like the dead. Yet, even given the differences, there is an evident identification of the petitioner with the dead in Sheol. This is established through direct statements (e.g. 'My life approaches Sheol' // 'I am reckoned with those who descend into the Pit'), the rhetoric of

---

[47] e.g. Isa. 38: 11, 18; Pss. 6: 6 (Eng. 5); 28: 1; 30: 10; 115: 17–18; Sir. 17: 27–8; and probably Ezek. 37: 11. On this, see further Olyan, ' "We are Utterly Cut Off": Some Possible Nuances of נגזרנו לנו in Ezek. 37: 11', *Catholic Biblical Quarterly*, 65 (2003), 43–57. [48] See n. 26.

[49] See my discussion in Ch. 1.

[50] The access of petitioners to the sanctuary is also clear in Solomon's prayer (1 Kgs. 8: 23–53). In v. 33, the sinning people may entreat Yhwh in the temple; other verses speak of supplicants praying in the direction of the temple.

being 'low' (שחח),[51] and the petitioner's mourning rites, which include sitting on the ground, an enactment of ritual descent to the underworld, as I have discussed.[52] The troubled petitioner is best described as occupying a niche between the living and the dead for the period of his supplication, for he shares characteristics with both.[53] In short, from a ritual standpoint, his situation is not unlike that of the mourner over the dead. It is perhaps captured best by Isa. 38: 14, a verse in which the ill petitioner, Hezekiah, king of Judah, makes bird-like sounds associated with the dead and, at the same time, calls upon Yhwh to save him, something the dead cannot do.[54]

As I have argued, the image of the petitioner approaching or residing in the underworld serves to emphasize his desperation and feelings of distance from the deity, and to bring into relief the decisiveness of Yhwh's anticipated intervention on

[51] As I have pointed out, the verb שחח, 'to be low', is employed to describe the ritual debasement of both penitential and non-penitential petitioner in psalms of individual and communal complaint (Pss. 35: 14; 38: 7 (Eng. 6); 44: 26 (Eng. 25)). Strikingly, the same verb is used in Isa. 29: 4 to compare besieged Jerusalem to the dead in the underworld: 'You will be low, from the underworld you will speak' // 'From the dust your word will be low' // 'Your voice will be like (that of) a ghost from the underworld' // 'From the dust your word will chirp' (ושפלת מארץ תדברי // ומעפר תשח אמרתך // והיה כאוב מארץ קולך // ומעפר אמרתך תצפצף). Just as the dead are low and speak in a lowly way, so the petitioner is low in imitation. On the chirping of the dead, see n. 54.

[52] The underworld associations of the ground as a locus for petition are well captured by the parallelism of עפר ('dust') and ארץ ('earth') in Ps. 44: 26 (Eng. 25). Cf. Isa. 29: 4, where עפר and ארץ are used together and unambiguously refer to the underworld. Note also Ps. 22: 30 (Eng. 29). The two terms occur separately with this meaning in a number of texts (e.g. Isa. 26: 19; Jonah 2: 7 (Eng. 6); Job 17: 16; Dan. 12: 2).

[53] See, similarly, Barth, *Errettung vom Tode*, 117, who reaches this conclusion without the same set of observations regarding the differences between the dead and the petitioner ('Der Bedrängte ist weder ein Toter noch ein im vollen Sinne Lebendiger; irgendwo in der Mitte hält er sich auf').

[54] For the association of bird-like sounds with the dead, see Isa. 29: 4 (the verb is צפצף). Cf. 8: 19, where the same verb is used of the sounds made by mediums and necromancers when they summon the dead. For the dead having a bird-like appearance, see Enkidu's dream in Gilgamesh vii, as noted by Blenkinsopp, *Isaiah 1–39* (AB 19; New York: Doubleday, 2000), 485. The motif of the bird-like appearance of the dead appears also in the Descent of Ishtar and Nergal and Ereshkigal. Feldman notes these correlations (*Defilement and Mourning*, 22). Bird-like moaning of a suffering petitioner is mentioned in Ludlul bēl nēmeqi, line 107 (Lambert, *Babylonian Wisdom Literature*, 36).

his behalf. Thus, it is not unlike the image of the drowning petitioner. Like the petitioner's mourning behaviours, the rhetoric of approaching or residing in Sheol debases the petitioner; it seems designed to attract the deity's attention to the petitioner's plea and secure his positive action for the petitioner's benefit. This subordination of the underworld imagery of the complaint psalms and the petitioner's mourning rites to the practical goals of entreaty is underscored by texts such as Pss. 88: 3–4 (Eng. 2–3) and 44: 25–7 (Eng. 24–6). Ps. 88: 3–4 (Eng. 2–3) reads: 'Incline your ear to my cry,' // '*For* my soul is filled with troubles,' // 'And my life approaches Sheol.' Ps. 44: 25–7 (Eng. 24–6) is similar: 'Why do you hide your face?' // '(Why) have you forgotten our affliction and our oppression?' // '*For* our soul is low in the dust,' // 'Our belly clings to the earth.' Both the mourning actions and the underworld associations of the supplicants in these psalms are ultimately intended to focus Yhwh's attention on their plight and provoke his positive action on their behalf. No matter how real the Sheol experience might be for the petitioner, the identification with the dead present in his behaviour and self-description functions mainly to serve the larger purposes of supplication. This stands in contrast to the identification of the mourner over the dead with the dead, which addresses very different social and ritual needs.[55]

[55] Anderson's understanding of the function of the underworld imagery of the psalms of complaint as well as the petitioner's mourning behaviour is somewhat different from mine (*A Time to Mourn*, 87–91). If I understand him correctly, he believes that the petitioner undertakes a ritual descent to Sheol during his petition, experiencing Yhwh as the dead experience him. Thus, during the period of entreaty, the petitioner is cut off from God and temple, and endures death ritually. There are problems with this formulation. First, as I have argued, the complaint psalms themselves do not suggest that the petitioner and the dead experience Yhwh in the same way, for the petitioner remembers Yhwh's saving acts and covenant loyalty, and more often than not, he is confident that Yhwh will deliver him. Even when Yhwh is said to be unresponsive to the petitioner's supplication, the supplicant can call upon Yhwh to save him, and does so, in contrast to the dead. The primary parallel between the petitioner and the dead is their common inability to praise Yhwh. This is certainly a significant point, emphasized by Anderson, but it goes beyond the evidence to claim that the petitioner is wholly cut off from Yhwh and the cult as are the dead. If this were so, there would be no point in petitioning Yhwh at all, and texts would not express confidence in his ultimate intervention. Furthermore, it is unlikely that the petitioner of the complaint psalms is cut off from the sanctuary as Anderson suggests. Petitioners in narrative and prophetic texts entreat the

COMFORTING AND PETITION

Just as the mourner for the dead could legitimately expect the company and support of comforters, so, apparently, could the individual petitioner. Psalm 69 illustrates this expectation well. In this text, a humiliated supplicant has called upon Yhwh to deliver him from his enemies who persecute him. In v. 21 (Eng. 20) he states:

> I awaited one to move back and forth (with me),[56] but there was none,
> Comforters, but I did not find them.

In the context of this psalm, the mention of a lack of comfort during petition is intended to underscore the degree of the petitioner's misery and isolation.[57] For the purposes of this study, the verse is significant because it suggests that having comforters during entreaty was a normal expectation. Ps. 77: 3 (Eng. 2) is less direct than Ps. 69: 21 (Eng. 20), but it too suggests that comforters could play a role in a petitioner's mourning. In this psalm, the petitioner speaks of seeking Yhwh in time of trouble, complaining to him and refusing to be comforted (מאנה הנחם נפשי). The statement that the supplicant refused comfort suggests that comforters attempted to play a characteristic comforting role such as bringing the petitioner's mourning to an end, but were rebuffed. In 2 Sam. 12: 17, the elders of David's household attempt to intervene to end David's petition to Yhwh on behalf

deity in the sanctuary, as I have demonstrated, and some psalms of individual complaint may have a sanctuary setting, though all discussion of their context must remain tentative. (It is generally agreed that communal complaints have a sanctuary locus.) Even Barth, who emphasizes the reality of the Sheol experience for the petitioner over against those who would understand it simply as rhetorical, and whom Anderson cites with approbation, acknowledges the role of the temple in petition (*Erretung vom Tode*, 93). I also note that the kind of household setting for the psalms of individual complaint advocated by scholars such as Gerstenberger and Albertz would be cultic in nature. On this, see the citations and discussion in n. 24 above.

[56] Where the MT reads נוד, an infinitive construct, which is awkward, LXX συλλυπούμενον suggests the participle *נד or perhaps *נד עמי. For reasons of English style, I have translated *נד 'one to move back and forth' rather than 'one moving back and forth'.

[57] Compare the repeated refrain 'she has no comforter' (אין מנחם לה) in Lam. 1: 2, 9, 17, 21, which appears to have a similar intent.

of his dying son by getting David to rise from the ground and eat food, but David is not willing to stop. These scenes are not unlike that of Gen. 37: 35, where Jacob's children attempt to comfort him (that is, get him to end his mourning over Joseph) but he refuses to do so.

Perhaps the richest description of the actions of one comforting a petitioner is to be found in Ps. 35: 13–14. Though the term 'comforter' (מנחם) does not occur in this passage, the text suggests that the narrator has played just such a role in the past for friends who are now disloyal: 'As for me, when they were sick, my clothes were sackcloth. I afflicted myself with fasting . . . I walked about like a person mourning (his) mother. I was bowed down low, a mourner' (ואני בחלותם לבושי שק עניתי בצום נפשי . . . התהלכתי כאבל אם קדר שחותי). The context for this mourning activity was the illness of friends, and therefore the rites must have had a petitionary purpose. Numerous psalms of individual complaint (e.g. Pss. 6: 3 (Eng. 2); 38) as well as other texts, both biblical and extra-biblical, suggest that illness is one basis for petition, and that those who are ill entreat the deity. In light of this, it seems very likely that the narrator of Psalm 35 was playing the comforter role when he mourned during the illness of his friends. Thus, one aspect of comforting in a petitionary context is to mourn with the petitioner or on his behalf, probably with the intent to increase the possibility that Yhwh will take note of the plea and act on it.[58] In contrast to individual supplication, in which comforters could play a role, communal entreaty, since it involves the entire populace, would have no comforting dimension unless foreign allies were to send their representatives as comforters. In this way, communal entreaty is much like corporate mourning for the dead, in that the whole population embraces the same ritual stance.

[58] Mesopotamian sources also bear witness to such mourning by supporters of a petitioner, among them family members. See e.g. the Sumerian composition 'A Man and his God', lines 63–7 (Kramer, ' "A Man and his God" ', 175, 179), as well as the prayer to Ishtar translated and discussed by Jacobsen, *Treasures of Darkness*, 148–9.

SOCIAL DIMENSIONS OF PETITIONARY MOURNING

Like texts that represent mourning the dead, petitionary mourning narratives are characterized by significant social dynamics. Bonds between individuals are initiated, affirmed, renegotiated, or terminated in contexts of petition. Distinct groups are formed or affirmed through shared participation in rites of penitence and entreaty. Rulers and ruled renegotiate their bond and externalize the state of their relations in settings of supplication, much as they do in contexts in which the dead are mourned. Not surprisingly, comforting and abstention from it are also fraught with social significance in petitionary settings, establishing, affirming, and severing relationships between individuals and groups.

Ezra 9–10 is an excellent illustration of the social dynamics of petitionary mourning. As I have discussed, Ezra begins his petition in the temple alone when he hears the report of the extent of the intermarriages in the community: He tears his garments, pulls out some of the hair of his head and beard, and sits on the ground, shattered (9: 3). While sitting devastated through the day, Ezra is joined by supporters: 'all who trembled at the words of the God of Israel concerning the sacrilege (מעל) of the exile community' (9: 4). After Ezra's penitential prayer to God on behalf of the community (9: 6–15), the narrative describes his continued rites of mourning before the sanctuary, and again notes the support group of individuals who gathered to him, weeping (10: 1). Ezra's followers may participate in the same set of rites that Ezra has embraced; at minimum, they weep, which indicates their identification with him. Their acts of entering Ezra's physical proximity and embracing his ritual stance realize and signal an affiliation between Ezra and his supporters and between the individual members of the newly formed group. The group itself is created in the context of penitential petition by the very behaviour of the individuals who choose to rally to Ezra and embrace mourning rites, thereby declaring their affiliation with him and with his cause. The mourning and petition of Ezra and his followers separate them ritually from all others who are worshipping in the sanctuary, and communicate to others their distinct political stance: Judaeans have broken commandments through their intermarrying with the peoples of the land, and these intermarriages represent a sacrilege. Eventually, Ezra and his supporters gain the cooperation of the majority of the 'exile community' according to the text, prevailing over their opponents, though some resist their campaign to compel the community to expel their foreign wives and the children born of the intermarriages (10: 15). Though the text says nothing about the ritual behaviour of the opponents, if it had, it is likely that the opponents would have been portrayed as eschewing mourning and petition as a way to communicate their stance vis-à-vis Ezra, his group, and their political position.

Such a scenario of resistance to mourning behaviour associated with penitential petition is precisely what we find in Jeremiah 36. In this narrative, Jeremiah's scribe Baruch reads Jeremiah's oracles of woe and promised destruction at a public fast in the Jerusalem temple (36: 10). Courtiers are informed of the scroll, and summon Baruch to read it to them. Though their reaction is one of dread, they do not tear their garments (36: 16). After advising Baruch to hide himself and Jeremiah, the courtiers tell Jehoiakim the king of the scroll, and the king destroys it by burning sections of it in a brazier as it is read to him (36: 23). The text then notes that the king and his servants hearing the words of the scroll 'did not fear nor did they tear their garments' (36: 24), though several courtiers urge the king not to destroy the scroll (36: 25). As with David in 2 Sam. 3: 31–7, the king sets the ritual agenda for his followers. His position is one of defiance, as his destruction of the scroll and his refusal to tear his garments make clear. The king's courtiers must follow his ritual example if they wish to remain loyal to him and signal their affiliation. This they do by refusing to mourn or express fear in the king's presence, though at least some courtiers reacted with dread to the words of the scroll when it was first read to them by Baruch, and these men also instructed Baruch to go into hiding with Jeremiah. Clearly, the courtiers who initially hear the words of the scroll sympathize with Baruch and Jeremiah and their message, but they are unwilling to affiliate with them and their political position by tearing their garments and assuming a penitential posture of entreaty. Instead, they wait for the king's reaction, and follow his example, for they apparently wish to privilege their link with the king above any competing social bonds (e.g. with Baruch and Jeremiah) and above their own private fears or preferences. In this narrative, refusal to mourn in a petitionary context not only communicates the king's position vis-à-vis Jeremiah and his message, but makes clear the hierarchical arrangement of the courtiers' patterns of affiliation and their affirmation of the reality of the king's political authority.

2 Sam. 15: 14–16: 13 is a third text that brings into relief a number of the social aspects of petitionary mourning rites. The section of the narrative of interest to us begins with David's order to his court to flee Jerusalem after he has heard of the initial success of his son Absalom's uprising in Hebron. The household and various courtiers and mercenaries leave the city with David, and as they ascend the Mount of Olives, they weep loudly, walking with their heads covered, probably a gesture of shame (15: 23, 30).[59] David is also said to weep as he walks along barefoot, with his head covered (15: 30). At the summit of the mountain, Hushay the Archite comes to meet David, 'with his garment torn and dirt upon his head'. After asking Hushay to return to Jerusalem to serve as a spy in Absalom's court and to counter the advice of the disloyal courtier Ahitophel, David moves on. He then meets Ziba, servant of Meribaal the Saulide, who provides a large supply of food and drink for the fugitives as well as several asses. After inquiring after the missing Meribaal, David and his followers continue on to Bahurim, where they are confronted by a Saulide named Shimi son of Gera, who curses David, stones him and his party, and throws dust at them (ועפר בעפר; 16: 13). He accuses David of blood-guilt in the matter of the House of Saul. As was the case in 2 Samuel 1 and 2 Sam. 3: 31–7, the public mourning rites of David's household, courtiers, and mercenaries in 2 Sam. 15: 14–16: 13 function to affirm their affiliation with the king and with one another over against others who do not share their political views. Thus, the distinct group of Israelites loyal to David at the time of Absalom's advance on Jerusalem is formed through the experience of mourning and flight. By coming out to meet David and his entourage as they

---

[59] The Hebrew word חפוי or חפו, a Qal passive participle, appears to mean 'covered', given the clearer meaning of Piel and Niphal forms of the root (e.g. 2 Chr. 3: 5, 7, 9; Ps. 68: 14 (Eng. 13)) and related forms in cognate languages. Covering the head is associated with shame in Jer. 14: 3–4, a text that speaks of a penitential communal response to drought.

flee the city, Hushay and Ziba both realize and advertise their loyalty to the king. (Hushay's torn garments and the dirt on his head have the same effect.) David's comment to Ziba about the absence of Meribaal indicates clearly that loyal retainers are expected to demonstrate their affiliation through their presence at times of adversity and calamity, not unlike the pattern of allies and vassals at the death of a ruler. Needless to say, the hostile behaviour and words of Shimi externalize his position vis-à-vis David in a dramatic way. The most interesting aspect of Shimi's anti-Davidic rites is his throwing of dust on the fugitives, given that those who embrace mourning normally strew dust or ashes on their own heads. Throwing dust on David and his supporters instead of on his own head may have been a particularly striking and effective way to communicate hostility and a lack of affiliation, as well as to suggest that the troubles that have come upon one's enemy are of his own making. Not surprisingly, this is precisely what Shimi suggests when he taunts David verbally.

As with comforting the mourner over the dead, the comforting of the petitioner stands out as a ritual scenario in which social relationships are made, remade, and broken. The petitioner's comforters embrace mourning behaviours on his behalf, most likely in order to increase the chance that Yhwh will notice the petition and act beneficently for the petitioner. Likewise, they rejoice with the petitioner when he is vindicated by Yhwh, as in Ps. 35: 27. By embracing the petitioner's self-debasing ritual behaviour, the comforter participates in a form of identification not unlike that of the comforter of the mourner over the dead. In this case, however, the identification most likely has a practical purpose (strengthening the petitioner's plea) in addition to affirming or creating ties with the petitioner in a public way and projecting those ties into the future. By separating ritually from those who rejoice, the comforter realizes and signals his affiliation with the petitioner in the petitioner's time of need. Comforting the petitioner, like comforting the mourner for the dead, is a practice that brings into relief and affirms pre-existing links between the petitioner and his closest affiliates, or creates new links. At the same time, the refusal of friends or allies to fulfil expectations and play the role of comforter, as in Pss. 35: 15; 38: 12 (Eng. 11); and 69: 21 (Eng. 20), would presumably result in the termination of social bonds. The call of the petitioner in some

of the psalms of individual complaint for the shaming and
punishment of disloyal friends certainly suggests such a severing
of ties (e.g. Pss. 35: 26; 109: 4–5, 29).[60]

Conclusions

Petitionary mourning, both communal and individual, penitential and non-penitential, shares a number of important characteristics with mourning the dead. These include the same set of
distinct rites, common idioms (e.g. derivatives of the verbs אבל
and ספד), and similar social dynamics (e.g. the creation, affirmation, re-negotiation, or termination of social relationships, and
the constitution of distinct groups). Both mourners for the
dead and petitioners expect comforters, and avoid rejoicing
behaviours for their period of mourning. The rites of petitioners
are even compared to those of mourners over the dead in a
number of texts, suggesting that mourning the dead is somehow
the model for petitionary mourning. Nonetheless, mourning
associated with entreaty represents a ritual configuration distinct
from mourning in death contexts. Its variety of specific purposes
(e.g. the supplication of penitents to reverse the deity's decision
to punish the community, or to cure illness; petition of a non-
penitent to secure an oracle or revelation) are unrelated to
mourning the dead. Similarly, petition's general purpose—to
attract the deity's or a human authority's attention to the plea
and secure his intervention—has no relationship to mourning at
the time of death. Unlike those mourning the dead, petitioners
are generally unpolluted, and therefore have access to a wider
range of loci than do mourners for the dead, loci that include the
temple sphere. Thus, much in contrast to those mourning the
dead, texts frequently locate the ritual activity of petitioners in
the sanctuary. Their lack of defilement also allows supplicants to
abandon mourning for rejoicing with relative ease and speed,
unlike those mourning the dead, who remain unclean for
seven days. Furthermore, petitionary mourning is less strictly
delimited in terms of time than is mourning the dead. Where
mourning in death contexts is restricted to a specific time period

---

[60] Other psalms of individual complaint contain calls for the punishment and
shaming of enemies, but these do not identify the enemies as former friends, in
contrast to texts such as Pss. 35: 12–14; 109: 4–5.

(usually seven days), petition may last a day, several days, or longer; it may even go on indefinitely until the petitioner's plea is answered. Debasement, which characterizes both the petitioner and the mourner over the dead, also differs in terms of purpose depending on the particular ritual context. Where the debasement of the mourner for the dead is intended to foster identification in order perhaps to establish a new and mutually beneficial social relationship with the dead, that of the petitioner is meant to serve the larger purposes of supplication. Even comforting, a characteristic of both mourning the dead and petition, differs with respect to purpose in each ritual context, for it seems likely that comforting in contexts of entreaty has the added goal of strengthening the petitioner's plea. In short, petitionary mourning is a distinct mourning type that shares various characteristics with mourning the dead and possesses unique features of its own.

Why use rites imported from a death context in petitionary settings? Though I can only speculate due to a lack of evidence, it seems likely that the self-diminishing power of mourning rites and their evident adaptability to new ritual settings must have led to their spread to non-death-related contexts such as entreaty which require the self-debasement of ritual actors. Once translated to a setting such as supplication, mourning rites took on new functions unrelated to mourning the dead (e.g. attracting the deity's or a human authority's attention to the petitioner's plea), while continuing to serve some of their original purposes (e.g. fostering identification between comforter and mourning supplicant).

The most striking and significant characteristic of petitionary mourning, a feature not shared with mourning the dead, is the petitioner's lack of defilement, which allows him to have access to the sphere of the sanctuary, in contrast to the mourner over the dead. Within the sanctuary sphere, texts suggest that petitionary mourning may replace rejoicing rites entirely for the whole community for a temporary period of time, as in the case of a communal fast. Alternatively, the supplication of individuals or small groups may occur while the temple's rites of rejoicing continue for others who are not petitioning. This is possible because of the complete ritual separation of petitioners from those who rejoice. Petitionary mourning is licit in the sanctuary sphere as long as there is no mixing of mourning and rejoicing behaviours in the same individual ritual actor(s). Thus, the sanctuary is a context in which petitionary mourning may replace rejoicing temporarily for the whole congregation, or entreaty may occur concurrently with rejoicing as long as mourning and rejoicing behaviours are not fused in any single ritual agent.

3

Mourning in Other Contexts

Two other types of biblical mourning remain to be considered, each of which differs significantly in terms of characteristics and purpose from both mourning the dead and mourning associated with entreaty. First, there are texts that represent mourning at the time of individual or communal calamity unconnected to death and with no evident petitionary aim. Easily recognizable mourning practices such as weeping, tossing dust on the head, and wearing sackcloth characterize the rites of persons or groups experiencing disaster in such texts, as they do the ritual behaviour of both the mourner over the dead and the petitioner. The texts in question also use typical mourning idioms such as derivatives of the verb 'to mourn' (אבל) or 'to lament'/'mourn' (ספד) in their descriptions of the ritual action of those experiencing personal or communal calamity (e.g. Esther 6: 12; Isa. 66: 10; Ezek. 27: 31). In addition, avoidance of rejoicing behaviours during mourning is characteristic of the ritual actors represented in these passages, as it is of mourners for the dead and petitioners. And like mourning the dead, non-petitionary mourning associated with catastrophe is sometimes characterized by the intoning of a dirge (e.g. over a destroyed city) by mourning professionals (e.g. Jer. 9: 16–18 (Eng. 17–19)) or by others (e.g. Ezek. 26: 16–18). Thus, these texts share a number of characteristics in common both with petitionary texts and with passages representing mourning over the dead. But they differ strikingly from descriptions of death-related mourning and those of petitionary rites in their lack of any discernible direct associations with death and any evident petitionary purpose. Though petitionary mourning at the time of a catastrophe serves primarily to direct the deity's attention to the plight of the petitioning individual or community and secure his positive action on behalf of the petitioner(s), mourning as described in non-petitionary calamity contexts must have other primary purposes. These might include marking those affected by the disaster off from others who are unaffected, and creating a ritual context in which they can enact and communicate their sorrow, shame, and personal or corporate diminishment as well as create, affirm, or modify social relationships. Thus, non-petitionary mourning associated with a catastrophe constitutes a third distinct mourning type over against mourning the dead, on the one hand, and petitionary mourning, on the other, sharing characteristics with each but standing alone nonetheless on account of its unique features. The other discrete mourning configuration to be considered in this chapter is represented in Lev. 13: 45–6. This text describes the ritual behaviour of the person afflicted with skin disease (צרעת), who utilizes mourning rites though no one has died and though his behaviour appears to have no evident petitionary purpose. Such mourning also differs from non-petitionary mourning at the time of disaster in that it is but one component of a larger series of ritual behaviours that serve primarily to isolate physically and socially the unclean, diseased person from those in the community who are unaffected. Thus, two additional mourning types may be recognized along with mourning the dead and petitionary mourning, and these will be the focus of this chapter.

NON-PETITIONARY MOURNING AT THE TIME OF A CALAMITY

The mourning behaviour of Haman in Esther 6: 12 is an excellent place to begin an investigation of mourning when disaster strikes that is not characterized by any evident petitionary purpose. After his plan to have himself honoured by the Persian king goes awry, Haman is forced by the king's order to honour Mordecai, his arch-enemy, publicly. He must lead Mordecai around the city's square, with Mordecai riding one of the king's horses, dressed in royal garb, and wearing a royal crown upon his head. As Haman does this, he must call out, 'So it shall be done for the man whom the king delights to honour.' After this scenario has come to pass, the text describes Haman's reaction: 'As for Haman, he hurried to his house in mourning and with (his) head covered' (והמן נדחף אל ביתו אבל וחפוי ראש).[1] Haman's mourning appears to be a marker of personal calamity, expressing his shame and his social diminishment; it has no discernible petitionary purpose. Haman's humiliation is evident from the fact that he has been forced to honour his rival Mordecai in public with the very tokens of distinction that he believed he himself deserved. Not only is Haman denied what he thinks is his just reward from the king; he must himself bestow it publicly upon another who has provoked his rage (3: 5; 5: 9) and whom we can safely assume he despises. Haman's wife and supporters describe this as the beginning of his 'fall', perhaps referring not only to Haman's coming loss of power and life, but also to his diminishment vis-à-vis Mordecai, whom he has been forced to honour (6: 13).[2] The absence of any petitionary purpose to Haman's mourning is indicated by the fact that his ritual behaviour is not directed toward the king, a deity, or anyone else who might be in a position to receive his entreaty and restore his honour. Instead, Haman retreats to the sanctuary of his own house and the company of his wife and supporters (אהבים), perhaps with the intention that they comfort him.[3] But instead of words of consolation from his intimates, Haman is told that this event marks the beginning of his decline. The lack of any evident petitionary dimension to Haman's mourning stands in contrast to some of the other mourning scenarios described in the Book of Esther. An example is the three-day fast of the Judaeans of Shushan ordered by Esther for her benefit[4] before her uninvited and risky appearance in the presence of the king (4: 1–2, 16–17). This fast must be petitionary in nature given that its intent is to benefit Esther. Presumably, it is directed toward Yhwh to secure his protection for her, though Yhwh is not mentioned directly in

---

[1] On the expression חפוי ראש, see the discussion of Ch. 2, n. 59.

[2] Haman's diminishment with respect to Mordecai is the focus of the LXX's interpretation (ηρξαι ταπεινουσθαι ενωπιον αυτου), where the Hebrew reads more ambiguously, allowing for both possibilities (החלות לנפל לפניו). Modern translations frequently opt only for the political sense of downfall (e.g. NRSV, NJPS).

[3] The mention of אהבים, literally 'lovers', or 'allies', is probably intended to suggest the milieu of comforting. Cf. Lam. 1: 2 אין לה מנחם מכל אהביה.

[4] The purpose of the fast is indicated clearly in the text: וצומו עלי.

this passage or anywhere else in the book for reasons that remain obscure.[5]

Tamar's reaction to her rape by Amnon is a second example of non-petitionary mourning behaviour associated with a personal catastrophe. As narrated in 2 Sam. 13: 1–22, Amnon, David's eldest surviving son, feigns illness in order to be alone with his half-sister Tamar whom he desires sexually. Though Tamar resists his physical assault with words of reason and common sense, Amnon is unwilling to listen to her and she is overpowered by him. Verse 19 describes her public behaviour after she has been forcibly turned out of Amnon's house: 'Tamar took ashes[6] (and put them) on her head, and the ornamented garment which she was wearing she tore. She set her hand upon her head and walked along, crying out as she walked.' When Tamar arrives at her brother Absalom's house, he is able to guess what has happened based only upon her appearance and her mourning behaviour: 'Has Amnon, your brother, been with you?' (v. 20). The text describes Tamar after this event as a 'devastated woman' (שממה) dwelling in the house of her brother Absalom (v. 20). That Tamar has been shamed is clear from her words to Amnon as she initially resists him: 'No, my brother! Do not force me, for such is not done in Israel! Do not do this sacrilege! As for me, where could I bear my reproach (חרפה)? And as for you, you would be like one of the outcasts in Israel' (vv. 12–13).[7] The description of Tamar as a 'devastated woman' (שממה) points to the source of her shame: her potential as a marriage partner has been drastically reduced if not eliminated both by her rape and by her expulsion from Amnon's house.[8] Yet, nothing in the

---

[5] The lack of explicit mention of Yhwh in the book has generated a number of explanations, and these are ably considered by M. V. Fox, *Character and Ideology in the Book of Esther* (Columbia, SC: University of South Carolina Press, 1991), 235–47.

[6] Or dust. See the discussion of the meaning of אפר in n. 8 of Ch. 1.

[7] For the translation 'sacrilege' for נבלה and 'outcasts' for נבלים, see McCarter, *II Samuel*, 323, with citations.

[8] Isa. 54: 1 is frequently cited by commentators to illuminate the meaning of שממה in 2 Sam. 13: 20. In this text, שממה is set in parallel with בעולה, 'married woman', suggesting that it means at minimum 'unmarried woman', and perhaps 'unmarriageable woman': כי רבים בני שממה // מבני בעולה אמר יהוה. The dialogue of 2 Sam. 13: 16 hints that marriage to Amnon could have served partially to ameliorate Tamar's social situation after the rape, presumably by preventing her from assuming the status of 'devastated woman', but Amnon was unwilling

narrative suggests any kind of petitionary purpose to Tamar's ritual behaviour after she has been raped by her half-brother. Like that of Haman, Tamar's mourning is not directed to the king or any other authority who might intervene on her behalf. She goes immediately to her brother Absalom's house, not unlike Haman's retreat to his own home and circle of supporters. In short, Tamar's mourning rites seem intended to express sorrow and shame, enact her new, debased status as a 'devastated woman', and invite support through comforting from her social intimates.

Descriptions of or allusions to corporate or individual mourning over a destroyed or conquered city or over the decisive defeat of an army in battle are sometimes characterized by a lack of any evident petitionary purpose.[9] In some respects, they resemble narratives of mourning the dead (e.g. on account of the use of the dirge in combination with mourning behaviours). Ezek. 26: 16–18 and 27: 28–36 are examples of such mourning over a destroyed city.[10] Both pericopes belong to a collection of materials in the Book of Ezekiel that prophesies the destruction of the Phoenician maritime city Tyre at the hands of Nebuchadnezzar, king of Babylon in the early sixth century BCE. Each text describes an imagined reaction to Tyre's destruction. According to Ezek. 26: 16–18, at Tyre's downfall, all the princes of the sea will descend from their thrones to the ground. They

to consider this option. For examples of biblical legal texts requiring the assailant to marry an unbetrothed virgin whom he has raped, see Exod. 22: 15–16 (Eng. 16–17) and Deut. 22: 28–9. These texts prescribe legal remedies for the social difficulties created by rape or seduction scenarios such as that narrated in 2 Samuel 13.

[9] Though not always. See the many descriptions or allusions to such calamity that incorporate supplication of some kind. Examples include Pss. 44; 74; 79; 80; 137; Lam. 1: 9, 11, 17, 20, 22; 2: 18–19; 3: 64–6; 5: 20–2. Gerstenberger takes up the subject of the presence of petition in some city laments and its absence in others. On this, see *Psalms, Part 2, and Lamentations*, 481–2. See also the comments of F. W. Dobbs-Allsopp, *Weep, O Daughter of Zion: A Study of the City-Lament Genre in the Hebrew Bible* (BO 44; Rome: Pontifical Biblical Institute, 1993), 92–4.

[10] On the genre 'lament for a destroyed city' ('Stadtuntergangsklage'), see the recent discussion of Albertz, *Die Exilszeit*, 124–30, as well as that of Dobbs-Allsopp, *Weep, O Daughter of Zion*, 30–96. On the relationship of lamentation over the dead and over destroyed cities, see Gerstenberger, 'Der klagende Mensch', 67.

will exchange their garments for mourning clothes(?)[11] and tremble, devastated on account of Tyre's destruction. The text goes on to quote a dirge they will intone over the city, part of which I translate here:

> How you have perished,
> You who were populated from the seas,
> The city that was praised,
> that was strong in the sea,
> she and her inhabitants . . .
> Now the coastlands tremble
> (on) the day of your downfall.
> The coastlands by the sea are dismayed by your end.[12]

Ezek. 27: 28–36 is similar. At Tyre's downfall, sailors will leave their ships and stand on shore. They will cry out bitterly over the city, tossing dust upon their heads and rolling in ashes or dust. They will shave a bald spot upon their heads, put on sackcloth, and weep bitterly over Tyre, lifting up a dirge over her. Like the narratives of Haman's and Tamar's mourning rites, neither the description of mourning and dirge recitation in Ezek. 26: 16–18 nor that of 27: 28–36 suggests any kind of petitionary intent on the part of the mourners. Witnesses to the imagined destruction of Tyre in both Ezek. 26: 16–18 and 27: 28–36 react with sorrow and shock to her downfall, and recall her greatness in their dirges.

Descriptions such as these of mourning over a destroyed city are not unlike characterizations of mourning rites over the dead found in texts such as 2 Sam. 3: 31–7 (the funeral of Abner). Sorrow is expressed through weeping and other mourning behaviours; the dead individual or destroyed city is eulogized by means of the intoning of a dirge; no petitionary element is discernible. A major difference between the two types of mourning is the role that shame or horror frequently plays in representations of mourning at the catastrophe of a city's fall,

---

[11] The word חרדות, 'trembling', may refer to mourning garments as some have argued, though this remains a speculation. See further the comments of M. Greenberg, *Ezekiel 21–37* (AB 22A; New York: Doubleday, 1997), 536, who renders 'tatters'.

[12] Understanding צאת of מצאתך as an infinitive construct from the root יצא, 'to go forth', with a meaning comparable to that of Exod. 23: 16, as Greenberg has argued (*Ezekiel 21–37*, 538), though I prefer 'end' to his more literal 'departure'.

something generally absent from scenarios of mourning the dead. Jer. 9: 18 (Eng. 19) serves as an excellent example of the potential centrality of humiliation in mourning at a city's demise: 'For the sound of lamentation is heard from Zion: "How we are destroyed, we are exceedingly shamed, for we have forsaken the land, for they have cast down our habitations."' Shame is the result of defeat, destruction, and expulsion; it is externalized through self-debasing rites of mourning.

Ezek. 7: 18 describes the mourning behaviour of fugitives who flee from an anticipated defeat and conquest of Judah by enemies who act on behalf of Yhwh. After mentioning the effects of plague, famine, and slaughter, the text describes the flight of terrified escapees to the mountains:

> They shall gird on sackcloth,
> Horror (פלצות) shall cover them.
> On every face (there shall be) shame (בושה),
> And on all their heads, a bald spot.

Though it is not clear whether these fugitives are the remnant of a defeated army or simply escapees from a conquered city, the shame and horror of defeat and conquest are certainly central motives for their anticipated mourning, as the verse suggests. From a literary standpoint, it is noteworthy how the poet uses parallelism and idiom to establish an intimate connection between the mourning behaviours of the fugitives and what they are intended to communicate. Horror is linked through the parallelistic structure of the poetry to sackcloth, shame to the bald spot. Horror is said to 'cover' (כסה) the mourning escapees in the same way sackcloth covers mourners in other texts (e.g. 2 Kgs. 19: 1–2=Isa. 37: 1–2; Jonah 3: 6, 8; 1 Chr. 21: 16). Shame finds its locus on the face as the bald spot does on the head. Sackcloth and bald spot thus become tokens of horror and shame in this passage.

The shame of defeat by the enemy is also a prominent theme in 2 Sam. 19: 4 (Eng. 3), which is unambiguous in its focus on the behaviour characteristic of a vanquished army. This verse, which I treated in Chapter 1 in my discussion of the hierarchical dimensions of public mourning, is part of a larger narrative in 2 Sam. 19: 1–9 (Eng. 18: 33–19: 8) concerning David's mourning for his dead, rebellious son Absalom after David's army's defeat of Absalom's forces. David's privileging of his private grief at a time of military victory prevents the expected rejoicing of his men and transforms their ritual behaviour in order that it conform to his. As v. 3 (Eng. 2) suggests, the army's rejoicing in the aftermath of victory is turned to mourning when they hear of the king's grief on account of Absalom. The mourning of David's men is compared by the text to that of a vanquished army that flees before its adversaries: 'So the army stole into the city on that day, as does an army humiliated (נכלמים) when they flee in battle.' The shame of defeat or conquest is connected directly to the mourning rites described in Ezek. 7: 18 and 2 Sam. 19: 4 (Eng. 3). Like the texts that speak of imagined mourning over a destroyed Tyre, these texts do not hint at any petitionary purpose to the mourning behaviour they describe.[13]

THE MOURNING OF THE INDIVIDUAL
AFFLICTED WITH SKIN DISEASE

Lev. 13: 45–6 prescribes a set of distinct ritual behaviours for persons afflicted with skin disease (צרעת).[14] Among the actions enjoined by this Priestly text are rites of mourning, as has often been noted by scholars. The verses read as follows: 'As for the individual afflicted with skin disease, his garments shall be torn (פרמים)[15] and as for his hair,[16] it shall be unbound (פרוע);[17] he shall cover his upper lip[18] and cry "unclean, unclean". All of the time

---

[13] Pace Gerstenberger, who has argued that all lament is intended to reach Yhwh ('Der klagende Mensch', 68, 72).

[14] Though modern translations usually render צרעת as 'leprosy', I prefer the more ambiguous and general 'skin disease', as the disease (or diseases) that biblical texts call צרעת has (have) yet to be convincingly identified. On this, see further the discussion with citations in Olyan, *Rites and Rank*, 146–7 n. 36.

[15] Compare the use of this verb in contexts that describe mourning the dead (Lev. 10: 6; 21: 10).   [16] Literally, 'head': וראשו יהיה פרוע.

[17] The same verb is used of the head in other mourning contexts (Lev. 10: 6; 21: 10). There is no consensus on the meaning of the idiom פרע ראש. Milgrom discusses the alternatives in *Leviticus 1–16*, 608–9, 803, and opts for the translation 'disheveled'.

[18] This action is also a mourning rite for the dead, as Ezek. 24: 17, 22 indicate. See also Mic. 3: 7, where the same idiom is used in a context of disaster, and 2 Sam. 19: 25 (Eng. 24), where the expression ולא עשה שפמו is used to describe the penitential mourning of Meribaal at David's return after Absalom's defeat.

that the affliction is in him he shall be unclean. He is unclean: he shall live alone; outside of the camp shall be his dwelling place.' Torn garments, unbound hair, and the covering of the upper lip are all attested as mourning rites in other biblical contexts, yet mourning behaviours are only one component of a larger constellation of ritual actions to be undertaken by the diseased person. In addition to mourning rites, the afflicted individual must announce to others that he is unclean, apparently in order to warn them to keep their distance from him, as his pollution is communicable.[19] He must also dwell outside the camp, physically separated from those who are unaffected by the skin disease. Thus, the mourning behaviour of the afflicted person can only be understood with reference to the other ritual practices prescribed for him, for they render his mourning distinct.

Though the diseased individual shares uncleanness with mourners who have been polluted by corpse contact, he differs in that he must call out 'unclean, unclean', presumably in order to keep others at a distance. As was pointed out long ago, this announcement would allow onlookers to distinguish the person afflicted with skin disease from a mourner for the dead, whom family and friends would normally approach to comfort.[20] It would also make it possible for witnesses to distinguish between the diseased person and the petitioner, who, like the mourner over the dead, expects comfort from intimates, or the non-petitioning person who has experienced individual or corporate calamity, who probably has similar expectations. In effect, individuals with skin disease, in contrast to persons mourning the dead, individual petitioners, and others utilizing mourning rites, are cut off from their intimates and allies; they lack the kind of concentrated community created by ritual contexts such as mourning the dead and petitioning. The afflicted individual must also reside outside of the camp according to this Priestly text, in contrast to the mourner defiled through corpse contact and other polluters.[21] Thus, both with respect to locus and social

[19] On this, see Milgrom, *Leviticus 1–16*, 804–5, who argues that according to P, skin disease is communicable both through physical contact and through proximity to a diseased person in an enclosed space.

[20] The point is made by Milgrom, ibid. 805, citing N. H. Wessely's commentary on Leviticus published in 1846.

[21] In contrast, see the position of H, which also excludes persons polluted due

interaction, the individual with skin disease stands apart from the mourner over the dead and from others utilizing mourning rites. The distinctiveness of his status is also evident with respect to the length of time he must mourn. Where the mourner for the dead mourns for a set period of time (seven days according to most texts), the diseased person continues his rites for as long as his affliction remains. In this respect he is much like the petitioner, who may petition as long as it takes to secure Yhwh's intervention on his behalf.[22]

SOCIAL DIMENSIONS: NON-PETITIONARY MOURNING ASSOCIATED WITH A CALAMITY AND THE MOURNING OF THE PERSON AFFLICTED WITH SKIN DISEASE

The social dimensions of non-petitionary mourning rites when catastrophe strikes are difficult to reconstruct on the basis of extant texts, which tend to tell us far less than we might like to know. Nonetheless, it seems likely that the social aspects of such mourning should differ little from what I have observed already with respect to mourning the dead and to communal and individual petition. As with communal petition or mourning the dead, collective mourning over a destroyed city or a military defeat would function to separate the mourners from others who do not share their sorrow or political and communal attachments. It would create a distinct group and define its membership both for members and outsiders. Such mourning would also provide a context in which comforters (e.g. the representatives of allies) could participate through identification with the mourners, thereby realizing and communicating their affiliation with the group that has experienced a calamity. Individuals such as Haman or Tamar separate themselves from the larger community by means of their mourning rites, which also function to

to corpse contact and persons with a diseased genital flow from the camp (Num. 5: 2–3; 31: 19).

[22] Obviously, I cannot agree with Anderson's claim that the person with skin disease 'resembles a mourner in every respect' (*A Time to Mourn*, 87 n. 81). The resemblance is more circumscribed than Anderson suggests, given the evident differences between the ritual behaviour of the mourner over the dead and the person afflicted with skin disease.

communicate sorrow, shame, and personal diminishment. Unhappily, the Esther and Samuel narratives are not explicit about the ritual behaviour of Haman's circle or Tamar's intimates. Nonetheless, it seems likely that as supporters, they too should participate in mourning in order to affirm their continued affiliation with the affected individuals, just as comforters identify with individual mourners over the dead and petitioners. As with mourning the dead and petition, non-petitionary mourning at the time of individual or collective calamity is a ritual setting in which social ties may be affirmed, forged, reconstituted, or broken. The refrain 'she has no comforter of all those who love her' (Lam. 1: 2) points to the severing of political ties between allies in the context of a city's destruction. In contrast, the mourning princes of the sea in Ezek. 26: 16–18 affirm their ties to Tyre through their envisioned self-debasing acts of mourning at the time of Tyre's destruction. The weeping of the murderer Ishmael in Jer. 41: 6 ought to be understood as a gesture of political and personal identification used cynically to establish the trust of unsuspecting pilgrims who mourn for Jerusalem and its temple in the aftermath of their destruction. By weeping as he approaches the pilgrims, Ishmael identifies himself ritually with them and their political position vis-à-vis the collective calamity that has befallen Judah. Thus, the weeping of Ishmael functions here in a similar way to that of Ezra's supporters in Ezra 10: 1, establishing and externalizing a socio-political relationship in a context of grief and mourning. But in the case of Ishmael, his secret intent appears to be to do away with the pilgrims.

The social dimensions of the mourning of the individual afflicted with skin disease differ markedly from those of mourning in death-related situations, petitionary contexts, and non-petitionary calamity settings. In all three other types of mourning, mourning rites separate an individual or group from others, and provide an important ritual context in which the affected persons and their intimates or allies can affirm, create, adjust, or sunder social ties. In contrast, the mourning behaviour of the skin-diseased person is a component of a larger constellation of rites intended to isolate the individual from all social interactions with unaffected persons, including intimates. Mourning behaviour in a context of death, petition, or calamity without entreaty is an invitation to social interaction for those who wish to actualize or maintain an affiliation with the affected party. Conversely, mourning on account of skin disease is one element of a series of rites that eliminate opportunities for the creation or perpetuation of social affiliations.

It is a commonplace to point out that the individual afflicted with skin disease resembles the dead or the corpse in a number of respects.[23] Even the biblical text itself compares the afflicted person to a diseased infant's corpse in Num. 12: 12, as the rabbis noticed long ago.[24] Entreating Moses on behalf of Miriam whom Yhwh has punished with skin disease, Aaron petitions as follows: 'Let her not be like one who is dead, whose flesh is half consumed when he comes forth from his mother's womb.' Yet, even given similarities to the dead and the corpse, is it legitimate to describe the diseased person as 'socially dead'? In Chapter 1, I raised this question with regard to the mourner over the dead. There I concluded that the biblical mourner's situation is not distinguished by the termination of social identity, the key attribute of social death in Patterson's or Middleton's usage. Nor can it be characterized by complete removal from the collective life of the community, the major feature of social death according to Hertz's definition. The individual with skin disease, in contrast, is entirely separated from the life of the community, though it is doubtful that he loses his social identity entirely. As I have pointed out, the diseased person has no comforters, in contrast to the mourner, the petitioner, and others utilizing mourning rites; no subsection of society joins him for the period of his disease. Given his separation from the cult, family and social circle, and given his separate physical locus, the afflicted individual might be legitimately described as socially dead according to Hertz's understanding. But it is more difficult to make a case for the social death of the person with skin disease if one employs the most common contemporary definition, for there is some evidence that that individual's social identity has not been entirely terminated. The evidence is found in 2 Kgs. 15: 5, which states

[23] See e.g. Feldman, *Defilement and Mourning*, 37–41; Anderson, *A Time to Mourn*, 87 n. 81. The diseased person resembles the dead because of his complete isolation from members of the community who are unaffected, and because of his mourning behaviours. He resembles the corpse on account of his ability to pollute without direct contact in a closed space.

[24] Feldman, *Defilement and Mourning*, 37–8.

that King Azariah, afflicted with skin disease for much of his reign, remained king in name at least, with his son Jotham acting as regent in the last years of his reign.[25] Thus Azariah retained his social position, even though he was isolated for an extended period of time due to skin disease.

Conclusions

Both non-petitionary mourning at the time of personal or corporate calamity and the mourning of the individual afflicted with skin disease share characteristics in common with mourning the dead and petitionary mourning, and also possess their own distinct features. Non-petitionary mourning at a time of catastrophe is characterized by the same set of rites, mourning idioms, and social dynamics as mourning the dead and mourning associated with entreaty. Like mourning in death contexts and settings of supplication, it too is characterized by ritual separation from rejoicing and the expectation of comforters. With mourning the dead, mourning at the time of disaster also shares the dirge form, in contrast to petitionary mourning and the mourning of the person afflicted with skin disease. Yet a lack of any direct association with death marks non-petitionary mourning at the time of calamity off from mourning the dead, and a dearth of any discernible petitionary purpose renders it distinct from mourning associated with supplication. Non-petitionary mourning at the time of personal or communal disaster appears to have as its purpose the ritual separation of those affected by the calamity from those who are unaffected. It is also apparently intended to allow for the creation of a ritual context in which those experiencing catastrophe may enact and communicate sorrow, shame, and personal or corporate diminishment. This ritual context is also a setting in which those affected and their intimates may affirm, modify, or create social relationships, as with mourning the dead and petitionary mourning.

Like the mourner over the dead, the petitioner, and the non-petitioner at the time of calamity, the individual afflicted with skin disease embraces familiar mourning rites, separating

[25] The biblical text says that Jotham was 'over the palace and judged the People of the Land'. On this, see further M. Cogan and H. Tadmor, *II Kings* (AB 11; New York: Doubleday, 1988), 168.

himself from rejoicing activities. He shares pollution in common with the mourner for the dead, though his uncleanness lasts as long as his disease, and may be perpetual, in contrast to that of the mourner in a death context, who is defiled for only seven days. Also, the long-lasting pollution of the person afflicted with skin disease, as well as his other non-mourning-related ritual acts (e.g. his calling out 'unclean, unclean'), function to isolate him socially, in contrast to all other types of mourner. Thus, his defilement is unlike the pollution of the mourner for the dead, who is not compelled to leave the community entirely and is normally joined by close associates who play the role of comforter. In contrast, the individual afflicted with skin disease receives no comforters and is at the centre of no community in mourning. In a word, he is cut off from society, and therefore there are no social dimensions to his mourning besides the dynamic of isolation.

As was the case with the petitioner, it is the self-debasing power of mourning rites and their adaptability to new ritual contexts unrelated to death that probably explain their adoption by non-petitioning individuals at the time of personal or corporate calamity and by persons afflicted with skin disease. Like the supplicant, the non-petitioning person reacting to catastrophe practices self-diminishment by means of mourning rites, but for purposes such as communicating shame and sorrow without any petitionary intent. The frequent emphasis on the humiliation of those mourning at the time of disaster strongly suggests a self-debasing dimension to their rites, although idioms of debasement (e.g. כנע, 'to humble oneself' or שחח, 'to be low') do not occur in descriptions of their ritual practices. Similarly, the diseased individual achieves his social isolation through a set of implicitly self-debasing rites that include mourning practices. Though Lev. 13: 45–6 does not suggest directly that these rites are intended to be self-diminishing, the strong association of mourning rites with debasement in other mourning contexts suggests a self-debasing function to the mourning of the individual afflicted with skin disease. The diseased person's other ritual behaviours—dwelling in isolation, calling out 'unclean, unclean' when near others—are probably best understood similarly.

4

The Constraints on Mourning Rites

Aside from conventional constraints placed on the length of the mourning period for the mourner over the dead, the Hebrew Bible also bears witness to several laws that seek to eliminate two common mourning behaviours, shaving and laceration, and so limit sanctioned mourning to ritual practices other than these. The biblical interdictions of shaving and laceration rites have long baffled scholars, and continue to elicit new explanatory proposals.[1] Shaving and laceration rites are prohibited for priests in

[1] e.g. Schmidt, *Israel's Beneficent Dead*, 166–78 for a recent attempt at a solution. (On Schmidt's proposal, see my discussion in n. 13 below.) The most common explanation in the literature for the proscription of these rites associates them with alleged Canaanite or other 'foreign' practices supposedly abhorrent to Yhwh (in particular, the ancestor cult). See e.g. B. A. Levine, *Leviticus* (JPSTC; Philadelphia: Jewish Publication Society, 1989), 143; E. Gerstenberger, *Das dritte Buch Mose: Leviticus* (ATD 6; Göttingen: Vandenhoeck & Ruprecht, 1993), 252, 285, who cites the Canaanite theory with some hesitation; and J. Milgrom, *Leviticus 17–22* (AB 3A; New York: Doubleday, 2000), 1690–1, 1693, 1796, 1802. Yet as Schmidt, C. Carmichael (*The Spirit of Biblical Law* (Athens, Ga.: University of Georgia Press, 1996), 129–30), and others have pointed out, these mourning practices are frequently represented as legitimate Israelite rites except in the three texts in question. Yhwh even orders the shaving of a bald spot for mourners in several texts (e.g. Isa. 22: 12; Amos 8: 10; Mic. 1: 16), and laceration occurs in contexts with no evident associations with the ancestor cult or any other practice that the text—or scholars—might construct as 'foreign' (e.g. Jer. 16: 6; 41: 4–5). Milgrom's attempt to defend the view that shaving and laceration represent 'pagan' practice by recourse to a text such as Isa. 15: 2 illustrates well the weakness of such a position. Isaiah 15, an oracle against Moab, speaks of the destruction of Moabite cities, and describes not only the shaving of a bald spot on every head and the shaving of every beard, but also wailing, weeping, and the girding on of sackcloth by Moabites mourning their calamity. If this text indicates that shaving a bald spot and shaving

Lev. 21: 5, and for all Israelites in Lev. 19: 27–8 and Deut. 14: 1.
Of the many mourning practices[2] witnessed in the biblical text,
only laceration and shaving are banned in any source, and their
interdiction is attested only in the Holiness Source and
Deuteronomy.[3] In contrast to their treatment in Holiness and
Deuteronomistic materials, laceration and shaving are represented as perfectly legitimate mourning rites in non-H and non-
D texts, as others have shown convincingly.[4] Therefore, it is
necessary to consider why they are proscribed in Holiness and
Deuteronomistic texts and nowhere else. I will begin my investigation by reviewing briefly the three texts in question, and go on
to ask what—if anything—distinguishes shaving and laceration
from other mourning rites. What, in other words, might have

the beard are 'foreign' practices as Milgrom suggests, then the same must be
true of weeping, wailing, and wearing sackcloth. Clearly, the text evidences
nothing more than the fact that shaving and laceration are components of a
larger repertoire of mourning rites shared by various peoples of ancient West
Asia, including the Israelites. Furthermore, there is no convincing evidence that
the rites in question have anything to do with an ancestor cult. When attested in
biblical texts, they are mainly associated with mourning the dead (e.g. Jer. 16: 6)
or mourning at a time of calamity (e.g. Jer. 41: 4–5); on occasion, they are a component of petitionary mourning (e.g. Mic. 4: 14 (Eng. 5: 1)). The proscribed
rites of Lev. 21: 5 follow upon a discussion of the limitations placed on priestly
mourning of dead family members; the text makes no mention of, or allusion to,
ancestral rites. Direct references to the dead in the prohibitions of Lev. 19: 28
(שרט לנפש) and Deut. 14: 1 (קרחה בין עיניכם למת) do not suggest an ancestor cult
context any more than they suggest a regular mourning context (cf. Lev. 21: 1
לנפש לא יטמא בעמיו; Num. 19: 11 הנגע במת לכל נפש אדם וטמא שבעת ימים).

[2] That these are rites associated with mourning can be shown from comparison with other biblical texts representing mourning practices (e.g. Jer. 16: 6; 41:
4–5) as well as extra-biblical materials (e.g. *CAT* 1.5 VI 11–25). An association
with mourning is also suggested by the mention of the dead in two of the
three texts in question (Lev. 19: 28; Deut. 14: 1) and the general mourning
context of Lev. 21: 1–6. See further Schmidt's helpful discussion (*Israel's
Beneficent Dead*, 167–71), and the comments of M. Noth, *Das dritte Buch Mose:
Leviticus* (ATD 6; Göttingen: Vandenhoeck & Ruprecht, 1962), 123, 134–5;
Gerstenberger, *Leviticus*, 252; Levine, *Leviticus*, 143; and B. Y. Schwartz,
תורת הקדושה: עיונים בחוקה הכוהנית שבתורה (Jerusalem: Magnes Press, 1999), 346–8,
among others. G. J. Botterweck is, however, not convinced that Lev. 21: 5
describes mourning rites ('נלח gillaḥ', *TDOT* 3: 7, 16).

[3] Ezek. 44: 20, an H-related text, also prohibits the shaving of the head for
priests, but does not mention laceration. On the relationship of Ezekiel to H, see
e.g. W. Zimmerli, *Ezechiel* (2 vols.; BKAT xiii; Neukirchen-Vluyn: Neukirchener, 1969), 1: 70*–78*.

[4] e.g. Schmidt, *Israel's Beneficent Dead*, 168–70.

motivated Holiness and Deuteronomistic circles to prohibit
these rites of mourning while accepting other mourning behaviours? After proposing what I believe distinguishes shaving
and laceration among rites of mourning, I will go on to consider
why they are proscribed for priests in Lev. 21: 5, and for all Israel
in Lev. 19: 27–8 and Deut. 14: 1. As others have argued, the
priestly ban likely antedates the interdiction for the whole
people, and I will propose a tentative explanation for the broad-
ening of the prohibition.

The three texts of interest read as follows:

They [the priests] shall not shave a bald spot on their head(s), nor shall
they shave the corner of their beard(s), nor shall they incise an incision
in their flesh.

(Lev. 21: 5)   לא יקרחה קרחה בראשם ופאת זקנם לא יגלחו ובבשרם לא ישרטו שרטת

You shall not round off the corner of your head(s), nor shall you destroy
the corner of your beard(s). You shall not set an incision for the dead in
your flesh, nor shall you impose the writing of a tattoo on yourselves. I
am Yhwh.

לא תקפו פאת ראשכם ולא תשחית את פאת זקנך ושרט לנפש לא תתנו בבשרכם וכתבת קעקע
(Lev. 19: 27–8)   לא תתנו בכם אני יהוה

Children shall you be to Yhwh your God. You shall not lacerate yourselves, nor shall you set a bald spot between your eyes for the dead.

(Deut. 14: 1)   בנים אתם ליהוה אלהיכם לא תתגדדו ולא תשימו קרחה בין עיניכם למת

Lev. 21: 5 prohibits priests from shaving a bald spot on the head,
shaving the corner (?) of the beard, and incising an incision in the
flesh. Shaving a bald spot on the head is a well-attested mourning rite (e.g. Isa. 22: 12; Jer. 16: 6; Amos 8: 10), as is manipulation (including shaving) of beard hair (e.g. Isa. 15: 2; Jer. 41: 4–5;
Ezra 9: 3). Incising an incision, a form of laceration, is explicitly
associated with the dead elsewhere—Lev. 19: 28, one of the three
texts under consideration here—and another idiom for laceration (the Hitpael of גדד) is closely associated with mourning in a
variety of biblical texts.[5] In addition to proscribing incisions for

---

[5] Laceration is most commonly described using the Hitpael of the verb גדד, as
in Deut. 14: 1; 1 Kgs. 18: 28; Jer. 16: 6; 41: 4–5; 47: 5; Mic. 4: 14. In almost all of
these examples, a mourning context for the act of laceration is clear. In contrast,
the nouns שרט and שרטת and verbal forms of the root שרט occur only in Lev. 21: 5;
19: 28; and Zech. 12: 3, and only in the former two passages do the noun and its
verbal reflexes relate to mourning.

the dead in language similar to that of Lev. 21: 5, Lev. 19: 27–8 forbids Israelites to 'round off' (נקף) the corner of the head (?), 'destroy' the corner of the beard, and tattoo the flesh. Rounding off the corner of the head, though obscure to us as a gesture, seems to refer to some form of shaving or hair-cutting. Destroying the corner of the beard is probably the same act as shaving the corner of the beard mentioned in Lev. 21: 5. Tattooing the flesh must differ from incising an incision though both appear to involve cutting the skin.[6] Finally, Deut. 14: 1 forbids Israelites to lacerate themselves (Hitpael נדד) or set a bald spot between the eyes for the dead.[7] The pairing of laceration and shaving as mourning gestures is not restricted to these three texts alone; there are several other passages in which the two acts together are represented as legitimate mourning rites (e.g. Jer. 16: 6, 41: 4–5). But these three texts are distinct for their prohibition of laceration and shaving.

What was it about shaving and laceration that led Holiness circles to ban them for priests, and later, Holiness and Deuteronomistic circles to proscribe them for all Israelites? In order to address this question, it is necessary to consider laceration and shaving as components of the larger complex of mourning rites that include acts such as sitting on the ground, tearing one's garment, strewing ashes or dust on one's head, wearing sackcloth, fasting, and weeping. As I have argued, these mourning rites function together to create and mark a distinct ritual status for the mourner, the petitioner, and others who utilize them. This status is abandoned when those embracing mourning practices replace them with rejoicing behaviours. A number of biblical texts suggest the possibility of rapid reversal from a stance of rejoicing to a posture of mourning, and vice versa. In Amos 8: 10, the Day of Yhwh is described. At that ominous time, Israel's joyous festivals will be transformed while in process: 'I

---

[6] The word קעקע, usually translated 'tattoo', occurs only in Lev. 19: 28. On this, see further N. Tur-Sinai, 'כתבת קעקע', *EM* 4: 378–80.

[7] The location of the bald spot in Deut. 14: 1 appears unusual at first blush. Most texts mentioning the shaving of a bald spot as a mourning rite locate it on the head, presumably where there is normally hair (e.g. Lev. 21: 5; Isa. 15: 2; Jer. 48: 37; Ezek. 7: 18; 29: 18; Amos 8: 10). On this, see Botterweck, 'גלח gillaḥ', 7. Shaving a bald spot between the eyes may be an idiomatic way of saying 'on the head', as Schwartz points out, citing the Ugaritic parallel qdqd // bn 'nm (תורת הקדושה, 348; for the parallel, see *CAT* 1.2 IV 21–2).

shall turn (והפכתי) your pilgrimage festivals into mourning,' //
'and all your songs into a dirge.' // 'I shall put sackcloth on every
loin,' // 'upon every head a bald spot . . .' Ps. 30: 12 (Eng. 11) is
similar in its description of a rapid transformation of mourning
into rejoicing: 'You turned (הפכת) my lamentation into dancing,'
// 'you removed my sackcloth and girded me with rejoicing . . .'.[8]
David's petitionary mourning for his sick son ends rapidly
through a series of ritual reversals in 2 Sam. 12: 20: He rises from
the ground, washes, anoints himself, and changes his clothes,
before going off to the sanctuary to worship and home to
dine. When one considers most of the rites that characterize the
activity of the mourner, it is clear that they are easily reversible:
the one who sits on the ground rises; the one covered with ashes
or dust bathes; the one fasting eats. The same observation
applies to rites that separate the mourner from the rest of the
community: sackcloth replaces normal attire; the head remains
unanointed; dirges replace joyful songs. Yet shaving and laceration do not fit this pattern.

Unlike other mourning practices that separate and mark the
mourner over the dead, the petitioner, and others who embrace
mourning, laceration and shaving are not easily reversible.
Laceration scratches or cuts the skin, and may cause bleeding
and scabbing that lasts for weeks; it may even leave long-lasting
or permanent scars on exposed body parts such as the arms.[9]
Shaving is at best only gradually reversible over an extended
period of time.[10] Thus, shaving and laceration stand out as
distinct among mourning rites because they are not easily or

---

[8] The verb הפך is sometimes used in other contexts to express rapid change
or transformation. See e.g. Exod. 7: 17, 20; Pss. 78: 44; 105: 29 (the Nile's waters
are turned into blood); Ps. 66: 6 (Yhwh turned the Sea of Reeds into dry
ground); Ps. 114: 8 (Yhwh brought forth water from the rock). See further, n. 45
in the Introduction.

[9] Such scars may be the subject of Zech. 13: 6, though this must remain
uncertain.

[10] This point is illustrated in 2 Sam. 10: 5, the case of David's humiliated
emissaries to the Ammonite court. The men, beards half-shaven and buttocks
(and possibly genitals) exposed in a mockery of mourning rites, are ordered not
to return immediately to Jerusalem, but to wait at Jericho until their beards
have begun to grow back. The exposure of their nakedness was without doubt
quickly remedied, but nothing could be done immediately about their half-
shaven beards.

rapidly reversible.[11] But there is more to say about the distinct
character of laceration and shaving as mourning practices.
Unlike the majority of mourning rites that can be reversed at
will, which last only as long as the mourner remains separated
from the community, the physical evidence of laceration and
shaving outlast the commonly attested, seven-day mourning
period.[12] It may even abide beyond the termination of a more
extended period of petition or mourning after personal or corporate calamity. At the end of seven days of mourning the dead,
sackcloth is removed and normal, quotidian clothing is donned;
fasting ceases and eating and drinking begins. A similar transformation occurs when petition or mourning activity related to
calamity ceases. But the shaved beard and the head with a bald
spot remain at the end of seven days and may last much longer;
they become conspicuous markers of mourning in a context
of non-mourning, as do lacerated arms or other body parts,
whose scars may be permanent. Thus, the carefully constructed
boundaries that separate the mourner from others are obscured
by the continued presence of shaved head or lacerated body parts
in non-mourning contexts. These blur the ritual distinction
between mourner and non-mourner, a distinction made and
marked by mourning rites, and threaten the continued viability
of the cult, which is grounded in a series of such distinctions.[13]

Now that the distinct character of shaving and laceration as
rites of mourning has been established, I shall go on to consider

---

[11] Schmidt anticipates me by noting in passing the irreversibility of laceration and shaving's long-lasting effects (*Israel's Beneficent Dead*, 177–8).

[12] I am not the first to make this observation. See Schmidt, ibid. 178 and n.
178.

[13] Though he notes in passing the long-lasting effects of laceration and
shaving, and observes that they outlast the mourning period, Schmidt, *Israel's
Beneficent Dead*, 178 argues that shaving and laceration are distinct because they
'offer an *unparalleled* identification of the living with the dead and an *unprecedented* reminder of death's intrusion upon the world of the living. Moreover, the
irreversibility of the markings embodies death's inevitability and its ever-
present threat.' I prefer to argue that their distinction resides not in any special
kind of identification they might foster, but in their lack of easy reversibility and
in the fact that they outlast the mourning period. We cannot know that shaving
or laceration fostered any greater identification with the dead in this culture than
did strewing ashes or dust on the head or sitting on the ground while weeping.
Yet we can establish that the effects of laceration and shaving go beyond seven
days.

what might have motivated their proscription for priests in Lev. 21: 5, and for all Israelites in Lev. 19: 27–8 and Deut. 14: 1. Priests find their primary locus in the sanctuary, where they present Yhwh's offerings at the altar and attend to other, specialized tasks such as blood manipulation. According to Lev. 21: 16–23 (H), priests with physical defects (מומים) such as blindness and lameness may not appear before Yhwh with offerings, nor may a blemished high priest approach the curtain at the entry of the holy of holies, the deity's throne room; to do so, says the text, would profane Yhwh's holy sanctuaries which Yhwh sanctifies (ולא יחלל את מקדשי כי אני יהוה מקדשם). Blemished priests may remain in the sanctuary and continue to eat holy foods as long as they do not approach Yhwh's primary loci (the altar and the holy of holies). It is clear from Lev. 21: 16–23 that Yhwh does not want to see physical defects on those who approach him *directly*, though he tolerates blemishes on those who do not (e.g. priests who do not serve at the altar). Yhwh's rejection of blemished priests who approach him directly finds parallels in the prohibition of shaving and laceration for priests in mourning in Lev. 21: 5. Just as Yhwh does not wish to see blemishes on the priests who approach him, so he does not wish to see permanent or long-lasting mourning markers such as a bald spot or lacerations on them.[14] The justification for the proscription of shaving and laceration in Lev. 21: 5 is remarkably similar to that offered in Lev. 21: 23 regarding blemished priests. Lev. 21: 23 states that the blemished priest shall not approach the altar or curtain because of his defect, that he not profane (חלל) Yhwh's holy sanctuaries which Yhwh sanctifies. Lev. 21: 6 exhorts the priests to be holy and not profane (חלל) the name of their God, 'for the offerings of Yhwh, the food of their God, they bring near . . .'[15] Thus, each passage justifies its particular restriction based on holiness, and the danger of its profanation, either by a blemished priest approaching the altar or by a priest with a permanent or long-lasting mourning marker doing so.[16]

---

[14] Lev. 21: 6, which justifies the restrictions of 21: 5, speaks specifically of priests *who present Yhwh's offerings*; it says nothing of the status of other priests who might not approach Yhwh directly and nothing of worshippers.

[15] On profanation, the legitimate or illegitimate transformation of something holy into something common, see the discussion in Olyan, *Rites and Rank*, 25–7.

[16] J. Tigay compares Lev. 21: 5–6 and 21: 23, noting the similarity of the

Why is Yhwh offended by the presence of a priest at his altar
with a permanent or long-lasting mourning marker? There are
two plausible answers to this question.[17] First, it is possible that
the shaved beard, the bald spot on the head, and lacerated limbs
or other body parts, are constructed as blemishes by this text, not
unlike lameness and blindness, though the text is not explicit in
this regard.[18] Just as the blind or lame priest cannot serve at the
altar, so the priest with a shaved beard or lacerated arms cannot.
Because these mourning markers are self-inflicted and can therefore be prevented, Lev. 21: 5–6 seeks to prohibit them for
priests.[19] Yet there is a second possible explanation for the interdiction of priestly shaving and laceration rites that does not
depend on assuming that these practices are constructed by the
text as blemishes. It also fits well within the pattern of the separation of mourning and rejoicing in each ritual actor that I have
discussed previously. Simply put, shaving and laceration are
proscribed for the priest in order to prevent him from mixing in
his person the rites of mourning and rejoicing. Such mixing
would occur when the priest has ceased mourning or petitioning,
and approaches the altar to carry out his customary, sacrificial
duties. For among the priest's responsibilities is officiating at
joyful sacrifice (e.g. the routine well-being (or peace) offering
(שלמים), during which the priest manipulates blood on the altar
and processes fat and organ meat according to P).[20] It is the
priest's continuing to bear on his person tokens of mourning

justification in each (*Deuteronomy* (JPSTC; Philadelphia: Jewish Publication
Society, 1996), 136).

[17] As I have noted, I do not consider the 'foreign practice' or ancestor cult
explanations plausible, nor do I find Schmidt's interpretation convincing. For
discussion, see further nn. 1, 13.

[18] Tigay, *Deuteronomy*, 136, argues that the mourning markers in question
are 'comparable' to blemishes (מומים), and therefore profaning to holiness. I note,
however, that such mourning markers do not occur in the list of blemishes in
Lev. 21: 18–20, nor are they ever referred to as blemishes in any text. Milgrom,
Leviticus 17–22, 1694, objects to Tigay's comparison on the grounds that the
results of shaving and laceration are only temporary and will eventually disappear. Though this observation is true with regard to shaving, it is not necessarily true of laceration, which can leave permanent scars.

[19] Milgrom anticipates me in noting the self-inflicted nature of these mourning markers, in contrast to the blemishes of Lev. 21: 18–20 (ibid. 1694).

[20] On the priest's manipulation of blood and fat and organ burning at the altar
in the context of שלמים sacrifices, see Lev. 3: 2–5, 8–11, 13–16.

when he has reverted to a ritual stance of rejoicing that would profane the name of Yhwh and threaten his own holiness[21] when he officiates at sacrifices (Lev. 21: 6). Similarly, blemishes on the priest serving at the altar profane the sanctuary according to Lev. 21: 23. The distinction between those who mourn and those who rejoice, so carefully maintained in the cult under normal circumstances, is threatened by the presence of a priest at the altar marked as a mourner in a sacrificial context of rejoicing. Which of these two interpretations accounts best for the data? Each has its appealing features, but the understanding of shaving and laceration as blemishes suffers from a notable weakness: these practices are never explicitly constructed as blemishes in any biblical text, so we cannot know that the law of Lev. 21: 16–23 is directly relevant to interpreting Lev. 21: 5–6. Understanding the prohibition as an attempt to prevent the inevitable and undesirable mixing of antithetical ritual behaviours in the same ritual actor, in contrast, explains the data well without depending on a questionable association.

Not surprisingly, other mourning practices that are easily reversible and do not outlast the mourning period are apparently permitted for priests, as these would neither be constructed as blemishes nor create situations in which mourning behaviour would be mixed with rejoicing in the same individual. Several texts, including Lev. 21: 1–5, speak of priestly mourning both directly and indirectly. Though Lev. 21: 1–4 forbids the priest to have corpse contact with all but the closest of kin and 21: 5 prohibits two types of shaving and incising an incision, they say nothing of other mourning rites. Yet other texts provide some insight into the mourning rites performed by priests. Ezek. 24: 16–17 suggests that for a priest such as Ezekiel, expected mourning behaviour would include actions such as weeping, the unbinding of the hair, the removal of shoes, and the covering of the upper lip.[22] Lev. 10: 6 may be read to suggest that practices

---

[21] The threat of laceration and shaving to the priest's holiness is implied by the emphatic call to the priests to be holy in v. 6, which follows immediately upon the proscriptions of v. 5. The text suggests that the practice of laceration and shaving would make priestly holiness impossible.

[22] The text describes a symbolic act of the prophet, Ezekiel's refraining from performing these actions at the death of his wife. The perplexed reaction of his audience suggests that they expected Ezekiel to perform these acts of mourning. On this, see further the discussion of M. Greenberg, *Ezekiel 21–37*, 509–

such as the unbinding of hair and the tearing of garments are normally permitted for priests.[23] Thus, several texts suggest that priests may perform mourning rites that are easily reversible, and leave no physical trace beyond the mourning period. These would not offend the deity or threaten the holiness of his name because they would no longer be in evidence when a priest leaves his mourning state to resume his normal cultic duties. The boundaries between mourning and rejoicing would therefore remain unchallenged; there would be no erosion of the ritual distinction between mourners and persons who enact rejoicing, no mourning markers in contexts where they do not belong.

It remains to explain the prohibition of laceration and shaving for all Israelites in Lev. 19: 27–8 and Deut. 14: 1. If the proscription originally applied to priests approaching Yhwh's altar, how did it come to be generalized to all Israelites in the Holiness Source and Deuteronomy?[24] The first thing to be noted is the parallel generalization of holiness to all Israel in both H and D. In the Holiness Source and in Deuteronomy, in contrast to other biblical materials such as the Priestly Writing, holiness is a quality shared by Israelites. Lev. 19: 2 addresses Israel as follows: 'You shall be holy, for I, Yhwh, your God, am holy.' Holiness passages such as Exod. 31: 13; Lev. 20: 8; 21: 8 describe Israel as sanctified by Yhwh continually: 'You shall keep my

10. Greenberg claims, incorrectly in my view, that 'self-wounding' mourning rites (i.e. laceration and shaving) were illegitimate in Israel (citing Lev. 19: 27–8; Deut. 14: 1–2), though texts such as Jer. 16: 6; 41: 4–5 suggest otherwise. The evidence for their illegitimacy is restricted to H and D.

[23] Lev. 21: 10–11 prohibits the high priest from all corpse contact, and the mourning rites of unbinding hair and tearing garments. Given the restrictions on priests in Lev. 21: 1–5, 21: 10–11 implies that the mourning actions forbidden to the high priest are permitted to priests, since 21: 5 says nothing about mourning rites other than shaving and laceration, and explicitly permits corpse contact for next of kin, in contrast to 21: 11. In contrast to these texts, Ezek. 44: 20 states that priests may neither shave their heads nor unbind their hair.

[24] As others have argued, it seems very likely that a restriction imposed on a single group (the priesthood) has been generalized to all Israelites. To argue the opposite thesis would, as Schmidt has pointed out, produce 'unnecessary redundancy' (*Israel's Beneficent Dead*, 171). See also K. Elliger, *Leviticus* (HAT 4; Tübingen: J. C. B. Mohr/Paul Siebeck, 1966), 289, who believes that Lev. 19: 27–8 may represent a 'democratization' of what was originally a rule restricting priests alone, and M. Fishbane, *Biblical Interpretation in Ancient Israel* (Oxford: Clarendon Press, 1985), 122.

statutes and do them; I am Yhwh, who sanctifies you (מקדשכם)'
(Lev. 20: 8). Similarly, Deut. 14: 2 describes Israel as 'a holy
people to Yhwh' their God.[25] Lev. 19: 2 heads a series of laws in
Leviticus 19, including the ban on shaving and laceration in 19:
27–8; though it does not say so explicitly, the text gives the
impression that obedience to these laws is a component part of
being holy. Deut. 14: 2 makes the connection between holiness
and the avoidance of laceration and shaving for the dead more
explicitly: Israelites should not shave a bald spot between the
eyes for the dead or lacerate themselves *because* they are a holy
people to Yhwh their God (כי עם קדוש אתה ליהוה אלהיך). Deut. 14: 2
and less explicitly, Lev. 19: 2, suggest that the mourning rites of
shaving and laceration are somehow a threat to the people's holiness, just as they apparently threaten the holiness of Yhwh's
name and that of the priests themselves according to Lev. 21: 6.
Therefore, the ban on the mourning rites of shaving and laceration for all Israel may find its explanation in the generalization of
holiness to the people of Israel as a whole.[26]

Once the people are conceived as holy, their holiness must be
protected from profanation caused by the presence of two kinds
of mourning markers on their persons. How might such mourning markers threaten to profane the holiness of the people? As
with the lacerated or shaven priest, it is possible that the issue is
one of blemishes as a threat to holiness, though this seems
unlikely, given H's lack of concern for blemishes on Israelite
worshippers.[27] The mixing of mourning and rejoicing in the
same ritual actor is a more likely explanation in my view, though
not an unproblematic one. The continued presence of mourning
markers such as a shaven beard or lacerated arms on a person
who has ceased mourning or petition would create difficulties in
a cultic setting in which the worshipper seeks to rejoice by
offering sacrifices to Yhwh or enacting other typical rejoicing

[25] Note also Exod. 19: 6 (D), where Israel is said to have the potential to
become a 'holy people' (גוי קדוש). It is clear that H texts both call upon Israel to
be holy (e.g. Lev. 19: 2) and assume Israel's holy state (e.g. Lev. 20: 8). On this,
see further the argument in Olyan, *Rites and Rank*, 121, 173–4 n. 3.

[26] Similarly, Tigay, *Deuteronomy*, 136–7 and now Milgrom, *Leviticus 17–22*,
1691.

[27] Though compare the saying of 2 Sam. 5: 8b, which probably excludes
blemished Israelites from the Jerusalem temple. On this, see Olyan, *Rites and
Rank*, 106–11.

behaviours. But would this not also be a problem even if the common Israelite worshipper were not constructed as a possessor of holiness? It seems to me that it would, for holy or not, the shaven or lacerated worshipper would be mixing mourning and rejoicing in his person when he brings sacrifices and offerings to the sanctuary at festivals and other times of rejoicing. In short, though the need to avoid the mixing of mourning and rejoicing in the same ritual agent is a plausible explanation for the prohibitions in question, it does not account for them on the basis of the extension of holiness to the people in the Holiness Source and Deuteronomy. This is a weakness, given that the attribution of holiness to the people parallels the extension of the proscription in H and D, and given that the holiness of Israel appears to be the motivating factor for the ban in Deut. 14: 1–2. Perhaps it was the very extension of holiness to the people in Holiness and Deuteronomistic circles that brought into relief the potential problems that abiding evidence of shaving and laceration could cause for worshippers in rejoicing situations, thereby resulting in the prohibitions of Lev. 19: 27–8 and Deut. 14: 1. On this point, however, we can only speculate.

Conclusions

Laceration and shaving, licit mourning practices in a variety of biblical materials, are prohibited for priests in Lev. 21: 5 and for all Israelites in Lev. 19: 27–8 and Deut. 14: 1. Their proscription in these Holiness and Deuteronomistic texts prompts us to ask what it is about them that makes them distinct and subject to special treatment by the Deuteronomistic and Holiness tradents. It is clear that they differ from other mourning rites in two important ways. First, unlike the majority of mourning practices that may be abandoned at will, shaving and laceration are not easily reversible. Once shaved, the hair of the head or beard grows back only gradually over an extended period of time. Similarly, lacerated body parts take time to heal, and laceration may leave permanent, exposed scars even after recovery is complete. Second, in contrast to other mourning rites, laceration and shaving are distinct in that they outlast the commonly attested seven-day mourning period for the dead, and may even remain in evidence longer than more extended periods of petition or mourning at a time of disaster. In a word, shaving and laceration have the potential to become mourning markers 'out of place', visible tokens of mourning on the bodies of those who have abandoned the mourning ritual stance and shifted to a posture of rejoicing. Such a mixing of mourning and rejoicing practices in the same ritual actor would blur the distinction between mourner and non-mourner, thereby obscuring the boundaries that separate the distinct ritual states and posing a threat to the continuity of the ritual order.

The proscription of these distinct, not easily reversible rites for priests was probably motivated by a desire to prevent the priest from mixing mourning and rejoicing rites in his person when he leaves a mourning context and returns to his normal duties. These include his routine officiating at rites of rejoicing such as the well-being (or peace) offering. It is presumably such a mixing of mourning and rejoicing in the same ritual actor that is understood by Lev. 21: 6 to profane Yhwh's holy name and threaten the priest's own holiness when he officiates at sacrifice. It is also possible that a desire to keep bodily defects out of the deity's presence motivated the ban on priestly laceration and shaving, though this seems less likely, for shaving and laceration are nowhere categorized as blemishes (מומים). The generalization of what appears to be an original priestly prohibition to all Israelites in Lev. 19: 27–8 and Deut. 14: 1 is paralleled by the attribution of holiness to all of Israel in the same two sources, and Deut. 14: 2 states explicitly that the people's holiness is the motive for the ban. Thus, it may be that the generalization of holiness to the people in D and H motivated the proscription of shaving and laceration for the whole people. The attribution of holiness to the whole people may have had the effect of focusing greater attention on potential difficulties caused by mourning tokens on the bodies of those who rejoice, though this must remain a speculation.

5

The Sanctioned Mixing of Mourning and Rejoicing

The variety of texts which describe mourning in sanctuary loci indicates that under normal circumstances, the rites of mourning and rejoicing are never combined in the same individual. This is the case even in cultic contexts where petitionary mourning behaviours occur as the rejoicing rites of the temple continue around the petitioner. In 1 Samuel 1, rejoicing persists in the Shiloh sanctuary during Hannah's individual supplication to Yhwh, but Hannah has separated herself ritually and physically from those who rejoice, and does not participate in acts of rejoicing such as eating and drinking during the period of her petition. Similarly, Ezra mourns on account of what he considers to be Judah's sacrilege, while the quotidian rites of the Jerusalem temple continue to take place around him. But neither he nor his supporters take part in such rites while they engage in penitential entreaty; they separate themselves ritually from those who enact the joyful rites of the sanctuary service. Rejoicing and mourning behaviours in a sanctuary context normally remain unmixed in each individual ritual actor, though they may occur simultaneously in different individuals except at certain times (e.g. during a pilgrimage festival or communal fast). This state of ritual separation allows one ritual posture to give way to the other under appropriate circumstances (e.g. the end of an individual petition). The ability to shift between the ritual stances of mourning and rejoicing preserves the ritual order itself, which is founded upon distinctions such as holy/common, clean/unclean, and rejoicing/mourning and dependent upon their careful maintenance for its perpetuation.

Though sanctioned petitionary mourning in temple settings is possible as long as petitioners do not fuse ritual stances, there is evidence that certain, specific occasions mandate one ritual behaviour or the other for the entire community. A collective fast such as that of 1 Sam. 7: 5–6, Joel 1–2, or 2 Chr. 20: 1–19 leaves no room for rites of rejoicing, as the whole Judaean community is obligated to engage in petitionary mourning behaviours in order to secure the deity's intervention on their behalf.[1] Similarly, the New Year as described in Neh. 8: 9–12 is a context in which the whole community is required to rejoice by means of eating festival foods, drinking sweet drinks, and sending portions to those who lack them. Mourning behaviour of any sort is strictly forbidden on such an occasion, as the passage makes clear. Evidence indicates that pilgrimage festivals such as Sukkot ('Booths') mandate rejoicing for the whole community (e.g. Lev. 23: 40 (H); Deut. 16: 14, 15; Neh. 8: 17), and according to Hos. 2: 13 (Eng. 11), other occasions such as the New Moon and Sabbath have similar requirements: 'I will bring all her joy to an end, her pilgrimage festivals, her New Moons, her Sabbaths, and all her festivals' (והשבתי כל משושה חגה חדשה ושבתה וכל מועדה). Similarly, victory in battle requires rites of rejoicing from the victors after the fact, as David learns in 2 Sam. 19: 1–9 (Eng. 18: 33–19: 8). Judith 8: 6, possibly a text of the second century BCE, suggests that where mourning the dead and obligatory rejoicing compete legitimately, rejoicing is privileged and mourning behaviour is abandoned temporarily.[2]

Yet the well-attested contrast between the rites of mourning and rejoicing and their cultic separation in each individual ritual

---

[1] The entire community's participation is indicated by the presence even of young children at the fast (e.g. Joel 2: 16; 2 Chr. 20: 13).

[2] In this passage, the widow Judith, who is presented as a paradigm of piety, fasts except on the Sabbath and the day before, the New Moon and the day before, festivals and days of rejoicing for Israel. The text claims that this behaviour lasted 3 and a half years. On the date of Judith, see Albertz, *Exilszeit*, 37, citing E. Zenger, *Das Buch Judit* (Gütersloh: Mohn, 1981), 431. In a later time, the rabbis will struggle with competing demands of mourning and rejoicing, striking a balance between public and private, rejoicing obligations and mourning obligations. See e.g. m. Moed Q 3. 5, which states that if a festival intervenes for the mourner who has been mourning for three days, he is not obligated to complete the seven-day mourning period. If he has mourned eight out of thirty days, he is not required to complete the thirty-day mourning period. See further, Semahot 7. 3 and b. Moed Q 14b, 19a.

agent is complicated by several texts that bear witness to the
sanctioned fusion of rejoicing and mourning behaviours in the
same individual in a temple or pilgrimage context. These texts
also complicate our understanding of the avoidance, under
normal circumstances, of either mourning or rejoicing at select
times when the other ritual behaviour is privileged (e.g. during
pilgrimage festivals, when rejoicing is obligatory). Both Jer. 41:
4–5 and Amos 8: 3 describe a mixing of normally distinct and
separate ritual modes of action. In the case of Amos 8: 3, the
fusion of rejoicing and mourning behaviours is foreseen in an
oracle of Yhwh to the prophet, so that it is clearly sanctioned. In
Jer. 41: 4–5, the combination of mourning and rejoicing rites
occurs during pilgrimage, presumably at the time of the fall
festival, a context in which rejoicing alone is expected of ritual
actors, and the text casts the pious pilgrims as a foil for the
scoundrel Ishmael who murders them.[3] Thus, the ritual behaviour represented in these two texts is strikingly different from
what is otherwise evidenced with regard to mourning and rejoicing, and therefore the texts require explanation. What is it about
the situations described by this pair of passages that allows for
such an apparent breakdown in the ritual distinctions in which
the cult is grounded? And what is such mixing of otherwise antithetical ritual modes intended to communicate?

Jer. 41: 4–5 is part of a larger narrative that tells of the murder
of Gedaliah the son of Ahikam, the Babylonian-appointed
governor of Judah after the conquest of Judah and Jerusalem in
587/6, by Ishmael son of Netaniah of the royal lineage. After
Ishmael's murder of Gedaliah and his associates in Mispah, and
before anyone had learned of the crime, Ishmael encounters a
group of northerners apparently on their way to Jerusalem: 'On
the day after the killing of Gedaliah, before anyone knew of it,
eighty men came from Shechem, Shiloh, and Samaria, their
beards shaved, their garments torn and lacerating themselves,
with cereal offering (מנחה) and frankincense (לבונה) in their pos-
session to bring to the House of Yhwh.' Ishmael, who weeps as
he approaches these unsuspecting men, invites them into the city

---

[3] In other words, nothing about the presentation of the pilgrims in Jer. 41:
4–5 suggests that their ritual actions are illegitimate in any way. In fact, they are
shown fulfilling pilgrimage expectations such as those of Deut. 16: 13–15 even
after the temple has been destroyed.

allegedly on behalf of Gedaliah, and then murders them.[4] What is most of interest to me in this narrative is the striking ritual behaviour of the eighty northerners. That they are pilgrims heading to the Jerusalem temple can hardly be disputed. They have come from far off bearing grain and incense, standard offerings for the House of Yhwh, and the text states specifically that the temple is their destination.[5] Presumably, they are going to Jerusalem to observe Sukkot ('Booths'), the fall pilgrimage festival, as the narrative states that the events took place in the seventh month (Jer. 41: 1).[6] By bearing these offerings on pilgrimage, the northerners enact routine rejoicing behaviours mandated for the fall festival.[7] Yet the pilgrims are on their way to a destroyed temple, and have taken on the appearance of mourners, presumably in mourning for that temple: they have shaved their beards, torn their garments, and they lacerate themselves.[8] In a word, they have fused in their persons the normally

---

[4] See my comments on the social dimensions of Ishmael's weeping in Ch. 3.

[5] Grain offerings and incense are mentioned together in the Bagohi letter from Elephantine (Cowley 31) as typical offerings formerly brought by worshippers to Elephantine's temple of Yhwh. On this document, see my discussion and translation below; for the Aramaic text, see the reference in n. 24. See also Neh. 13: 5, 9, which mention the grain and incense offerings stored in the Jerusalem temple complex, and Jer. 17: 26, which speaks of grain and incense among the characteristic offerings brought to the House of Yhwh in Jerusalem in a rejoicing context. Cf. similarly Isa. 43: 23. Num. 29: 14 discusses the required grain offering of the fall festival and its preparation from the perspective of P. See also Lev. 2: 1, 2 (P) on frankincense as a component of the typical grain offering.

[6] Gedaliah was murdered in the seventh month according to Jer. 41: 1. On the fall festival's pilgrimage requirement for all males, see Exod. 23: 16–17; 34: 22–3; Deut. 16: 13–17. It is a commonplace among scholars to note that the pilgrims are on their way to Jerusalem bearing offerings, and that the fall festival is the reason for their pilgrimage. See e.g. A. Weiser, *Das Buch des Propheten Jeremia* (ATD 20; Göttingen: Vandenhoeck & Ruprecht, 1960), 356; W. Rudolph, *Jeremia* (HAT 12; Tübingen: J. C. B. Mohr/Paul Siebeck, 1958), 231–3; McKane, *Jeremiah*, 2: 1027. It is difficult to imagine why else pilgrims from various northern cities would undertake such a journey to the Jerusalem temple bearing offerings in the seventh month.

[7] Both Lev. 23: 40 (H) and Deut. 16: 14, 15 command rejoicing during the fall festival, with Deut. 16: 15 specifically excluding all non-rejoicing activity: 'You shall only rejoice' (והיית אך שמח). Neh. 8: 17 notes the 'exceedingly great rejoicing' (שמחה גדולה מאד) characteristic of the fall festival observed by the returnees to Jerusalem.

[8] On shaving as a mourning rite, see Olyan, 'What do Shaving Rites

incompatible and antithetical rites of mourning and rejoicing into a single, novel ritual constellation as they journey to Jerusalem on pilgrimage.[9] They mourn for the destroyed sanctuary even as they undertake the obligatory seasonal pilgrimage bearing offerings.[10]

What is this unprecedented fusion of rejoicing and mourning behaviours in the context of pilgrimage intended to communicate? It can only mean that the distinctions between the contrasting states of cultic rejoicing and mourning have completely broken down, and therefore the ritual order has collapsed. With the temple lying in ruins, such a loss of ritual distinctions, expressed as a fusion of normally separate ritual behaviours, is not difficult to conceive. There no longer exists a separate, sanctified cultic sphere with its distinct set of ritual requirements, among them the separation of rejoicing and mourning in the individual ritual agent. Movement between the ritual states of mourning and rejoicing is no longer possible, because a distinct sphere for rejoicing has ceased to exist. The pilgrims, by their actions and appearance, signal the demise of the sanctuary and the ritual distinctions separating rejoicing from mourning. Mourning is enacted together with rites associated with rejoicing in a ritual context (pilgrimage) formerly reserved for rejoicing alone.[11] Though the New Year in Neh. 8: 9–12 is a ritual context

Accomplish and what do they Signal in Biblical Ritual Contexts?', *JBL* 117 (1998), 616–17. On laceration and mourning, see Schmidt, *Israel's Beneficent Dead*, 166–78.

[9] Ishmael, the only actor in the text who confronts the northern pilgrims, secures their trust and avoids suspicion by weeping as he approaches them. He joins them in their mourning, suggesting that their grief is the result of national catastrophe rather than any personal loss, given that Ishmael presumably does not know them, and would therefore be under no obligation to play the role of comforter. Cf. Schmidt, ibid. 171, who speculates unconvincingly that the men are in mourning for lost loved ones. On the comforter role in diplomatic and personal contexts, see e.g. 2 Sam. 10: 2–3; Jer. 16: 7; Job 2: 11–13, Anderson, *A Time to Mourn*, 84–7 and my previous discussions in Chs. 1, 2, and 3.

[10] Baruch Schwartz has suggested to me that the pilgrims are evidently continuing to fulfil the requirement for all males not to appear empty-handed at the fall festival (Deut. 16: 16–17), even though the sanctuary has been destroyed and has ceased to function (oral communication, 13 Mar. 2002). The fact that meat offerings are unmentioned in Jer. 41: 4–5 may relate to the destruction of the sanctuary, though this remains unclear.

[11] The pilgrimage route to the sanctuary is represented by biblical texts in much the same way as the sanctuary itself, and the pilgrimage process is

in which the penitential impulse of the assembly is suppressed because it is not contextually appropriate, such is not the case with the fall festival described in Jer. 41: 4–5, a ritual setting with comparable rejoicing requirements (see Deut. 16: 15). Not only mourning, but mourning fused with acts of cultic rejoicing is apparently sanctioned under these particular and peculiar circumstances. Though many commentators have noted the mourning behaviour of the pilgrims in this text, they have not to my knowledge explored, problematized, or even noticed the mixing of ritual behaviours it describes.[12] Yet this fusion of rites is clearly the most interesting characteristic of Jer. 41: 4–5, setting it apart from the typical text representing mourning rites.

Amos 8: 3 is similar to Jer. 41: 4–5 in a number of ways, though it differs with respect to certain details of context. Instead of describing the ritual actions of worshippers in response to the disastrous loss of a temple as in Jer. 41: 4–5, Amos 8: 3 envisions such disaster in Israel's future by means of an image of a polluted, chaotic cult site:[13]

described much like the ritual process of rejoicing in the sanctuary. The way to the temple, like the temple itself, is holy, and forbidden to those who are polluted (Isa. 35: 8); the journey is characterized by self-sanctification and rejoicing with song, joyful cries, and musical instruments (Isa. 30: 29; 35: 10). One might thus imagine pilgrimage space and activity as an extension of sanctuary space and activity.

[12] A typical treatment is that of J. Bright, *Jeremiah* (AB 21; Garden City, NY: Doubleday, 1965), 254. In his comments, Bright notes that the northern pilgrims on their way to Jerusalem are mourning for the destroyed temple, but has nothing to say about the fact that they fuse mourning and rejoicing behaviours in their pilgrimage. See similarly A. Weiser, *Jeremia*, 356; W. L. Holladay, *Jeremiah 2* (Hermeneia; Minneapolis: Fortress, 1989), 297; G. P. Couturier in R. E. Brown, J. A. Fitzmyer, and R. E. Murphy (eds.), *The New Jerome Biblical Commentary* (Englewood Cliffs, NJ: Prentice Hall, 1990) 293; Schmidt, *Israel's Beneficent Dead*, 171; and McKane, *Jeremiah*, 2: 1019. Even Anderson has nothing noteworthy to say about Jer. 41: 4–5 or Amos 8: 3, the other text that appears to describe a fusion mourning and rejoicing. Amos 8: 3 is not treated, and Jer. 41: 4–5 is mentioned only in passing in a footnote devoted to laceration (*A Time to Mourn*, 62 n. 6). After developing my argument, I discovered that Pedersen, in contrast to others, noted the 'remarkable' mixing of mourning and rejoicing behaviours in this text. However, he understood the behaviour of the northerners to be typical of atonement fasts, which is clearly not the case, as I have pointed out (*Israel: Its Life and Culture*, 4: 458–9).

[13] I shall speak of the sanctuary in the singular for simplicity's sake, though it is obvious that the verse speaks of a single temple in the first colon, and a plurality of sanctuaries in the second.

'They shall wail (והילילו)[14] the songs of the temple (שירות היכל) on that
day',[15] an oracle of the Lord Yhwh.
'Many will be the corpses in every sanctuary (מקום)[16] . . .'[17]

The poetic association of corpses and sanctuaries is striking, as
the presence of corpses signals profound pollution and the ruin
of sanctified cultic places.[18] The polluted temple imagined in this
verse is the context in which mourning and rejoicing behaviours
are fused, as in Jer. 41: 4–5. This is indicated by the first colon, in
which unspecified Israelites (perhaps temple singers?) shall wail
(והילילו)the songs of the temple (שירות היכל). The expression 'songs
of the temple' must refer to the joyous liturgical hymns associated with sanctuary and pilgrimage rites in so many texts, also
called 'songs of Yhwh' or 'songs of the House of Yhwh' (see e.g.
Isa. 30: 29; Amos 5: 23; 8: 10; Ps. 137: 4; 1 Chr. 6: 16 (Eng. 31);
25: 6, 7).[19] The verb ילל, 'to wail', is commonly found in descriptions of mourning behaviour, as a number of other texts show

[14] It is also possible to understand והילילו as a masculine plural imperative.

[15] The popular emendation שירות ('songs') > שרות ('female singers') is not particularly compelling, as the text as it stands yields good sense in a context of
sanctuary destruction. Nor is the proposed emendation reflected in the versions.
Though the verb ילל is otherwise attested as transitive only in Ezek. 30: 2, the
noun שירות as the object of ילל is hardly reason enough to amend the text. The
feminine form שירה occurs commonly in the singular, though the plural here in
Amos 8: 3 is a *hapax legomenon*. The common attestation of the singular שירה is
yet another reason that militates against emendation, as שירות would be the
expected plural of שירה. For the emendation שרות, see e.g. NJPS and H. W. Wolff,
Dodekapropheton 2: Joel und Amos (BKAT xiv/2; Neukirchen-Vluyn: Neukirchener, 1969), 366. My understanding of והילילו שירות היכל of Amos 8: 3 is
similar to that of J. L. Mays, *Amos* (OTL; Philadelphia: Westminster, 1969),
140–2. Cf. also RSV and NRSV ('The songs of the temple shall become wailings
in that day . . .').

[16] The word מקום occurs with the meaning 'sanctuary' in a number of biblical
texts, and is an appropriate parallel term for היכל, 'temple'. For מקום as 'sanctuary', see the texts listed by NKB 2.627.

[17] What follows, השליך הם, is very likely corrupt, and contributes nothing of
interest to this investigation in any case.

[18] 2 Kgs. 23: 15, 16 speak of the destruction of the Bethel sanctuary by means
of the introduction of bones or corpses.

[19] Such songs are clearly associated with pilgrimages and contrasted with the
mourning dirge in Amos 8: 10: 'I shall turn your pilgrimage festivals into
mourning' // 'And all your songs (כל שיריכם) into a dirge (קינה).' Though not all
songs are to be associated with rejoicing rites and contexts (e.g. Deut. 31: 19),
the expressions 'song of Yhwh' or 'song of the Temple' or 'song of the House of
Yhwh' do seem to suggest such an association consistently.

(e.g. Jer. 48: 20; 49: 3; Joel 1: 5, 11, 13; Mic. 1: 8; Ahiqar C 1. 1. 3. 41).[20] One normally sings temple songs joyously and wails and intones dirges in a context of lamentation and mourning. Thus, to wail temple songs is a striking image that fuses mourning and rejoicing behaviours, not unlike the activity of the pilgrims of Jer. 41: 4–5, who bear the offerings of pilgrimage but in the guise of mourners. The fusion represented by the wailing of songs of rejoicing signals the collapse of the distinctions between the two ritual states, as does the fusion of mourning behaviours and pilgrimage rites in Jer. 41: 4–5. This is not surprising, given the ruined, polluted sanctuaries envisioned in the next colon. Just as the destruction of the Jerusalem temple results in the fusion of mourning behaviours and pilgrimage rites of rejoicing after the fact in Jer. 41: 4–5, the anticipated defilement of the sanctuaries of the north results in a similar fusion of ritual behaviours in Amos 8: 3.[21]

[20] For the text in Aramaic, see Porten and Yardeni, *Textbook of Aramaic Documents*, 3: 30.

[21] Several other texts might appear at first blush to represent the fusion of mourning and rejoicing behaviours, but upon closer examination, this is clearly not the case. 1 Maccabees presents a scene in which temple offerings are brought to an assembly at Mispah at which mourning rites are enacted for petitionary purposes (3: 46–53). At Mispah, the people ask Yhwh what they are supposed to do with the offerings, given that the temple is polluted and the cult has ceased. It seems to me that this pericope draws upon several earlier biblical texts, including Jer. 41: 4–5 (Mispah, offerings), Joel 1–2 (petition at time of disaster), and 1 Sam. 7: 5–11 (Mispah, offerings, petition). As a result, it reads as a pastiche of sorts. There does not, however, appear to be a fusion of mourning and rejoicing in the manner of Jer. 41: 4–5 and Amos 8: 3 in this context. All joyful activity has ceased, the context is a petitionary fast and not a festival (cf. Jer. 41: 4–5), and nothing is actually done with the offerings. Even if Yhwh were offered sacrifices, as he is at other fasts (e.g. 1 Sam. 7: 5–11; Lev. 23: 27; Num. 29: 7–11), fusion would not be the result, since sacrifice in a petitionary context is not constructed as rejoicing (joyful songs of praise are absent, the offerer fasts and petitions rather than eats). Similarly, the cultic scene described in Ezra 3: 12–13 is not truly analogous to what is represented in Amos 8: 3 and Jer. 41: 4–5. In this passage, many rejoice with joyful shouts at the establishment of the new temple in Jerusalem just as one might expect, while others weep, apparently in disappointment. Though the result is a cacophony that can justifiably be described as a case of 'ritual infelicity' ('the people could not discern the sound of the joyful shouts from the sound of the weeping . . .'), the scenario described differs from those of Jer. 41: 4–5 and Amos 8: 3, in that individual ritual actors do not mix mourning with rejoicing behaviours in their persons, and the behaviour is not sanctioned. On 'ritual infelicity', see the

Jer. 41: 4–5 and Amos 8: 3 share in common the context of a
destroyed sanctuary, and I have argued that the loss of the sanctuary lies behind the images of fused rites of mourning and
rejoicing in the cultic settings mentioned in each text. But is such
a combination of rites an obligatory response to the destruction
of a cult site? An examination of other texts that describe the
response of worshippers to the loss of their sanctuary suggests
that it is not. Two texts in the Book of Zechariah are relevant to
this discussion: Zech. 7: 1–7 and 8: 18–19. Zech. 7: 1–7 concerns
the continued observance of fast days, one of which marks the
anniversary of the destruction of the Jerusalem temple in the
fifth month. The text characterizes the yearly observance in
memory of the temple's destruction as one of weeping, fasting,
and lamentation. Nowhere in this passage is there any hint of the
fusion of mourning and rejoicing behaviours witnessed in Jer.
41: 4–5 or Amos 8: 3.[22] This impression is confirmed by Zech. 8:
18–19, in which four yearly fast days, among them the fast for the
temple in the fifth month, will be transformed into observances
marked by rejoicing:

> The word of Yhwh of hosts came to me as follows:
> Thus says Yhwh of hosts:
> 'As for the fast day of the fourth month,
> and the fast day of the fifth month,
> and the fast day of the seventh month,
> and the fast day of the tenth month,
> they shall become joy (ששון) for the House of Judah,
> and rejoicing (שמחה) and festivals (מעדים טובים) . . .'

That this text can speak of the transformation of fast days into
days of rejoicing indicates clearly that in the view of the author,
the distinctions that characterize mourning and rejoicing remain
in force. Mourning and rejoicing are distinct and separate sets of
ritual behaviours. Those who observe fast days with mourning
rites can assume a rejoicing posture with the necessary changes
in the community's circumstances. The reason for the predicted
transformation of fasts into festivals is likely the anticipated

helpful discussion of Wright, *Ritual in Narrative*, 112–18, whose focus is the
Aqhat epic from Ugarit.

[22] Nor does the text suggest that the mourning rites were observed in the
setting of the sanctuary, though such a locus is certainly possible.

rebuilding of the temple and the restoration of the cult, a central theme of Zechariah 1–8.[23]

Another text of interest that concerns communal observances after the destruction of a temple hails from the Elephantine archive from Upper Egypt. The text is a letter in Aramaic written by Judaeans in the Elephantine fortress to Bagohi, governor of Judah. The letter was written in 407 BCE and concerns the destruction of the temple of Yhwh in Elephantine three years before. In it, the Judaean communal leaders tell of the successful plot of the priests of the Egyptian god Khnum and the local governor Vidranga to destroy the Judaean temple. Three years after the destruction of their sanctuary, the Judaeans in Elephantine are still mourning their loss, and their leaders appeal to Bagohi to intervene on their behalf with the Persian authorities in Egypt so that the temple of Yhwh may be rebuilt. What is interesting for our purposes is the behaviour of the Judaeans of Elephantine at the time that the letter was written:

From the month of Tammuz (in) the fourteenth year of Darius the king to this day, we have been wearing sackcloth and we have been fasting. Our wives are like widows, we do not anoint ourselves with oil, and wine we do not drink. Also, from that time until this day, the seventeenth year of Darius the king, cereal offering, frankincense, and burnt offering they have not made in that temple.[24]

As in Zech. 7: 1–7 and 8: 18–19, the people observe mourning rites to mark the loss of their sanctuary.[25] The rites may have taken place at the locus of the temple, though nothing in the text indicates this. The people fast (presumably at set times), abstain from anointing themselves, and from drinking wine. In addition, the letter points out that offerings of grain, incense, and meat have ceased in the temple. In this text, there is no evidence that mourning and rejoicing were fused in any way by the Judaeans at Elephantine who undertook ritual observance of their communal loss. Offerings are apparently not brought to the site of the

---

[23] Other passages in Zechariah 8 allude to the anticipated restoration of the cult. See e.g. 8: 3, 9, 20–3.

[24] This is my translation of Cowley 31. For the text in Aramaic, see Porten and Yardeni, *Textbook of Aramaic Documents*, 1.72.

[25] Anderson compares the prolonged communal mourning of Zech. 7: 1–7 and 8: 18–19 with that described in the Bagohi letter in his discussion of the ritual movement from mourning to rejoicing (*A Time to Mourn*, 110–12).

ruined sanctuary, as they are in Jer. 41: 4–5, and the letter makes no allusion to the persistence of any other rejoicing behaviours after the destruction of the temple. As in Zech. 7: 1–7 and 8: 18–19, a strict separation of mourning and rejoicing behaviours is evident. With the destruction of the sanctuary, cultic rejoicing has ceased entirely, replaced by mourning.

Other biblical texts describing the aftermath of the Jerusalem temple's destruction present a similar scenario of mourning without evidence of cultic rejoicing. In Lam. 1: 4, the personified 'ways of Zion' (דרכי ציון) mourn, without pilgrims. In 2: 10, the elders of Zion sit on the ground in silence, wearing sackcloth and with dust on their heads. Ps. 137: 1–4 is yet another example of mourning in the aftermath of the destruction of temple and city. The text refers to exiled Judaeans mourning the destruction of Zion by the rivers of Babylon. Stringed instruments are hung on trees, and the mocking demand of the captors for words of song and rejoicing is ignored, most likely in part because of the mourning context and in part because of the locus in an alien land.[26] A later text of interest is 1 Maccabees, which describes the plundering and defilement of the Second Temple by the Seleucid king Antiochus IV Epiphanes and his minions. Several passages in this text imitate earlier biblical descriptions of temple destruction and subsequent mourning rites (e.g. 1: 39 echoes Amos 8: 10). They present scenes of mourning after the plundering and defilement of the temple (1: 25–8, 39–40; 2: 14), though with no suggestion that the mourning behaviours described are fused with rites of rejoicing.

Clearly, the fusion of rejoicing and mourning behaviours witnessed in Jer. 41: 4–5 and Amos 8: 3 is not an obligatory response to a sanctuary's destruction. On the contrary, many texts, among them Zech. 7: 1–7; 8: 18–19 and the Aramaic letter to Bagohi from Elephantine, suggest that mourning alone is a

---

[26] Worship in an alien land may be impossible according to Ps. 137: 4 for any number of reasons. First, foreign lands are unclean according to a number of biblical texts, and as such, they would be inappropriate loci for cultic worship. See e.g. Hos. 9: 3; Amos 7: 17; Ezek. 4: 9–15. Other texts suggest that in the view of some Israelites, the worship of Yhwh is restricted to his territory alone, and not possible outside the land of Israel (e.g. 1 Sam. 26: 19; cf. 2 Kgs. 5: 17; Ezek. 11: 15). Finally, exiles who were supporters of the Deuteronomistic ideology of cultic centralization would have found it difficult to conceive of a temple of Yhwh outside of Jerusalem.

perfectly acceptable response to a loss of such great magnitude. Even with the cult in ruins, the distinctions between mourning and rejoicing can remain in force. How then might one understand the passages that speak of the fusion of the rites of mourning and rejoicing? Perhaps texts such as Jer. 41: 4–5 and Amos 8: 3 simply represent the way ritual actors might interpret catastrophe *in the most profound and striking terms possible*. As I have noted, the fusion of mourning and rejoicing not only marks disastrous loss poignantly; it implies that no return is possible to the way things were. Once the distinctions that produce a cultic order are lost, the cultic order itself ceases to exist. In contrast, texts such as Zech. 7: 1–7; 8: 18–19 and the Elephantine letter, by preserving the distinct spheres of mourning and rejoicing, allow for possible reversal should circumstances change. But they do so by presenting a less extreme, and therefore, somewhat less compelling image of disaster. Why might some texts treating the destruction of a sanctuary represent the cultic order as potentially restorable (e.g. Zech. 7: 1–7; the Bagohi letter), while other texts describing the same set of circumstances suggest that the cultic order has ceased to exist forever (e.g. Jer. 41: 4–5)? Perhaps the different ways of representing ritual activity in the aftermath of a temple's destruction simply reflect two very different interpretations of the implications of that disastrous event.

Conclusions

Various biblical texts suggest that under normal conditions, mourning and rejoicing behaviours are never combined in the individual ritual agent. One rejoices or one mourns, keeping the two ritual postures separated and distinct, and moving back and forth between them as required. Mourning and rejoicing may occur simultaneously in different ritual actors in a single cultic setting, except on certain occasions such as communal fasts or pilgrimage festivals, when one ritual stance becomes mandatory for all. Yet several texts challenge the pattern of separation of ritual behaviours in the individual ritual actor that I have identified, and also the pattern of devoting certain times such as pilgrimage festivals or communal fasts to one ritual behaviour to the exclusion of the other. These texts, Jer. 41: 4–5 and Amos 8: 3, both portray the fusion of mourning and rejoicing behaviours in individual ritual agents. In the case of Jer. 41: 4–5, this mixing of ritual modes apparently occurs in the context of pilgrimage at the fall festival, a context normally devoted entirely to rejoicing. The fusion of mourning and rejoicing behaviours represented in these texts is not insignificant, for it signals the collapse of the ritual order on account of the loss of the ritual distinctions that ground the cult. But what is it about these passages that allows for this unusual, sanctioned fusion of normally distinct and separated ritual modes? Each of these texts describes rites that occur in the context of a destroyed sanctuary. In Jer. 41: 4–5, the mourning pilgrims are on their way to the site of the Jerusalem temple after it has been demolished by the Babylonians. Amos 8: 3 envisions a future time of calamity in which the temple's songs of rejoicing will be wailed in a polluted sanctuary. It can only be the destruction of the sanctuary and the loss of a distinct, sanctified ritual space that allows for this sanctioned response of mixing otherwise separate and incompatible ritual modes. Though other texts suggest that fusion of this type is not a mandatory response to such catastrophe, it may be that those responsible for Jer. 41: 4–5 and Amos 8: 3 seek to present a more extreme and pessimistic interpretation of the cult's future prospects. By representing the complete collapse of the ritual order through the image of mourning fused with rejoicing in the same ritual actors, they may be suggesting that there can be no hope of restoration. In contrast, mourning alone, a well-documented alternative ritual response to the destruction of a sanctuary, leaves open the possibility of a return to cultic activity, since the distinctions between mourning and rejoicing remain in effect.

Conclusion

RITUAL DIMENSIONS OF MOURNING

Four types of mourning are represented in biblical texts, each with its own distinctive characteristics. Mourning rites are embraced by the mourner over the dead, by the petitioner (whether a penitent or not), by the non-petitioning individual at the time of personal or corporate catastrophe, and by the person afflicted with skin disease. Though explaining the interrelationship between these mourning types is key to developing an understanding of the ritual dimensions of biblical mourning, scholars have seldom sought to identify and map different mourning configurations let alone illuminate their common and unique attributes.[1] Addressing this deficiency in the history of research has been a major focus of this study. Apart from identifying four kinds of mourning in biblical texts, I have argued that mourning the dead is the form of mourning upon which the other types are modelled, and that all mourning shares debasement in common, though it functions differently in each mourning configuration. The interrelationship between the four types of mourning is best described and analysed by comparing their spatial aspects, their chronological dimensions, the pollution or purity of their respective ritual agents, and the ease or difficulty of reversion from each type to a ritual stance of rejoicing. Comparing the nature and function of debasement, the dynamics of comforting, and the role of other characteristics (e.g. the presence or absence of the dirge) among the four mourning types also contributes significantly to an understanding of mourning as a ritual activity. Comparison and contrast bring into relief the

---

[1] On this, see the discussion and citations in n. 5 in the Introduction.

common attributes and differences among the four configurations of biblical mourning.

The four mourning types share a number of traits in common. Most significantly, the same set of distinct ritual behaviours are used by the mourner over the dead, the petitioner, the non-petitioning person marking catastrophe, and the individual stricken with skin disease. In addition, all four kinds of mourner eschew rites of rejoicing during their period of mourning. Several other characteristics are shared by at least two of the four mourning configurations. The same technical vocabulary (derivatives of the roots אבל and ספד) is at times utilized to describe the ritual behaviour of the mourner for the dead, the petitioner, and the non-petitioning individual experiencing disaster. (Lev. 13: 45–6, the one text that represents the mourning behaviour of the person afflicted with skin disease, does not use any derivative of these verbs, but this is probably only due to chance.) Furthermore, the mourner over the dead, the petitioner, and the non-petitioning person at a time of catastrophe could expect the support of comforters.[2] Finally, both persons mourning the dead and those responding ritually to the ruin of a city make use of the dirge form to express sorrow and to eulogize the dead or the destroyed city.

Debasement is a common characteristic of all four mourning configurations, though it has distinct functions in each context in which it occurs. I have argued that the mourner for the dead debases himself by means of mourning rites in order to honour the dead through identification with him. Such debasement may be intended to establish a new, mutually beneficial and ongoing relationship between the mourner and the dead. In contrast, the ritual diminishment of the petitioner functions to attract the deity's or a human authority's attention to his plight and secure his decisive intervention. It may also communicate shame, repentance, and concession of authority in the case of the penitent, and shame in the case of the non-penitential petitioner. Texts representing the mourning activity of individuals at the time of personal or corporate calamity tend to suggest that feelings of humiliation motivate their self-debasing acts. Finally, the ritual self-diminishment of the person stricken with skin disease,

---

[2] The individual afflicted with skin disease, in contrast, had no comforters on account of his mandated social isolation.

suggested by his utilization of the same set of mourning rites which have debasing functions elsewhere and his other, distinct ritual behaviours, contributes to the realization and communication of his social isolation. Texts also suggest the important role of debasement in comforting. Comforters of the mourner over the dead and the non-petitioning person at a time of disaster debase themselves in order to foster identification with their intimate or ally. Those who comfort the petitioner debase themselves not only to identify with the petitioner, but probably also to increase the effectiveness of the petitioner's entreaty. Thus, debasement is a pervasive trait of mourning and comforting in their various manifestations, serving a variety of purposes depending on the context. Though debasement is a characteristic shared in common among the mourning types, it functions to distinguish type from type due to its differing functions in each mourning configuration.

The purity status of ritual actors who utilize mourning rites tends to determine their spatial range. The mourner over the dead is polluted by corpse contact or by proximity to a corpse; similarly, the person afflicted with skin disease is defiled by his condition. As a result, neither can approach the sanctuary for the period of his pollution. According to the Priestly Writing, the individual with skin disease is excluded not only from sanctified loci, but also from all centres of communal settlement as long as he is infected and polluting (Lev. 13: 46). In marked contrast to the mourner over the dead and the individual afflicted with skin disease, texts suggest that the petitioner and the non-petitioning individual experiencing disaster are unrestricted with respect to loci, since neither is typically polluted in a way that would exclude access to the sanctuary.[3] Thus, the petitioner or the mourner at the time of calamity has full access to the sanctuary, as various texts demonstrate (e.g. Ezra 9–10; Joel 1–2).

Similar distinctions among the four types of mourning emerge when their temporal characteristics are considered. The mourner for the dead mourns for part of a day, one day, seven days, or thirty days, depending on the text. In each case, there is not only a required minimum period of mourning, but also a

---

[3] On the penitent polluted by means of transgression, see my discussion in Ch. 2, n. 3. As I have noted, Num. 5: 11–31 suggests that defilement from sin does not result in exclusion from sanctified loci.

predetermined terminus beyond which mourning may not continue. In contrast, petitionary mourning, the non-petitionary mourning practices of the person who experiences catastrophe, and the rites of the individual afflicted with skin disease, are not temporally limited in the same way. The mourning of the person with skin disease is completely open-ended; it may continue for as long as the disease is present, which may be until death. A petitioner may entreat the deity continuously until his supplication has been answered; alternatively, he may fast and enact other petitionary mourning rites for more limited time periods (e.g. a day, three days, or three weeks). Those mourning disaster may do so as long as they deem necessary, though their observances may also occur on a single day at set intervals (e.g. yearly fasts, such as the fast in the fifth month in commemoration of the temple's destruction).

Finally, the ease or difficulty of reversing the mourning stance to a ritual posture of rejoicing differs among the various mourning configurations. The petitioner or the non-petitioning mourner at the time of a catastrophe may abandon mourning and revert to rejoicing quickly and with little trouble, as long as he does not bear the physical evidence of laceration and shaving, rites that are not immediately reversible. In contrast, the mourner over the dead, polluted by corpse contact, must wait seven days and undergo elaborate purification procedures before he can assume a rejoicing stance. Similarly, the individual afflicted with skin disease cannot abandon mourning until the disease is healed, a time period has passed, and he has undergone extensive rites of purification. Shaving and laceration would also complicate the return of the mourner for the dead to rejoicing, since traces of these acts would continue to be present in his person after his mourning period has ended. (No text speaks of the use of laceration and shaving by individuals afflicted with skin disease.)

Such differences with respect to the function of debasement, range of loci, purity status, temporal requirements, ease or difficulty of reversibility, and other characteristics (e.g. comforting), produce four unique configurations of mourning. In the case of the person with skin disease, additional mandatory ritual behaviours (e.g. calling out 'unclean, unclean') accompanying his mourning rites function to mark his mourning off as distinct from mourning the dead and the other types of mourning. Thus, each kind of mourner can usually be distinguished from the others, as the following examples illustrate. An individual in the sanctuary with the appearance of a mourner cannot be mourning the dead or mourning as a result of skin disease; he is most probably a petitioner there to entreat the deity. Similarly, the ritual behaviour of a person who cries 'unclean, unclean', who mourns ceaselessly without comforters, and who avoids settled areas, indicates that he is clearly afflicted with skin disease. A mourner who shuns the sanctuary sphere for seven days, is joined by comforters while he mourns, ceases mourning after the seven days have passed, and undergoes rites of purification before returning to the temple sphere is evidently mourning the dead. Distinct and recognizable configurations of mourning emerge therefore from a consideration of commonly shared characteristics and differences among the mourning types.

That mourning the dead is the paradigmatic form of mourning is suggested by texts that compare petitionary mourning and the rites of persons experiencing calamity to mourning the dead (Jer. 6: 26; Joel 1: 8; Ps. 35: 13–14). The fact that mourning the dead is never likened to other forms of mourning is also an indicator that it serves as the model for the other mourning configurations. Given the apparent prototypical status of mourning the dead, how might we explain the utilization of mourning rites in non-death-related contexts? As an historical reconstruction of the emergence of mourning unrelated to death is impossible due to a dearth of evidence, we must be content to speculate about what might have motivated persons with no death connection to embrace mourning rites for their own purposes.[4] As I have argued, it seems likely that the debasing function of mourning practices and their adaptability led to their use in new contexts requiring the diminishment of ritual agents. In these novel settings, self-diminishing mourning rites served new and distinct purposes, though some of their original functions seem to have been preserved as well. For example, in the context of

---

[4] Because phenomena such as petitionary mourning are not restricted to Israel alone, diachronic explanations for the spread of mourning that focus on internal, Israelite developments are unconvincing. For an example of this kind of explanation, see my discussion below, in n. 5, on Podella's reconstruction. On petitionary mourning outside of Israel, see Ch. 2, n. 5.

entreaty, texts suggest that mourning rites are intended to attract
the attention and secure the intervention of the deity or another
authority on behalf of the petitioner, and may also communicate
shame, repentance, and concession of authority. Though none of
these functions is native to mourning the dead, the identification
practised by the petitioner's comforter is much like that of the
mourner's comforter on which it is modelled, though it has
probably taken on a new, context-specific purpose (strengthening entreaty) in addition to its other aims. Thus, the identification dimension of comforting in contexts of mourning the
dead is translated into a new ritual scenario—entreaty—with
appropriate modifications. It is the adaptable character of
mourning rites and their power to debase that best explains their
application to new ritual settings with no direct relationship to
mourning the dead.[5]

---

[5] Though Podella also believes that mourning rites came originally from
death contexts, he presents a wholly speculative historical sketch of their spread
to petitionary situations allegedly under the influence of prophetic critique of
the cult and Deuteronomistic ideas. Podella believes that two characteristics of
mourning rites were responsible for their utilization in petitionary contexts:
their power to create social solidarity and their ability to protect the living from
the threat of death (*Šôm-Fasten*, 271–2, for a summary statement). As I
have mentioned, Podella's historical reconstruction, which focuses on alleged
internal Israelite developments, cannot explain the phenomenon of petitionary
mourning in Mesopotamian and other non-Israelite contexts successfully, and
therefore, it is unconvincing. Given the ubiquity of such rites, any explanation
of the spread of mourning to non-death-related contexts cannot be particular to
Israel. Even if Podella's thesis were plausible, it only attempts to account for
mourning in contexts of entreaty, while any successful explanation will have to
account for all mourning phenomena. For the sake of argument, let us consider
whether Podella's two characteristics potentially have a wider application. If we
look at other mourning contexts, they do not explain the embrace of mourning
successfully. One of Podella's two characteristics that allegedly account for the
spread of mourning to petitionary situations, its power to create social solidarity, would have no application whatsoever to the individual stricken with
skin disease whose rites function to isolate him socially. His second characteristic, protection from the threat of death, assumes that all those who embrace
mourning rites are threatened by death, a view I reject as implausible on the
basis of the various settings in which mourning occurs, including a number of
petitionary contexts. (On this, see my discussion below.) Thus, Podella's explanation cannot be used to account for non-petitionary and non-death situations
in which mourning occurs; it does not explain all petitionary contexts in which
mourning rites are utilized; and its historical contextualization is wholly speculative, and inapplicable to contexts outside of Israel. Gerstenberger explains the

Yet some scholars have argued that it is the threat of death that lies behind the employment of mourning rites in contexts unrelated to the dead. K. Spronk, for example, states that those who embrace mourning practices in non-death-related contexts do so to 'indicate that they feel themselves threatened by death'.[6] I am not convinced by this claim, for it does not account well for the variety of contexts and circumstances in which mourning rites are utilized. A number of examples of mourning in non-death-related contexts have no evident associations with the threat of death or the realm of the dead, even indirectly. Daniel's employment of mourning rites to seek a vision from Yhwh is one such case (Dan. 10: 2–3, 12). The mourning is petitionary in nature, but there is nothing in this text to suggest that Daniel perceives himself to be threatened by death in any way; he simply wants guidance and insight from Yhwh.[7] The mourning of Haman after his public humiliation is another pertinent example (Esther 6: 12). Though Haman responds to his shaming by mourning, nothing in the text suggests that he is threatened by death; rather, he reacts to his humiliation at the hands of his arch-enemy. It is true that some petitioners in the psalms of complaint speak of approaching the underworld during their time of suffering, and it must also be acknowledged that all who embrace mourning rites very likely resemble the dead in terms of appearance. But these characteristics alone do not suggest that the threat of death is the general motivation for the mourning of petitioners and others whose mourning is unrelated to death contexts. The rhetoric of approaching the realm of the dead in some of the psalms of complaint, as I have argued, is subordinated to the larger purposes of petition, and in any case, it is not evidenced in all petitionary settings. Resemblance to the dead on account of the embrace of mourning rites is an inevitable

use of a shared set of rites in both death settings and contexts of entreaty by what he believes is the common aim of supplication and lament for the dead: reaching Yhwh ('Der klagende Mensch', 68). The problem with this explanation is that there is no evidence that lament for the dead and related mourning rites have any petitionary intent whatsoever. The same is true of the rites of the person afflicted with skin disease and the mourner at the time of catastrophe who does not petition, though Gerstenberger does not mention these ritual actors.

[6] *Beatific Afterlife*, 246. See also the role of the threat of death in Podella's formulation (*Ṣôm-Fasten*, 273).

[7] See the words of the angel to Daniel in 10: 12: נתת את לבך להבין.

by-product of the borrowing of such rites in non-death-related contexts; it cannot be said to indicate that every ritual actor who mourns feels threatened by death. In short, though all mourning retains some death associations due to its origin in a death-related context, one would be hard pressed to make a convincing case that the threat of death has motivated mourning in all of the various contexts in which it occurs. Debasement is a more cogent explanation for the utilization of mourning rites outside of death-related contexts than is the threat of death, which may be evidenced in some settings in which mourning occurs, but certainly not all.

The resemblance of persons who utilize mourning rites to the dead, a by-product of the adoption of mourning practices in settings unrelated to death, contributes to their debasement in a variety of ways. For the individual stricken with skin disease, whose constellation of rites is intended to isolate him from all social interaction, shared appearance with the dead has the effect of underscoring his extreme pollution and his separation from the sanctuary and all community. For the dead are cut off from the living and from Yhwh, and corpses, like the diseased person himself, are profoundly polluting. The tendency witnessed in Num. 12: 12 to compare the afflicted individual to a corpse, however widespread it might have been, would probably have been strengthened by his resemblance to the dead. For the petitioner, sharing an appearance with the dead, like other debasing characteristics and acts, would function mainly to attract the deity's attention and secure his intervention on his behalf. Other functions such as the communication of repentance, shame, and concession of authority would also be strengthened by means of such a resemblance to the dead. Like the rhetoric of approaching Sheol in the psalms of complaint, the petitioner's appearance underscores the urgency of his petition in its various aspects. He has debased himself exceedingly in order to secure Yhwh's intervention on his behalf, whether it be in order to rescue him from enemies, to heal him from illness, or to provide guidance by means of an oracle. For the non-petitioner at the time of disaster, shared appearance with the dead would contribute to his self-diminishment for the purpose primarily of externalizing sorrow, horror, and shame. Thus, the ramifications of sharing an appearance with the dead can only be understood by considering the role of shared appearance in each specific mourning setting, for like debasement in general, its significance differs from context to context.

Before turning to the social dimensions of biblical mourning, I shall consider the patterns in the relationship of mourning to rejoicing that I have discerned in this study. Anderson's argument that mourning and rejoicing are distinct and antithetical ritual stances is certainly correct. However, Anderson did not investigate the problem of mourning in sanctified loci, nor did he consider texts in which mourning and rejoicing are apparently fused in the same ritual agent, nor did he make the constraints on mourning a subject of his study. Yet, a consideration of these topics is essential to understanding the ritual dimensions of mourning, allowing us both to test and to sharpen the thesis that mourning and rejoicing are opposed and incompatible ritual behaviours.

Mourning in the sanctuary is odd at first blush, and demands explanation, given the well-evidenced ritual incompatibility of mourning and rejoicing and given that rejoicing is arguably the ritual activity par excellence of the cult. It also presents a challenge to scholars who have emphasized the incompatibility of death and its tokens with the temple and its sanctified sphere.[8] If mourning and rejoicing are incompatible, and rejoicing is the primary ritual activity of the sanctuary, and even petitionary mourning bears some death associations, how is it possible that sanctioned mourning can occur in a temple setting? Two patterns of mourning by petitioners in the standing sanctuary are discernible. In Joel 1–2 and other representations of communal fasts, petitionary mourning in the temple replaces rejoicing for the whole community for the period of petition. In other texts such as Ezra 9–10 and 1 Samuel 1, petitionary mourning temporarily takes the place of rejoicing for an individual or group in a sanctuary setting in which cultic rites of rejoicing continue for the larger community. Though mourning occurs in the sanctuary in both patterns, in neither case is mourning combined with rejoicing in the same ritual actor. Fasting communities abandon all rejoicing rites for the period of their fast, and individual supplicants or groups of petitioners mourn while

---

[8] e.g. Feldman, *Defilement and Mourning*, 57, 59.

eschewing the rejoicing behaviours of others around them. In all cases, mourning petitioners have access to the sanctuary because they are not defiled in a manner that would disqualify their entry. Thus, texts suggest that legitimate petitionary mourning rites are possible and may even be commanded in sanctuary settings as long as mourning and rejoicing remain unmixed in individual petitioners. It is not petitionary mourning in the sanctuary per se that is problematic; various texts represent this as a routine phenomenon. Rather, it is the mixing of the two ritual postures in the same individual that must be eschewed. This scrupulous avoidance of combining mourning and rejoicing rites in the same person allows one ritual mode to continue to give way to the other as circumstances demand, since each ritual stance remains distinct from the other. Thus, the ritual order itself, founded on a series of distinctions such as rejoicing/mourning, clean/ unclean, holy/common, is preserved and perpetuated through their careful maintenance.

It seems likely that the proscriptions on the rites of shaving and laceration witnessed in Lev. 21: 5; 19: 27–8; and Deut. 14: 1 are intended to prevent just such a mixing of mourning and rejoicing in priests or worshippers after they have ceased mourning and returned to a posture of rejoicing. Unlike other mourning rites, laceration and shaving are not easily reversible, and would typically outlast the seven-day mourning period for the dead and most periods of petition or mourning associated with personal or corporate calamity. Thus, the mourner may abandon his mourning or petition, but lacerated body parts or a bald spot on the head, distinctive mourning tokens, would continue to mark him as a mourner in rejoicing contexts such as sacrificial worship, leading to an unacceptable mixing of mourning and rejoicing in his person. As I have pointed out, such a fusion of mourning and rejoicing would threaten the integrity of the distinctions that undergird the ritual order, and therefore it is not surprising that several biblical legal texts proscribe shaving and laceration.

A striking fusion of mourning and rejoicing rites in the same ritual agents is evidenced in Jer. 41: 4–5 and Amos 8: 3. These texts differ from the petitionary texts just discussed in that they each describe ritual behaviour in the context of a temple's destruction. With the demise of the sanctuary, Jer. 41: 4–5 and

Amos 8: 3 suggest that the distinctions between the contrasting ritual states of mourning and rejoicing have completely broken down, and that the ritual order itself has therefore collapsed. The sanctuary sphere, formerly sanctified, separated from common territory, and protected scrupulously from pollution, has ceased to exist as an independent entity. As a result, suggest these texts, the sanctuary's distinct ritual requirements, among them the separation of mourning and rejoicing in the same ritual agent, no longer exist. With the fusion of mourning and rejoicing in the same individual, reversion from mourning to rejoicing and vice versa is no longer conceivable. No return is possible to the former ritual patterns. This interpretation of the significance of the destruction of a sanctuary is striking and compelling, but it is only one possible reading of such a situation. As I have argued, many other texts that describe the ritual behaviour of individuals in the aftermath of a sanctuary's demise suggest that mourning alone is a perfectly legitimate response to such calamity. A response of mourning, rather than fusion of the two ritual modes, leaves open the possibility of reversion to rejoicing should future circumstances warrant it. In short, mourning alone after the destruction of a sanctuary preserves the ritual distinctions upon which the cult is founded, in contrast to the fusion of mourning and rejoicing witnessed in Jer. 41: 4–5 and Amos 8: 3.

Texts that represent mourning in the sanctuary suggest that the separation of mourning and rejoicing rites in the same ritual actor is the operative principle upon which the ritual order is founded, rather than the separation of rites in terms of the locus in which they occur. Calendrical considerations are a secondary influence shaping patterns of ritual behaviour (e.g. rejoicing is mandatory on a festival; mourning is required on a fast day). That different ritual agents can enact both mourning and rejoicing simultaneously in a sanctuary sphere at times other than obligatory feasts or fasts suggests that we ought to question schematizations such as Anderson's that tend to dissociate petitionary mourning behaviour from the temple.[9] The central issue

---

[9] e.g. Anderson states that '[t]he ritual movement from mourning to joy has mirrored a spatial movement from Sheol to Temple, from the absence of God to the presence of God', implying that petitioners are dissociated from the temple for the period of their petition. Similarly, Anderson states that 'just as

is not separation of antithetical ritual behaviours in terms of the place they occur; rather, it is the separation of such rites in the individual ritual actor along with appropriate observance of times devoted exclusively to one mode of ritual action or the other. Consideration of the texts that represent a fusion of mourning and rejoicing behaviours brings into relief the degree to which the cultic order is founded on the separation of the two ritual postures in individual ritual agents. The mixing of mourning and rejoicing is both emblem and cause of the ritual order's breakdown.

SOCIAL DIMENSIONS OF MOURNING

Mourning in its various configurations has profound social implications, as rites in general are a context for the continual creation and recreation of the social order and for its potential transformation. Bonds linking individuals, groups, and political entities such as states are affirmed, created, re-negotiated, or terminated in mourning contexts, just as they are in ritual settings such as pilgrimage, joyful sacrifice at the sanctuary, festival meals in the home, public assemblies, or the reception of messengers at court. Treaty relationships between political entities, or between a ruler and his people, may be embraced, affirmed, recast, or ended in public mourning settings. A king's authority is put to the test by his people's response to his own precedent-setting ritual behaviour. Social rank may be conferred and embraced in contexts of mourning, or contested by individuals or collectivities. Groups representing distinct political positions may come into being, be perpetuated, be reconstituted, or be terminated in mourning settings. Mourning, like other ritual phenomena, also has a communicative dimension. The rites of the mourner not only create his ritual separation from others, but externalize it for all to see. At the same time, mourning publicizes the social relationships it engenders, confirms, recasts, or terminates.

Existing social bonds are affirmed in a variety of mourning

mourning attire can restrict one's access to the royal court, so also for the divine court', suggesting that the tokens of mourning are incompatible with the sanctuary (*A Time to Mourn*, 91, 92).

contexts such as those represented in 2 Sam. 3: 31–37, 2 Sam. 15: 14–16: 13, and Ezek. 26: 16–18. In 2 Sam. 3: 31–7, the description of Abner's funeral, David's followers weep in response to his order to mourn Abner, Saul's general, thereby confirming and externalizing their loyalty to and affiliation with the king and his political purpose. It is likely that the mourning rites of David and the Judaeans are intended to affirm publicly the treaty which David had established with Abner just before Abner's murder by Joab. Such an avowal by means of an appropriate funeral and mourning rites realizes and communicates the state of good relations David desires between Abner and the north, on the one hand, and himself and Judah, on the other. Comparable social dynamics in the very different context of flight and supplication are evidenced in 2 Sam. 15: 14–16: 13, the narrative of David's escape from Jerusalem at the time of his son Absalom's revolt. Like David himself, those who leave Jerusalem with David enact mourning as they walk, weeping loudly with heads covered. Their ritual behaviour, and that of other loyal subjects such as Hushay and Ziba who meet the fugitives on their ascent from the city, affirm and publicize their loyalty to and affiliation with David. The behaviour of David's faithful followers stands in marked contrast to those who avoid the king and his company at this time of need, or those such as Shimi the Saulide who actively taunt them. David's questioning of the absence of Meribaal indicates clearly that crises such as these were contexts in which loyalty and affiliation were to be actively demonstrated. Finally, the mourning and dirge-intoning of the princes of the sea in Ezek. 26: 16–18 after the envisioned destruction of Tyre illustrates how non-petitionary mourning associated with catastrophe can also function to affirm previously existing social relationships. These allies of Tyre realize and communicate their loyalty to the city even in the aftermath of its destruction.

New social relationships between groups or individuals are created in mourning settings, as Ezra 9–10 and Jer. 41: 6 illustrate. In Ezra 9–10, Ezra practises penitential mourning rites in the sanctuary in response to widespread intermarriage in the Judaean community, something he understands as a sacrilege. His ritual behaviour attracts a group of supporters that grows larger over time according to the narrative. Ezra's sympathizers establish and externalize an affiliation with him and his political

programme through the acts of gathering around him and weeping as he mourns. Their ritual actions serve to bring their distinct
group into being, for in effect, they not only create an affiliation
with Ezra as they weep, but also with each other. Jer. 41: 6 illustrates how mourning with the apparent intent to affiliate might
be manipulated to serve dastardly ends. In this passage, Ishmael,
who has already murdered Gedaliah, the pro-Babylonian
governor of Judah after the fall of Jerusalem, weeps as he
approaches a group of unsuspecting northern pilgrims who
mourn the destruction of the temple as they travel to its site in
Jerusalem. By weeping, Ishmael apparently seeks to win the
trust of these strangers and establish an affiliation with them. In
effect, his actions communicate that he shares their interpretation of the event as a catastrophe for Israel and Judah, and has
friendly intentions. When Ishmael approaches the pilgrims,
he invites them to come to Gedaliah in Mispah. This ruse is
intended to move the pilgrims into an area Ishmael controls, so
that he and his followers might murder them, which is precisely
what transpires.

Aside from affirming previously existing social bonds and
engendering new ones, mourning is also a context for the inten-
tional termination of previously established ties. 2 Samuel 1, 2
Samuel 10, and several other texts describe or allude to cases of
such changing affiliations. In 2 Samuel 1, David and his men
hear the news of the Philistine victory over Israel at Mt. Gilboa,
and the deaths of Saul and his son Jonathan in battle. By mourning in response to the news, David and his followers establish a
new affiliation with Saul and Israel, thereby terminating their
treaty bond with their overlord Achish, the Philistine king of
Gath. As has been widely noted, allies are expected to rejoice at
the military victory of their covenant partner; they do not mourn
for the defeated enemy. By mourning Israel's defeat and their
slain, David and his men in effect change sides, actively
affiliating with Israel and against the Philistines, their former
treaty partners. 2 Samuel 10 provides another example of
mourning as a context for the rescission of a treaty and the social
relationships dependent upon it. The text describes the humiliation of David's emissaries who have been sent to Ammon as
comforters at the death of the Ammonite king Nahash. The
narrative is an excellent illustration of the way in which covenant

bonds may be terminated in a mourning setting through the dishonouring of participants representing the treaty partner. David's representatives, accused of being spies, are shamed by having half their beards shaven off and their buttocks (and perhaps, genitals) exposed and by being expelled from the Ammonite court. Such acts of aggression against David's embassy bring to an end the treaty between Ammon and Israel, and recast the relationship between the two as one of adversaries rather than allies. This political realignment is accomplished through humiliating ritual actions in a context of national mourning at the passing of a king. Aside from these settings of public mourning rites over the dead, a number of texts suggest that the ritual context of petition could also serve as a setting for the severing of social ties. Several psalms of complaint speak of the refusal of intimates to comfort petitioners (e.g. 38: 12 (Eng. 11); 69: 21 (Eng. 20)); others even mention the rejoicing of former friends over a petitioner's suffering (e.g. 35: 15). The petitioner's call for the humiliation and punishment of disloyal friends in some psalms of complaint certainly suggests a termination of relations.

Several texts suggest a hierarchical dimension to public mourning and other ritual contexts that involve the participation of the ruler. Whether the context is mourning the dead, rites in the aftermath of military victory, or response to a prophetic announcement of doom, the king's ritual behaviour determines that of his followers. Those who choose to remain loyal to the king and communicate their affiliation follow his lead ritually, no matter what their private feelings might be, and no matter what they might otherwise wish to do. This is so even in contexts where the king's ritual behaviour might be inappropriate to the occasion. By embracing the ruler's ritual behaviour, his subjects affirm the reality of his political authority. 2 Sam. 3: 31–7 is one narrative in which this hierarchical dimension is prominent. At Abner's death, David commands his followers to mourn for Abner, and this they do, weeping as he weeps. Even Abner's killer Joab is ordered to mourn by David. By obeying David and following his lead ritually, David's followers realize and publicize their loyalty to him, affirming the reality of his authority over them. A second example of the precedent-setting nature of the king's ritual behaviour is 2 Sam. 19: 1–9 (Eng. 18: 33–19: 8), the description of the aftermath of David's rebel son Absalom's defeat by David's forces. In this instance, it is the ruler's inappropriate ritual acts that determine those of his followers. Though David's army is victorious, the rebel Absalom has been killed, and rejoicing over the victory is expected, David privileges his private grief over his public obligations, mourning over his dead son. When the army hear that David is mourning, his ritual behaviour determines theirs. They mourn, says the text, as a defeated and humiliated army mourn, all because of the king's precedent-setting ritual action and their desire to confirm and perpetuate their relations with him. A third example of a ruler's ritual behaviour determining that of his followers is Jeremiah 36. In this instance, it is the defiant refusal of the king to mourn after hearing a prophetic announcement of doom that shapes the ritual response of his courtiers. Though the text makes clear that at least some of the king's followers sympathize with the prophet Jeremiah and are in dread of his message, their public response to the oracles of doom is the same as that of the king: they refuse to tear their garments. Thus, Jeremiah 36 shows courtiers with multiple, competing affiliations privileging their ties to the king over their relationship to Jeremiah and over their private fears. Their loyalty to the king and his political stance and the reality of the king's political authority are brought into relief by their refusal to mourn in response to the prophet Jeremiah's words.

Comforting the mourner is an activity with significant social dimensions. Through ritual acts of self-debasing identification, comforters of the mourner over the dead, the petitioner, and non-petitioning individuals or groups experiencing calamity realize and communicate their loyalty and their ties of affiliation to those who mourn, and project these into the future. The contexts of mourning the dead, entreaty, and calamity bring the social ties of the mourner into relief, affording the mourner and his intimates the opportunity to create a distinct, temporary community of their own, ritually separated from others who do not share their mourning. Thus, contrary to Feldman's claim that the mourner over the dead is socially isolated, mourning the dead, entreaty, and non-petitionary mourning associated with catastrophe function to privilege the mourner's social relationships. Yet the person afflicted with skin disease is the exception to this pattern. Though he mourns, he has and can have no comforters, for his mourning is only a component of a larger constellation of rites intended to isolate him socially. Of the four types of mourner, he is the only one who is cut off from community. Therefore, Feldman's claim regarding the isolating effects of mourning is applicable to the individual with skin disease, though not to others who mourn. The person stricken with skin disease, in contrast to other mourners, is socially dead according to Hertz's understanding of social death; his separation from collective life is total. Yet even he cannot be described as socially dead according to the more contemporary definition employed by Middleton, Patterson, and others, for at least one text (2 Kgs. 15: 5) suggests that he has not entirely lost his identity and place in the social order.

BIBLIOGRAPHY

ADLER, H. P., *Das Akkadische des Königs Tusratta von Mitanni* (AOAT 201; Neukirchen-Vluyn: Neukirchener; Kevelaer: Butzon & Bercker, 1976).

ALBERTZ, R., *Persönliche Frömmigkeit und offizielle Religion: Religionsinterner Pluralismus in Israel und Babylon* (Calwer Theologische Monographien 9; Stuttgart: Calwer, 1978).

—— *A History of Israelite Religion in the Old Testament Period* (2 vols.; Louisville: Westminster/John Knox, 1994).

—— *Die Exilszeit: 6. Jahrhundert v. Chr.* (Biblische Enzyklopädie 7; Stuttgart: Kohlhammer, 2001).

ALSTER, B., 'The Mythology of Mourning', *Acta Sumerologica*, 5 (1983), 1–16.

ANDERSON, G. A., *A Time to Mourn, A Time to Dance: The Expression of Grief and Joy in Israelite Religion* (University Park, Pa.: Pennsylvania State University Press, 1991).

ARTZI, P., 'Mourning in International Relations', in B. Alster (ed.), *Death in Mesopotamia* (Mesopotamia: Copenhagen Studies in Assyriology 8; Copenhagen: Akademisk Forlag, 1980), 161–70.

BARTH, C., *Die Errettung vom Tode in den individuellen Klage- und Dankliedern des Alten Testaments* (2nd edn.; Zurich: Theologischer Verlag, 1987).

BAUMANN, A., "אבל 'ābhal', *TDOT* 1: 44–8.

—— 'ילל yll', *TDOT* 6: 82–7.

BAYLISS, M., 'The Cult of Dead Kin in Assyria and Babylonia', *Iraq*, 35 (1973), 115–26.

BELL, C., *Ritual Theory, Ritual Practice* (New York: Oxford University Press, 1992).

—— *Ritual: Perspectives and Dimensions* (New York: Oxford University Press, 1997).

BIRD, P., 'The Place of Women in the Israelite Cultus', in P. Miller *et al.* (eds.), *Ancient Israelite Religion: Essays in Honor of Frank Moore Cross* (Philadelphia: Fortress, 1987), 397–419.

BLENKINSOPP, J., *Ezra-Nehemiah* (OTL; Philadelphia: Westminster, 1988).

—— *Isaiah 1–39* (AB 19; New York: Doubleday, 2000).

BLOCH, M., and PARRY, J. (eds.), *Death and the Regeneration of Life* (Cambridge: Cambridge University Press, 1982).

BLOCH-SMITH, E., *Judahite Burial Practices and Beliefs about the Dead* (JSOTS 123; Sheffield: Sheffield Academic Press, 1992).

BORGER, R., *Babylonisch-assyrische Lesestücke* (Rome: Pontifical Biblical Institute, 1963).

BOTTERWECK, G. J., 'גלה gillah', *TDOT* 3: 5–20.

——and RINGGREN, H. (eds.), *Theologisches Wörterbuch zum Alten Testament* (10 vols.; Stuttgart: Kohlhammer, 1970–).

————(eds.), *Theological Dictionary of the Old Testament* (11 vols.; Grand Rapids, Mich.: Eerdmans, 1974–).

BRIGHT, J., *Jeremiah* (AB 21; Garden City, NY: Doubleday, 1965).

BROWN, R. E., FITZMYER, J. A., and MURPHY, R. E. (eds.), *The New Jerome Biblical Commentary* (Englewood Cliffs, NJ: Prentice Hall, 1990).

CARMICHAEL, C., *The Spirit of Biblical Law* (Athens, Ga.: University of Georgia Press, 1996).

COGAN, M., and TADMOR, H., *II Kings* (AB 11; New York: Doubleday, 1988).

COMAROFF, J. and J. (eds.), *Modernity and its Malcontents: Ritual and Power in Post-Colonial Africa* (Chicago: University of Chicago Press, 1993).

The Compact Edition of the Oxford English Dictionary (2 vols.; Oxford: Oxford University Press, 1971).

COWLEY, A. E., *Aramaic Papyri of the Fifth Century B.C.* (Oxford: Clarendon Press, 1923).

DANFORTH, L. M., and TSIARAS, A., *The Death Rituals of Rural Greece* (Princeton: Princeton University Press, 1982).

DIETRICH, M., LORETZ, O., and SANMARTÍN, J. (eds.), *The Cuneiform Alphabetic Texts from Ugarit, Ras Ibn Hani, and Other Places* (Münster: Ugarit Verlag, 1995).

DOBBS-ALLSOPP, F. W., *Weep, O Daughter of Zion: A Study of the City-Lament Genre in the Hebrew Bible* (BO 44; Rome: Pontifical Biblical Institute, 1993).

DURKHEIM, É., *Les Formes élémentaires de la vie religieuse: Le Système totémique en Australie* (Paris: Librairie Générale Française, 1991).

EBERSOLE, G. L., 'The Function of Ritual Weeping Revisited: Affective Expression and Moral Discourse', *History of Religions*, 39 (2000), 211–46.

ELLIGER, K., *Leviticus* (HAT 4; Tübingen: J. C. B. Mohr/Paul Siebeck, 1966).

Encyclopaedia Judaica (10 vols.; New York: Macmillan, 1971–2).

Enṣiqlopedya Miqra'it (9 vols.; Jerusalem: Mosad Bialik, 1950–88).

FELDMAN, E., *Biblical and Post-Biblical Defilement and Mourning: Law as Theology* (New York: KTAV/Yeshiva University Press, 1977).

FERRIS, P. W. Jr., *The Genre of Communal Lament in the Bible and the Ancient Near East* (SBLDS 127; Atlanta: Scholars Press, 1992).

FISHBANE, M., *Biblical Interpretation in Ancient Israel* (Oxford: Clarendon Press, 1985).

FOSTER, B., *Before the Muses* (2 vols.; Bethesda, Md.: CDL Press, 1993).

FOX, M. V., *Character and Ideology in the Book of Esther* (Columbia, SC: University of South Carolina Press, 1991).

GADD, C. J., 'The Harran Inscriptions of Nabonidus', *Anatolian Studies*, 8 (1958), 35–92.

GEERTZ, C., *The Religion of Java* (New York: Free Press, 1960).

—— 'Thick Description: Toward an Interpretive Theory of Culture', in idem, *The Interpretation of Cultures* (New York: Basic Books, 1973).

GENNEP, A. VAN, *Les Rites de passage* (Paris: Émile Nourry, 1909).

—— *The Rites of Passage*, trans. M. B. Vizedom and G. L. Caffee (Chicago: University of Chicago Press, 1960).

GERSTENBERGER, E., 'Der klagende Mensch: Anmerkungen zu den Klagegattungen in Israel', in H. W. Wolff (ed.), *Probleme biblischer Theologie: Gerhard von Rad zum 70. Geburtstag* (Munich: Kaiser, 1971), 64–72.

—— *Der bittende Mensch: Bittritual und Klagelied des Einzelnen im Alten Testament* (WMANT 51; Neukirchen-Vluyn: Neukirchener, 1980).

—— 'The Lyrical Literature', in D. A. Knight and G. M. Tucker (eds.), *The Hebrew Bible and its Modern Interpreters* (Chico, Calif.: Scholars Press; Philadelphia: Fortress Press, 1985), 409–44.

—— *Psalms, Part 1: With an Introduction to Cultic Poetry* (FOTL xiv; Grand Rapids, Mich.: Eerdmans, 1988).

—— *Das dritte Buch Mose: Leviticus* (ATD 6; Göttingen: Vandenhoeck & Ruprecht, 1993).

—— *Psalms, Part 2, and Lamentations* (FOTL xv; Grand Rapids, Mich.: Eerdmans, 2001).

GILDERS, W. K., 'Representation and Interpretation: Blood Manipulation in Ancient Israel and Early Judaism' (Ph.D. diss., Brown University, 2001).

GREENBERG, M., *Ezekiel 21–37* (AB 22A; New York: Doubleday, 1997).

GRIMES, R., *Deeply into the Bone: Reinventing Rites of Passage* (Berkeley and Los Angeles: University of California Press, 2000).

GRUBER, M., 'Mourning', *EJ* 12: 485–93.

HALLO, W. H., 'Lamentations and Prayers in Sumer and Akkad', *CANE* 3: 1871–81.

HERTZ, R., 'Contribution à une étude sur la représentation collective de la mort', *L'Année Sociologique*, 10 (1905–6), 48–137.

—— 'A Contribution to the Study of the Collective Representation of Death', in idem, *Death and the Right Hand*, trans. R. and C. Needham (Glencoe, Ill.: Free Press, 1960), 27–86.

HIRSCHBERG, H. Z., 'אבל', *EM* 1: 40–5.

HOLLADAY, W. L., *Jeremiah 2* (Hermeneia; Minneapolis: Fortress, 1989).

HUMPHREYS, S. C., 'Death and Time', in S. C. Humphreys and H. King (eds.), *Mortality and Immortality: The Anthropology and Archaeology of Death* (London: Academic Press, 1981), 261–83.

HUROWITZ, V. A., 'Joel's Locust Plague in Light of Sargon II's Hymn to Nanaya', *JBL* 112 (1993), 597–603.

HVIDBERG, F. F., *Weeping and Laughter in the Old Testament* (Leiden: Brill; Copenhagen: Nyt Nordisk Forlag/Arnold Busck, 1962).

JACOBSEN, T., *The Treasures of Darkness: A History of Mesopotamian Religion* (New Haven: Yale University Press, 1976).

JAHNOW, H., *Das hebräischen Leichenlied im Rahmen der Völkerdichtung* (BZAW 36; Giessen: Töpelmann, 1923).

JANZEN, W., *Mourning Cry and Woe Oracle* (BZAW 125; Berlin: de Gruyter, 1972).

KERTZER, D. I., *Ritual, Politics & Power* (New Haven: Yale University Press, 1988).

KLAWANS, J., *Impurity and Sin in Ancient Judaism* (New York: Oxford University Press, 2000).

KNOHL, I., *The Sanctuary of Silence: The Priestly Torah and the Holiness School*, trans. J. Feldman and P. Rodman (Minneapolis: Fortress Press, 1995).

KOEHLER, L., and BAUMGARTNER, W., *The Hebrew and Aramaic Lexicon of the Old Testament* (5 vols.; Leiden: Brill, 1994–2000).

KRAMER, S. N., ' "A Man and his God": A Sumerian Variation on the "Job" Motif', in M. Noth and D. Winton Thomas (eds.), *Wisdom in Israel and in the Ancient Near East* (VTSup 3; Leiden: Brill, 1955), 170–82.

KUTSCH, E., ' "Trauerbräuche" und "Selbstminderungsriten" im Alten Testament', in idem, *Kleine Schriften zum Alten Testament*, ed. L. Schmidt and K. Eberlein (BZAW 168; Berlin and New York: de Gruyter, 1986), 78–95.

LAMBERT, W. G., *Babylonian Wisdom Literature* (Oxford: Clarendon Press, 1960).

LEACH, E., *Culture and Communication* (Cambridge: Cambridge University Press, 1976).

LEVINE, B. A., *In the Presence of the Lord: A Study of Cult and Some*

Cultic Terms in Ancient Israel (Studies in Judaism in Late Antiquity 5; Leiden: Brill, 1974).

LEVINE, B. A., *Leviticus* (JPSTC; Philadelphia: Jewish Publication Society, 1989).

—— 'Silence, Sound, and the Phenomenology of Mourning in Biblical Israel', *JANES* 22 (1993), 89–106.

—— *Numbers 1–20* (AB 4; New York: Doubleday, 1993).

—— and DE TARRAGON, J.-M., 'Dead Kings and Rephaim: The Patrons of the Ugaritic Dynasty', *JAOS* 104 (1984), 649–59.

LEWIS, T. J., *Cults of the Dead in Ancient Israel and Ugarit* (HSM 39; Atlanta: Scholars Press, 1989).

—— 'How Far Can Texts Take Us? Evaluating Textual Sources for Reconstructing Ancient Israelite Beliefs about the Dead', in B. Gittlen (ed.), *Sacred Time, Sacred Place: Archaeology and the Religion of Israel* (Winona Lake, Ind.: Eisenbrauns, 2002). 169–217.

LINCOLN, B., *Emerging from the Chrysalis: Rituals of Women's Initiation* (New York: Oxford University Press, 1991).

LIPINSKI, E., *La Liturgie pénitentielle dans la Bible* (Lectio Divina 52; Paris: Cerf, 1969).

LOHFINK, N., 'Enthielten die im Alten Testament bezeugten Klageriten eine Phase des Schweigens?', *VT* 12 (1962), 260–77.

LUTZ, C. A., *Unnatural Emotions: Everyday Sentiments on a Micronesian Atoll & Their Challenge to Western Theory* (Chicago: University of Chicago Press, 1988).

MCCARTER, P. K., Jr., 'The Apology of David', *JBL* 99 (1980), 489–504.

—— *II Samuel* (AB 9; Garden City, NY: Doubleday, 1984).

MCKANE, W., *A Critical and Exegetical Commentary on Jeremiah* (2 vols.; ICC; Edinburgh: T. & T. Clark, 1996).

MAYER, G., 'ידה ydh', *TDOT* 5: 427–43.

MAYS, J. L., *Amos* (OTL; Philadelphia: Westminster, 1969).

METCALF, P., and HUNTINGTON, R., *Celebrations of Death: The Anthropology of Mortuary Ritual*, (2nd revised and expanded edn.; Cambridge: Cambridge University Press, 1991).

MIDDLETON, J., 'Lugbara Death', in M. Bloch and J. Parry (eds.), *Death and the Regeneration of Life* (Cambridge: Cambridge University Press, 1982), 134–54.

MILGROM, J., *Leviticus 1–16* (AB 3; New York: Doubleday, 1991).

—— *Leviticus 17–22* (AB 3A; New York: Doubleday, 2000).

MORAN, W. L., 'The Ancient Near Eastern Background of the Love of God in Deuteronomy', *CBQ* 25 (1963), 77–87.

—— *The Amarna Letters* (Baltimore: The Johns Hopkins University Press, 1992).

MORRIS, I., *Death-Ritual and Social Structure in Classical Antiquity* (Cambridge: Cambridge University Press, 1992).

MOWINCKEL, S., *The Psalms in Israel's Worship*, trans. D. R. Ap-Thomas (2 vols.; Oxford: Blackwell, 1962).

NOTH, M., *Das dritte Buch Mose: Leviticus* (ATD 6; Göttingen: Vandenhoeck & Ruprecht, 1962).

OLYAN, S. M., 'Honor, Shame, and Covenant Relations in Ancient Israel and its Environment', *JBL* 115 (1996), 201–18.

—— 'What do Shaving Rites Accomplish and what do they Signal in Biblical Ritual Contexts?', *JBL* 117 (1998), 611–22.

——*Rites and Rank: Hierarchy in Biblical Representations of Cult* (Princeton: Princeton University Press, 2000).

—— ' "We Are Utterly Cut Off": Some Possible Nuances of נגזרנו לנו in Ezek. 37: 11', *Catholic Biblical Quarterly*, 65 (2003), 43–57.

PARPOLA, S., *The Standard Babylonian Epic of Gilgamesh* (State Archives of Assyria Cuneiform Texts 1; Helsinki: The Neo-Assyrian Text Corpus Project, 1997).

PATTERSON, O., *Slavery and Social Death: A Comparative Study* (Cambridge: Harvard University Press, 1982).

PEDERSEN, J., *Israel: Its Life and Culture* (4 vols.; London: Oxford University Press; Copenhagen: Povl Branner, 1926–40).

PHAM, X. H. T., *Mourning in the Ancient Near East and the Hebrew Bible* (JSOTS 302; Sheffield: Sheffield Academic Press, 1999).

PODELLA, T., *Ṣôm-Fasten: Kollektive Trauer um den verborgenen Gott im Alten Testament* (AOAT 224; Neukirchen-Vluyn: Neukirchener; Kevelaer: Butzon & Bercker, 1989).

PORTEN, B., and YARDENI, Y. (eds. and trans.), *Textbook of Aramaic Documents from Ancient Egypt* (4 vols.; Jerusalem: Hebrew University, 1986).

PRITCHARD, J. B. (ed.), *The Ancient Near East in Pictures Relating to the Old Testament* (2nd edn. with supplement; Princeton: Princeton University Press, 1969).

RADCLIFFE-BROWN, A. R., *The Andaman Islanders* (Cambridge: Cambridge University Press, 1933).

RAINEY, A. F., 'Dust and Ashes', *Tel Aviv*, 1 (1974), 77–83.

RAPPAPORT, R. A., *Ritual and Religion in the Making of Humanity* (Cambridge: Cambridge University Press, 1999).

RUDOLPH, W., *Jeremia* (HAT 12; Tübingen: J. C. B. Mohr/Paul Siebeck, 1958).

SAKENFELD, K. D., *The Meaning of Hesed in the Hebrew Bible: A New Inquiry* (HSM 17; Missoula, Mont.: Scholars Press, 1978).

SASSON, J. M. (ed.), *Civilizations of the Ancient Near East* (4 vols.; Peabody, Mass.: Hendrickson, 2000).

SCHARBERT, J., 'ספד, sāpad', *TDOT* 10: 299–303.

SCHMIDT, B. B., *Israel's Beneficent Dead: Ancestor Cult and Necromancy in Ancient Israelite Religion and Tradition* (Winona Lake, Ind.: Eisenbrauns, 1996).

SCHWARTZ, B. Y., תורת הקדושה : עיונים בחוקה הכוהנית שבתורה (Jerusalem: Magnes Press, 1999).

SCURLOCK, J., 'Ghosts in the Ancient Near East: Weak or Powerful?', *HUCA* 68 (1997), 77–96.

—— 'Death and the Afterlife in Ancient Mesopotamian Thought', *CANE* 3: 1883–93.

SEGAL, Z., ספר בן סירא השלם (Jerusalem: Mosad Bialik, 1958).

SEYBOLD, K., *Das Gebet des Kranken im Alten Testament: Untersuchungen zur Bestimmung und Zuordnung der Krankheits- und Heilungspsalmen* (BWANT 5.19; Stuttgart: Kohlhammer, 1973).

SPRONK, K., *Beatific Afterlife in Ancient Israel and in the Ancient Near East* (AOAT 219: Neukirchen-Vluyn: Neukirchener; Kevelaer: Butzon & Bercker, 1986).

TIGAY, J., *Deuteronomy* (JPSTC; Philadelphia: Jewish Publication Society, 1996).

TOORN, K. VAN DER, *Family Religion in Babylonia, Syria & Israel: Continuity & Change in the Forms of Religious Life* (SHCANE 7; Leiden: Brill, 1996).

TROMP, N. J., *Primitive Conceptions of Death and the Nether World in the Old Testament* (BO 21; Rome: Pontifical Biblical Institute, 1969).

TROPPER, J., *Nekromantie: Totenbefragung im Alten Orient und im Alten Testament* (AOAT 223; Neukirchen-Vluyn: Neukirchener; Kevelaer: Butzon & Bercker, 1989).

TURNER, V., 'Betwixt and Between: The Liminal Period in Rites de Passage', in idem, *The Forest of Symbols: Aspects of Ndembu Ritual* (Ithaca: Cornell University Press, 1967).

—— 'Liminality and Communitas', in idem, *The Ritual Process: Structure and Anti-Structure* (New York: Aldine De Gruyter, 1995).

TUR-SINAI, N., 'כתבת קעקע', *EM* 4: 378–80.

VANDERKAM, J., 'Davidic Complicity in the Deaths of Abner and Eshbaal: A Historical and Redactional Study', *JBL* 99 (1980), 521–39.

VANONI, G., 'שמח śāmaḥ', *TWAT* 7: 808–22.

WÄCHTER, L., 'עפר 'āpār', *TDOT* 11: 257–65.

WALTKE, B. K., and O'CONNOR, M., *An Introduction to Biblical Hebrew Syntax* (Winona Lake, Ind.: Eisenbrauns, 1990).

WEISER, A., *Das Buch des Propheten Jeremia* (ATD 20; Göttingen: Vandenhoeck & Ruprecht, 1960).

WESTERMANN, C., *Das Loben Gottes in den Psalmen* (3rd edn.;

Göttingen: Vandenhoeck & Ruprecht, 1963).

—— *Genesis* (BKAT 1; Neukirchen-Vluyn: Neukirchener, 1982).

—— *Die Klagelieder: Forschungsgeschichte und Auslegung* (Neukirchen-Vluyn: Neukirchener, 1990).

WILSON, R. R., *Sociological Approaches to the Old Testament* (Philadelphia: Fortress, 1984).

WOLFF, H. W., 'Der Aufruf zur Volksklage', *ZAW* 76 (1964), 48–56.

—— *Dodekapropheton 2: Joel und Amos* (BKAT xiv/2; Neukirchen-Vluyn: Neukirchener, 1969).

—— *Hosea* (Hermeneia; Philadelphia: Fortress, 1974).

WRIGHT, D. P., *Ritual in Narrative: The Dynamics of Feasting, Mourning, and Retaliation Rites in the Ugaritic Tale of Aqhat* (Winona Lake, Ind.: Eisenbrauns, 2001).

XELLA, P., 'Death and the Afterlife in Canaanite and Hebrew Thought', *CANE* 3: 2059–70.

ZENGER, E., *Das Buch Judit* (Gütersloh: Mohn, 1981).

—— 'Das Buch der Psalmen', in E. Zenger (ed.), *Einleitung in das Alte Testament*; 3rd edn. (Kohlhammer Studienbücher Theologie 1.1; Stuttgart: Kohlhammer, 1998), 309–26.

ZIMMERLI, W., *Ezechiel* (2 vols.; BKAT xiii; Neukirchen-Vluyn: Neukirchener, 1969).

INDEX OF BIBLICAL
REFERENCES

GENERAL INDEX